Crimes Without Punishment

Crimes Without Punishment

Humanitarian Action in Former Yugoslavia

Michèle Mercier

Foreword by Cyrus Vance

Pluto Press

LONDON · EAST HAVEN, CONNECTICUT

First published as *Crimes sans châtiment*, 1994
by Bruylant, Brussels and L.D.G.J., Paris

First English edition published 1995 by Pluto Press
345 Archway Road, London N6 5AA
and 140 Commerce Street, East Haven, Connecticut 06512,
USA

British Library Cataloguing in Publication Data
A catalogue record for this book is available from the British
Library

ISBN 0 7453 1080 X hbk

Library of Congress Cataloging in Publication Data
Mercier, Michèle, 1946–
    [Crimes sans châtinant. English]
    Crimes without punishment : humanitarian action in former
Yugoslavia / Michèle Mercier : foreword by Cyrus Vance.
        p.   cm.
    First published 1994 by CICR Presse, Brussels — T.p. verso.
    Includes bibliographical references (p.   ) and index.
    ISBN 0-7453-1080-X (hbk.)
    1. International Committee of the Red Cross. 2. Yugoslav War.
1991– — Civilian relief — Bosnia and Hercegovina.
3. Yugoslav War.
1991– — Civilian relief — Croatia.
HV568.M4213 1996
949.702'4—dc20   95–36109
                                                         CIP

Designed and produced for Pluto Press by
Chase Production Services, Chipping Norton, OX7 5QR
Typeset from disk by Stanford DTP Services, Milton Keynes
Printed in the EC by J.W. Arrowsmith, Bristol

Contents

Maps

Figures

Acknowledgements

It is impossible to mention by name all the representatives of the humanitarian and political organizations whom I have met in the field or elsewhere, who have enabled me to appreciate more accurately the conditions in which the war in former Yugoslavia is being waged; men and women working for the United Nations, the UNHCR, UNICEF and WHO, *Médecins sans Frontières* and other NGOs. Their help has been invaluable.

Without the extraordinary degree of friendship and accessibility shown me by the ICRC's locally engaged employees, whether Croat, Montenegrin, Bosnian, Serbian or Slovene, by its drivers, delegates of both sexes, doctors and nurses, and by the officials continually travelling between Geneva headquarters and the field, it would have been impossible to understand the humanitarian issues involved. I owe them my most grateful thanks.

I have particularly appreciated the unfailing trust placed in me by all the officials of the International Committee of the Red Cross (ICRC) in commissioning me to write this book, and the freedom allowed me throughout my research and the period of its composition, bearing in mind the fluctuating situation in former Yugoslavia and the still-unresolved conflict there. I am especially grateful to Cornelio Sommaruga, President of the ICRC, and to the Executive Board of the ICRC.

Throughout, I have been fortunate enough to have the guidance and advice of François Bugnion, the ICRC's Deputy Director of the Department of Principles, Law and Relations with the Movement, whose historical exactitude and passion for clarity have been an inspiration to me. The political and humanitarian vision of Thierry Germond, at the time the ICRC's Delegate General for Western and Central Europe, has also been invaluable, as have the information and advice of his Deputy, André Collomb, and all those working with the 'Europe zone'.

My documentary research has been greatly facilitated by Françoise Patry, the cheerfully efficient research assistant in the ICRC's Archives Division, while the care and efficiency of Charles Pierrat and Missak Pechtimaldjian in following the various stages of preparation of this book were much appreciated. Lastly, my warm thanks go to Joëlle Kuntz, Jacques Givet and Isabelle Vichniac, for their friendship in so kindly reading the manuscript throughout its gestation.

Foreword

The conflict in the former Yugoslavia, now almost three years old, has thus far defied all outside initiatives to bring it to a halt. The combined efforts of the major powers, the European Union and the United Nations have not yet succeeded in securing peace with justice for its suffering peoples. As I write these lines, new initiatives are underway combining military force with diplomacy in the long search for a negotiated settlement to the hostilities. We trust that steadiness of purpose will prevail and that a just settlement will be attained.

Few conflicts in recent times have broken out with such a plethora of advance warning. For years Western statesmen, journalists and analysts had watched Yugoslavia and worried about what would happen after Tito departed the scene. But when the breakup of Yugoslavia turned violent in June 1991, no outside institution or country was prepared to take effective action to restore peace. Advance warning was also given at the end of 1991 that premature, selective recognition of certain Yugoslav republics would lead to further conflict in Bosnia and Herzegovina. The hostilities, in short, were foreseeable and were foreseen.

What could not be foreseen was the unbridled ferocity of the conflict – one in which civilians rapidly became not only victims of the violence, but the prime targets of such violence. The media quickly transmitted to a shocked world accounts and images of atrocities that had not been seen in Europe for decades.

From the outset it was the humanitarian agencies, led by the International Committee of the Red Cross, which responded to these breaches of international humanitarian law. The ICRC, as ever, was present and was soon joined by the United Nations High Commissioner for Refugees and other governmental and non-governmental agencies. ICRC delegates shared the hardships of innocent civilian victims, helped them as well as military prisoners, and looked after the homeless and the expellees. Delegates died and were injured performing their humanitarian duty.

Beginning with my first mission for the United Nations to the former Yugoslavia in October 1991, until May 1993 when I relinquished the Co-Chairmanship of the Steering Committee of the International Conference on the Former Yugoslavia, I was in constant contact with the men and women of the ICRC at all levels in ex-Yugoslavia, Geneva and New York.

I am proud to bear witness to the brave and vital work of the men and women of the ICRC. Unarmed except for their commitment and their courage, they emerge from the tragedy of former Yugoslavia as standard bearers of the world's conscience. Michèle Mercier's valuable book tells their story. I hope it will be read by citizens and statesmen alike.

Cyrus Vance
April 1994

Preface

In December 1992, when war was raging in Bosnia-Herzegovina and any hope for a political and military settlement of the crisis still seemed only a utopian dream, the International Committee of the Red Cross (ICRC) decided to make an interim assessment of its activities in the region in a way new to it. It was not so much the idea of the assessment itself which was unusual – such things are no novelty to officials directing humanitarian operations – but the anticipation of a need to make known publicly its view of the most important events of a war whose outcome was as yet unknown. In this it was running a risk, for nobody knew when and how the bloody strife now ravaging former Yugoslavia would end. But the humanitarian agencies' experience is already so vast that conclusions have to be drawn from it even though these may seem short-sighted.

The public debate now taking place on the limits and extent of humanitarian commitment in armed conflicts, given difficult conditions in the field and the rules of multilateral diplomacy, will continue for so long as there is a clash of interests; that is, for decades to come. Meanwhile the emergency continues and the humanitarian agencies have to find a place for themselves in the scheme of things or try to change that scheme.

This book contains a wealth of testimony from people who have lived in the context of former Yugoslavia since the early 1990s. I am thinking in particular of representatives of governmental and non-governmental humanitarian organizations, correspondents of the international press whom I have met on the spot, and local journalists who are struggling to uphold some shreds of professional integrity. Special mention is due to the delegates, both men and women, of the ICRC, on whose unique experience this book is based.

As well as interviews with eye-witnesses of the Yugoslav tragedy (which comprise the majority of unsourced quotations in this book), this book draws on the considerable public documentary sources obtainable from NGOs such as Amnesty International and *Médecins sans Frontières*, from United Nations bodies such as the Security Council, the Human Rights Commission and the United Nations Office for Refugees, and from the media, particularly the printed press, which produces a regular flow of in-depth commentary. The archives of the ICRC have also been a mine of information.

Inevitably, this book is only an attempt to make an interim assessment of the main questions that assailed humanitarian agencies between 1991 and 1993, and still do so at the time of publication. Only time will bring better understanding of the reasons for the successes and failures of humanitarian effort in contemporary conflicts, and show whether the conclusions drawn from its grave setbacks in former Yugoslavia are valid. For this we must wait until the arbiters of the world's destiny rate humanitarian effort higher on their list of priorities; but we must not wait until the rules that states have adopted to create islands of humanity in war are still further trampled underfoot.

Introduction

The humanitarian organizations have not emerged unscathed from the conflict in which so many men, women and children have perished. Is there still any point in trying to mitigate man-made chaos by humanitarian aid? No idle question, for former Yugoslavia provides an especially edifying and indeed exemplary instance of the juxtaposition of barbarous conduct on the one hand, bravery and impotent heroism on the other. In these conditions humanitarian aid has to contend with the most abject political conduct and the inexhaustible indifference of governments.

When the world emerged from the devastation and physical and moral ravages of the Second World War, and from the shame provoked by the discovery of the atrocities in Nazi concentration camps, it was thought for a time that international humanitarian law might be on the brink of a golden age. In a surge of idealism it produced the Universal Declaration of the Rights of Man, followed by the modern version of the Geneva Conventions, containing major additions designed to protect civilians in enemy hands. The international community believed that it could impose a new way of life. This state of grace was brief. The barely healed wounds of the Second World War were reopened by the Korean War, the Vietnam War, the wars of liberation of colonial countries, civil war in Biafra and in Lebanon, and many other conflicts.

The philosophers – and it is no part of their plan to replace good with evil – tell us that to open the door to the wind of change we must learn to unlearn. And in studying the region of former Yugoslavia, which is still digging deeper and deeper into the rubble of its own history, those responsible have to determine where, when and how everything went wrong, and put forward new answers to the barbarism that rules there.

The excesses committed in the conflicts of former Yugoslavia since 1991 have thrown into harsh relief the basic questions the politicians and humanitarian agencies were already asking themselves concerning their respective roles, whether or not those roles should be merged, their priorities, and how to cope with changes in international customs. Those drawing up an inventory of this kind must not let themselves be hypnotized by the crisis in one area. They also have to decide what the recent conflicts have to teach them, valuable pointers to the changes of direction adopted in humanitarian work.

For the linking of humanitarian activities with politics and military intervention does not date from the Bosnian conflict, and the change to humanitarian aid backed by force did not take place overnight. Whilst recognizing that it is unrealistic and inappropriate to attempt total separation of politics from humanitarian action, the International Committee of the Red Cross (ICRC) (for more than a century the principal architect of humanitarian law and humanitarian activities in armed conflicts) uncompromisingly favours a clear division of labour between charitable and political organizations. Its determination to achieve this grows daily, for now that chaos has been adopted as a way of settling disputes, and many more humanitarian organizations are active than before, the situation in the field is increasingly ambiguous. The cards are dealt out to more and more players. Formerly, the ICRC was usually left to cope on its own with the humanitarian consequences of conflicts, particularly civil war. Now it works elbow to elbow with many United Nations agencies and non-governmental organizations. This is all to the good as regards sharing the burden, but it compels the ICRC to declare even more clearly than ever that whilst it will always co-operate with all the institutions concerned, it has a right to work independently. While this is not a contradiction in terms, it is terribly difficult to put into practice. Indeed, there is a great risk of appearing to be swimming against the stream if the ICRC does not endorse the new majority-held views which aim to build a humanitarian order closely linked to the wishes of the superpowers.

The predominant role of the United Nations in the settlement of the Afghan conflict foreshadowed the major changes that were to characterize UN practice as regards direct intervention in the internal affairs of a state, with the prompting of its reinvigorated Security Council. The United Nations General Assembly of 1988 marked another turning point in international practice. Resolution 43/131 conferred full recognition of the 'right of intervention' and opened new avenues to all the organizations involved, closely or otherwise, in humanitarian operations. Taking advantage of the ambiguity of a quarrel between the old school, which respects state sovereignty, and the modern school whose new moral order rejects geographical and political frontiers, the resolution refurbishes a right that the Geneva Conventions of 1949, which are universal texts, have long recognized under the title of 'right to humanitarian assistance' due to all victims of armed conflict. According to Claire Brisset, this makes of the right of humanitarian intervention nothing more than an empty phrase, a 'portmanteau word', used by all and sundry to soothe consciences perturbed by this new disorder that has invaded the world.[1]

The Gulf War of 1991, the first large-scale international conflict since the collapse of the Berlin Wall, highlighted all the benefits and all the evils that can be conferred simultaneously in a single country by applying the right of intervention as its inventors conceived of it. Its benefits were the use of force to come to the help, in *ad hoc* operations, of tens of thousands of people in danger from hostilities, cold and hunger, as in Iraqi Kurdistan. Its evil effects were indifference to the fate of the Shiite Arab population of southern Iraq, whose survival was no less precarious because they were isolated in unhealthy areas that were continually bombarded and cut off from any international aid. From December 1992 onwards the Somali war was the theatre of even more grotesque and highly publicized military-cum-humanitarian operations that cast a permanent cloud over this kind of intervention.

In former Yugoslavia the situation is different. Where more emphatic intervention by the forces of protection was expected it did not take place. The safe areas that might have given asylum to minorities, on whom excesses of every kind were routinely committed, were not set up in time because troops were not available to protect them. The United Nations in its present form could not mobilize the forces needed for a large-scale protection operation without subcontracting with a state or community of states willing to send troops. In countries where such means existed, political will was lacking. *A fortiori*, any purely military plan of intervention put forward by a part of public opinion to cut short the death agony of a republic was nipped in the bud.

The aberrations of the international community, starting with the first conflict of 1991 and growing steadily since the outbreak of hostilities in Bosnia-Herzegovina, justify the fear that the patterns of behaviour usually regulating relations between states may disappear. Governments, whatever their complexion, are criticized for abdicating their responsibilities. Ignorance, helplessness and refusal to deal with the root causes characterize the international scene, which is totally out of touch with conditions in the field. 'The United States have taken two years' vacation from Europe, and the whole of the western world has withdrawn from the scene. Nobody seems to want to know what is happening', says a very knowledgeable American journalist. No one will either realize or remember that these conflicts have not broken out by chance, but there has been no lack of warning signs of the disasters to come.

The Yugoslav upheavals prior to the open crisis are directly due to the turmoil, caused by the decline of communism in eastern Europe, which Mikhaïl Gorbachev's last-minute reforms were powerless to contain. Besides the Berlin Wall, two other props of the precarious Yugoslav mosaic, namely the Communist Party and the external threat, suddenly collapsed. The Red Army withdrew first from Hungary and then from Bulgaria, giving free rein to the aspirations to independence of the Yugoslav republics, until then prudently quiescent under the wing of the Party. Together with these stirrings came the breakup of the USSR, the full consequences of which are still unknown.

The Yugoslav conflict is also the outcome of the political decomposition peculiar to the Yugoslav Federation, whose pace quickened when Tito's regime came to an end. Tito had installed a system intended to ensure at least a constitutional balance between the various republics (each of which enjoyed a high degree of autonomy) together with the coexistence of the various communities. This model system progressively fell to pieces, so giving the élite of the communities, particularly Slovene and Croat, the impression that it was working for the benefit of the largest group, the Serbs. This is the source of the movement for autonomy, soon succeeded by the secessionist movement, of the Croats and Slovenes, and the resultant tension with Serbia, which was increasingly unwilling to comply with the demands of a federal system.

In this festering political situation, the ICRC offered its services to the federal government of Yugoslavia to visit the political prisoners, mainly Kosavars, imprisoned in several republics. The ICRC is better known as the guardian of the Geneva Conventions, and therefore for its work in theatres of war. But particularly since the 1960s it has also distinguished itself by its work for political detainees in every continent of the world.[2] Its delegates, who now number about a thousand men and women serving in some fifty delegations all over the world, devote themselves in an infinite number of ways to mitigating the suffering caused by war and political disturbances. They compile lists of persons deprived of liberty, talk to them regularly in private, transmit letters between them and their families, and urge the prison authorities to improve the conditions in which such prisoners are confined. They also give emergency assistance to communities in need of material aid, provide medical care where local infrastructures are insufficient, and keep health centres supplied with basic drugs. And they enable members of dispersed families to get in touch with each other again and correspond by means of Red Cross messages where normal postal communications are interrupted.

To carry out all these tasks, ICRC delegates rely on the experience of thousands of locally recruited persons, without whose help humanitarian activities would be infinitely less effective. In former Yugoslavia they have been able to draw on a reserve of exceptionally well-qualified persons who regarded the help they gave to a humanitarian organization not only as a useful paid job but also as a means of retaining their human dignity, jeopardized by their compatriots' barbarous methods of waging war. For example, a doctor of nuclear physics has become a driver, a professor of Germanic languages a telephone operator and receptionist, and an executive in a service industry a field officer. Their personal loyalty is all the more remarkable because they are working in their own country, and in order to be able to operate efficiently, they have to keep their emotional reactions under strict control.

After 35 months of uninterrupted service in former Yugoslavia, humanitarian aid workers inevitably ask themselves a chain of crucial questions. However used they have become to accommodating their views to circumstances, they are appalled at having day after day to accept the price of politicians' lies, decipher statements by officials expert in duplicity and preach to deaf ears the virtues of a humanitarian approach. One of the most pointed questions is how far the belligerents can be trusted to honour their undertakings. It arose in the very first conflict between Croatia and federal Yugoslavia. The tragic fate of Vukovar in Slovenia, the best known of the many towns to be blockaded and incessantly bombarded in the second half of 1991, imposes a radical change in the way of approaching the parties to the conflict. The international treaties regulating the conduct of armed conflicts[3] require that the warring parties be enjoined to agree on undertakings explicitly applicable to the conflict in which they are engaged. Although the Geneva Conventions do not *ipso facto* apply,[4] the obligation for the ICRC to remind the belligerents to observe the rules of behaviour in battle requires its officials to engage in ongoing negotiations in Geneva and in the capital cities of the region. Also, in New York, former Yugoslavia has been the subject of extreme activity at United Nations headquarters since the end of 1991, especially immediately after the meeting of the Security Council on 31 January 1992, which was held for the first time in its history at the level of Heads of State or Government. This summit meeting mandated the new Secretary-General, Boutros Boutros-Ghali, to study how best to 'strengthen and make more efficient within the framework and provisions of the Charter the capacity of the United Nations for preventive diplomacy, for peacemaking and for peace-keeping'.[5]

It was therefore 'with a sense of moment'[6] that the Secretary-General presented his 'Agenda for Peace' to Member States of the United Nations.

Although June 1992 was not a happy month for Bosnia-Herzegovina, being drawn daily deeper into war, it was in that month that reinforcements were sent to the United Nations Protection Force on the eve of the reopening of Sarajevo airport. This lifeline, often severed and restored, links the capital of Bosnia-Herzegovina with the outside world and helps to ensure the survival of a population that in one way after another has suffered more than any other, and has endured the longest siege in the modern history of the western world. Television and newspaper reports of daily life in Sarajevo have convinced the rest of the world that it can do nothing to end the war. The United Nations, as guarantor of international security, symbolically invokes Chapter VII of its Charter, which authorizes the use of force when all peaceful attempts to resolve a serious crisis have failed and its own credibility is at stake. Since the awakening of the 1990s the eyes of the world have been fixed on New York, and its hopes pinned to the United Nations, to which so many appeals have been made that it can hardly answer them. In Bosnia-Herzegovina the UN has reacted on a grand scale. It has deployed considerable logistic facilities to enable the United Nations High Commission for Refugees (UNHCR), its special agency responsible for the entire system, to carry out a vast operation in aid of displaced and besieged persons. Within a very short time the dangerous conditions required that the aid convoys should be escorted. This was the beginning of the militarization of humanitarian assistance. Parallel with this, political negotiations having failed time after time, charitable organizations were granted more and more resources so as to hide the tragic shortcomings of the western world. It was as if humanitarian aid began 'to look perilously like an ideological ritual, which is not asked to face up to the (nasty and depressing) complexity of reality, but to take its place and appease our souls'.[7]

Little remains to be said, or written, about humanitarian aid. Politics have taken it hostage and used it as an alibi. But nothing has been settled. There is only a welter of disparate opinions and proposals, a rush to be the first to invent the new 'international humanitarian brigades', which would blazon around them all the virtues of political-cum-diplomatic-cum-humanitarian action like three-way commandos. Other agencies, including very obviously the ICRC, claim the 'right to autonomy' for humanitarian organizations, not necessarily leading insidiously to superb isolation but leaving the door open to collective pressure and collective approaches whenever the gravity of the situation requires it. When at the International Conference for the Protection of War Victims in Geneva, on 30 August and 1 September 1993, the President of the ICRC affirmed that he was convinced that 'the efficacy and credibility of humanitarian action and the degree to which it is accepted by belligerents are a direct corollary of that independence', and added that it was essential 'to draw a clear distinction between the role of states in peace-keeping operations and the role of neutral and impartial humanitarian organizations' should be clearly established, he was supported by the Secretary-General of the United Nations, who stated that it was 'essential and urgent, in view of ... conflicts of which our conscience disapproves and which the law condemns, to keep finding new ways of better protecting civilian

populations'. He added that since 1991 the UN's operations for
the maintenance of peace had included 'a humanitarian assistance
component, in addition to the restoration of democracy'. At the
same conference the United Nations High Commissioner for
Refugees, Sadako Ogata, was moved by her Commission's
experience in the thick of the fighting to declare that 'it is essential
that the independent, non-political and impartial nature of humanitarian action be forcefully reaffirmed, preserved, perceived as such
and respected by all'. From these speeches it is clear that those in
daily touch with the harsh realities of humanitarian operations, in
fields as arduous and abrasive as Somalia and former Yugoslavia,
know that nothing is more likely to lead humanitarian organizations into deadlock than to confuse their role with that of
governments.

International humanitarian law in its present state, seen against
the troubled background of contemporary conflicts, earns a no less
critical appraisal. Tahar Ben Jelloun calls it

> an asset which should neither be negotiated or used as a strategy
> to obtain power. This law implies the giving of one's time,
> energies and abilities without counting the cost or expecting
> anything in return. This is what gives it its beauty and grandeur.[8]

Nevertheless the question arises whether the time has come to apply
humanitarian law in its strictest form, such as is found in the
Geneva Conventions and their Additional Protocols, or whether
it is preferable to extract its quintessence and, using the simplest
of approaches, go back to first principles and adopt a streamlined
law, such as that of the ten articles that composed the very first text
of the Geneva Convention of 22 August 1864 for the Amelioration
of the Condition of the Wounded in Armies in the Field. Or should
the ICRC throw its weight behind the adoption of a new and more
trenchant code of law that would, for example, propose a set of
mandatory rules for the protection of civilians subjected to blockade,
or would go so far as to forbid the use of blockade as a weapon of
war? A code that would wholeheartedly encourage the establishment of safe areas, much vilified in the Bosnian conflict, but in the
view of the ICRC the least unsatisfactory way of safeguarding
civilians subjected to 'ethnic cleansing'?

Another possible choice would be to adjust international humanitarian law more closely to human rights, but politics have too
obviously exploited the human rights issue for this choice to be a
popular one. This is clear from various official declarations at the
last world conference on human rights in Vienna, 14–25 June
1993, that it was essential to preserve the principle of state sovereignty. Nevertheless, the two approaches are complementary and
will remain so.

An ideal form of humanitarian law has, therefore, still to be reached. Meanwhile the cornerstone of the existing law has been thrown on the rubbish heap. The first article of each of the four Geneva Conventions explicitly states that every signatory (that is, nearly every state in the world) undertakes 'to respect and to ensure respect for' the rules they contain. But whilst all parties daily accuse each other of breaches of humanitarian law, the countries or political entities that would have the power to put a stop to such breaches are totally incapable of doing so. This is one of the most dismaying phenomena of failure for humanitarian workers in former Yugoslavia who, day after day since July 1991, have been faced with the belligerents' shameful behaviour.

The officials of the charitable organizations who have to ensure the security of their teams in the field have opted for multilateral diplomatic approaches whilst keeping in touch with both political and military leaders and with local commanders; for so long as there is any doubt whether the leaders of the parties to the conflict are in control of their troops and until they receive confirmation of that control, these officials have no other choice and can obtain no guarantees. They send out onto the roads of Bosnia-Herzegovina delegates who know that there is little room for humanitarian aid in this war of broken promises and who are well aware that they are seen as actors in a tragic and elaborate deceit. Disturbed and disorientated by dealing with people very similar to themselves, unlike other victims in the southern hemisphere to whom they are accustomed, the field workers, both men and women, feel themselves becoming more and more vulnerable, and sometimes cannot contain their tears. Who could forget those television pictures of a soldier of the United Nations Protection Force sobbing at the sight of women and children who had been massacred?

Nobody is prepared for the outrages of war, neither its direct victims nor their murderers, neither the politicians nor the humanitarian aid workers. All of them, whatever their responsibilities, are now wondering what they could or should have done when, in their heart of hearts, they very well knew.

CHAPTER 1

Horror at First Hand

Behind the official statements of an institution like the International Committee of the Red Cross (ICRC) are the individual men and women, the delegates whose subconscious becomes overloaded with all they have lived through without finding any safety-valve except in action. None, that is, except to talk about all they have thought and gone through, sharing a little of their emotional overload with another of their kind. They talk about the routine difficulties of a humanitarian mission in war-torn terrain, but above all about the doubts and questions that assail them. They may be fiercely critical of authority, they may be moralists, but all they say springs from thought fired by action, by what the 'good Samaritan' of old felt when he met people who were suffering, by the clash of their humanitarian ideals and the harsh realities of politics and war. The following eye-witness accounts, gathered in heart-to-heart talks, illustrate the eternal conflict of certainty and doubt experienced by humanitarian aid workers in action.

Illusion – Should we draw a lesson from the horrors of the war in former Yugoslavia or simply put them out of our minds as soon as possible, as if they were an isolated phenomenon that should never have happened? To tackle the humanitarian consequences of a conflict other means have to be used, and unfortunately these are military. Humanitarian aid alone simply cannot cope. It is completely unrealistic to try to settle the problem by humanitarian aid. That solves nothing. It only touches the fringe, as if you were trying to cure cancer with an aspirin. We are not allowed to visit a prison unless its governor over the way sends permission that we should be let in and allowed to do our work. There is nothing wrong with the approach, but we lack strength – military strength. What are we doing in March 1993 in Huambo, Angola? Nothing. Not because our approach is wrong, but because in the circumstances we need to be able to use force. We were not in Pol Pot's Cambodia, where we could not even try to stop the worst from happening. Right back in the Second World War, hostilities came to an end because the Allies intervened, not because of any humanitarian approach, which in extreme situations is useless by itself. So when all is said

1

and done, Yugoslavia is not such a special case as all that. The only difference is that here we are on the spot, we see it all for ourselves whereas elsewhere we don't get there until afterwards. We are nearer horror than ever before, and it's not hard to bring us to a halt. Enough to say 'Don't take the Split–Zenica road today, they're shelling it', and we don't take it. Delegates are all the more frustrated because they are seeing the trouble from the inside, although we know well enough that the mere fact of being there can't stop the worst from happening. It's an illusion to believe that it can, but it doesn't prevent humanitarian aid workers from doing their job. Within limits.

* * * * * * * *

Morality – When the peace plan collapsed the time was supposed to have come for a down-to-earth moral message to take its place. But how are we to use our 'moral strength'? Is it any help to us unless we have a monopoly? And how do we set about preaching a message to humanity as a whole when people can only see things as a fight between Goodies and Baddies?

* * * * * * * *

Identity – Humanitarian action only starts when politicians are at their wits' end at not being able to reach political settlement. When that happens Europe and the United Nations usually fall back on humanitarian action. That's why humanitarian action is on a tremendous scale here and even includes a military component. It's armoured and if it's fired on it returns the fire. The first result for the ICRC is that it is no longer a spearhead organization. In present circumstances a convoy whose passage is opposed has to be armoured and you have to be ready to accept casualties. United Nations people get shot, the UN accepts the casualties, and that's that. I don't think the ICRC could do that. The UN has invented humanitarian aid backed by force, as opposed to humanitarian aid by consensus, and nowadays the spearhead organizations are the ones that practise humanitarian aid backed by force. Our way of humanitarian aid by consensus doesn't work, but I do think it will work in the long run, and that we should not change our way of doing things. The second result is that humanitarian action is unpopular with all the parties. The Serbs would like the West to be rather less in evidence, and the Bosnians would like to see a little more of it. Both of them share a hearty dislike of the West. Here you can see relief convoys being brought to a halt by mobs of civilians, you can see women and children you want to help stopping released prisoners from going on their way, certainly because they have been put up to it. We are operating in an environment where nothing that comes from abroad has ever been good news. That's what makes our work so difficult.

* * * * * * * *

Suffering (1991) – We have got rather too used to the sort of situation we find in Africa, where people are dying of starvation. Here in former Yugoslavia suffering is not a stage between life and death where ICRC action automatically saves lives. Nevertheless, when people suddenly find themselves homeless, they suffer intensely. And that suffering easily turns into violence!

The plight of displaced persons in this country is utterly unlike the hardships of exodus in much more fragile countries. Geographical proximity has amplified it. All the same I don't think Europeans suffer either less or more than anybody else. Human beings suffer in the same way but express their suffering in different ways. It depends on the culture they belong to.

* * * * * * * *

The visual image (1992) – When I saw the first ICRC convoys I thought I was watching a film written by Hemingway during the Spanish Civil War. They were made up of dingy old lorries emitting clouds of blue smoke. Most of them were hired and there were no flags. They were gradually replaced by other lorries. These had other problems but they were at least white with red crosses. Before then, you could pass an ICRC convoy without realizing it.

* * * * * * * *

The atmosphere (winter 1991–92) – The atmosphere was already pretty menacing then. It was winter, it was cold, and war in a cold climate makes more of an impression on you. But you don't feel it unless you are in the middle of the battle areas. It made me think of First World War stories, people in Paris making merry on champagne when a mere hundred kilometres away on the Marne soldiers were tearing each other's guts out. It has always struck me that in war the brutality is localized. First of all you are driving through a lovely, peaceful landscape; you can see a chap fishing from a boat, a little stream between the willows, children coming home from school and farmers getting in the harvest. Then all of a sudden, without warning, you see Stalingrad. The shock comes from contrast, and it leaves you pretty well shaken. Nearby life's normal again – lines of cars waiting at petrol stations. People are living right near the war, you don't know whether you can relax or whether you have to keep on your guard. It's unsettling.

* * * * * * * *

Hesitations – We said we would go back to Sarajevo only on condition that we were given a complete and convincing explanation of why the attack was made and that the persons responsible for it were named. That is what the official statement said. But we never had any reply. We could have tried going back there sooner, but we could hardly do so without knowing what we were going to do there and in what conditions, for meanwhile the international organizations had become extremely concerned about Sarajevo. ICRC headquarters were so shaken by the death of our colleague that they went on treating Sarajevo as very much a special case. If we had gone back there earlier on we should no doubt have been spared a lot of harsh criticism, but our return would also have constituted a kind of alibi intended to soothe public opinion and public opinion should not be soothed. For one of the perverse effects of humanitarian activities is that they make prickings of conscience slower in coming. That in itself is enough to put off any attempts to find a solution.

In October 1992, more than four months after the humanitarian convoy was attacked, a delegate said that the ICRC had committed an historical error in not returning to Sarajevo. It took us until February 1993 to get fully operational once again, with armoured vehicles and flak-proof waistcoats. The United Nations asked us to return. General MacKenzie gave us every guarantee that he would provide logistic support for the resumption of our activities in the capital. We were pressed to organize medical evacuations and resume visits to prisoners. We promised to come back very soon. But the decision was hard to take and late in coming, even though the security arguments in favour of resuming work at Sarajevo seemed to us to be good for all sorts of other regions where our delegates were active again. We went back to Sarajevo on tiptoe and started again from square one. The town had changed, we no longer had any offices or living accommodation, the old reference marks had vanished and we had to rebuild our network of contacts.

* * * * * * * *

Survival – In a single week we saw thousands of people. Our visits to the camps at Trnopolje, Omarska and Manjaca did not leave us unscathed. Even the experienced delegates, who had seen plenty of horrors, were overwhelmed. Were we more affected because the people we were seeing were Europeans, people like ourselves, or because the stories they told were beyond belief? A bit of both. In the evening, when we left the camps at Banja Luka, where a curfew was in force and there were frequent bursts of fire from automatic weapons, we had little reason to be pleased with ourselves. We kept going over our visit in our minds, seeing dozens and dozens of people who wanted only one thing: to speak, and talk about their experiences. And the best sort of therapy we could offer them was just to listen. In other circumstances we'd have put questions to them and asked for fuller details, but the urgent thing with these distressed people was to let them tell their tale without making them feel that they were being cross-examined.

I remember one day when we distributed cigarettes to nearly 4,000 prisoners. The camp guards made all the men lie flat on their stomachs on the ground (this was right at the beginning of the visits and blankets had not yet arrived). They were lying in lines, very close together, on dry fern fronds. We had to walk between the lines and put packets of cigarettes into the prisoners' hands, which were crossed behind their backs. Then they were allowed to sit up again and they thanked us by loudly applauding. It was extremely touching.

Some of the prisoners had no strength left. They wanted to die. Others still had a little spark of life left, and just not being ill any more and having a little more to eat since we arrived made them believe they would soon be set free. It was difficult to take down the names of all the prisoners. We lost track of some of them, either because they were transferred without our knowledge or had been exchanged under local arrangements. In other parts of the world, such as Sri Lanka, if a prisoner has his name on a list, he is safe. Not so in Bosnia-Herzegovina. Many things happened there without our knowledge, in spite of all our attempts to get the authorities to render us a proper account.

* * * * * * * *

Destitution – On the capture of Vukovar, thousands of people were evacuated by bus. I saw many of these families when they arrived at the hotel which put them up for a night or two. These old people reminded me so much of the region I come from, Friuli in northern Italy. They don't speak the same language, but they're like the people I grew up amongst. It's almost the same country, geographically speaking. When I saw these old people who had lost everything they possessed I thought of my own village, and I lacked the distance that protects us emotionally when dealing with people from a completely different origin. I could identify with their sufferings, and this made everything much harder to bear.

* * * * * * *

Frustration – Everything's happening very quickly and it changes all the time. We can't keep up with events. 'Ethnic cleansing' stops and starts again. They're making a thorough job of it. Whatever we do we can't protect people, and sometimes our being there puts them in even worse danger. At the end of 1992 the 'cleansing' slowed down only because the snow came. When the winter ended it started again, worse than ever.

* * * * * * *

Dilemma – I arrived at a turning point in the operation, at a time when neither the United Nations nor the ICRC had any wish to be seen or felt as taking part in anything connected with 'ethnic cleansing'. What I found in the field was total despair among the delegates who could do nothing to help people. They felt that to leave them in their villages was to condemn them to death and trying to protect them there would be useless. The only thing that seemed of any use was to help them to make for a safe place until some political arrangement enabled them to return. It seemed to us hypocrisy for the political negotiators to say that nothing should be done that might possibly encourage 'ethnic cleansing'. We saw only one way out – to help people to get away and at the same time denounce 'ethnic cleansing'.

* * * * * * *

Despondency – Mostar, autumn 1992: it's raining and everything is shrouded in grey. We have just shown two new delegates their offices, miserable ones in the basement of a high-rise building of working-class flats, surrounded by a protective wall of sandbags three metres high. Dreadful. The next day we went over to the old Muslim town, which was completely in ruins. This old town once contained monuments of immense historic value. Now they are all reduced to charred rubble. And yet people go on living in these half-burnt-out houses. The bank in the main street is burnt out and burned banknotes are scattered over much of the street. There must be tens of millions of dinars' worth of them. A little farther on, the conservatory of music is perched high up on a sort of promontory opposite what was once a very fine hotel. From the skeleton of this conservatory comes music; someone in there, heard but not seen, is playing the piano. It was too much for us. We were all in tears.

* * * * * * * *

Hatred in Sarajevo. The idea of hatred made me crazy because I knew that there was no possible way of eradicating it. Everyone around me, the people I know, the people in Sarajevo who have the same education as I, they too know that it cannot be stopped. It was no longer possible to do away with formulas like 'If you are pro-Muslim you're a fundamentalist' or 'If you are not anti-Serb you must be a "Chetnik"'.[1] I think former Yugoslavia was the ideal breeding ground for attitudes like these. It was a country that was neither altogether a part of the communist bloc nor of the western world. It was beginning to destroy itself bit by bit. It had to reach rock-bottom. It was easy to use the pretext of nationality, though for Bosnians born in the Sixties like ourselves, there had never been any question of nationality. But whoever fired the first shot probably never thought things would go so far. Now [March 1993] in Sarajevo everybody's fed up to the back teeth. After a year of living in conditions worthy of the Middle Ages, people don't care a damn whether the town is to be separated into two, or who's going to rule the country. All they want is for the fighting to stop. This is what everybody has been thinking since February 1993.

The only way to keep sane in Sarajevo is to work. I have seen so many people, especially the young ones and particularly the girls (most of the men have gone) just hanging about doing nothing, whilst the older people tried to find something to do around the house or went out to fetch water. The young people are crazy because they've got nothing to do. Their nerves are on edge. Whatever you say to them they'll go for you. If anybody had asked me a few years ago what I'd be most afraid of in war, I should have said being hungry or fighting. Now I say unhesitatingly: boredom. Here you spend your whole life in an area of 500 square metres. That's all. You die of boredom, it kills your mind. And I wonder how long we shall be able to hold out like this, mentally and physically. There were already cases of nervous breakdown in June 1992, and more a little later. I myself never saw a corpse in my life until May 1992, nor did I hear a shot fired until April. I hadn't the least idea how I'd react. Things have been all right so far, but I don't know when I shall break down. At the beginning of the war, every morning when I went to work, I didn't know until the evening where my mother was nor whether she was all right. Luckily I got her to leave the town. She left in the November 1992 convoy and she's now a refugee in Ljubljana. I couldn't stand the worry every day of having no news of her. It was getting me down.

* * * * * * * *

Solidarity in Sarajevo – It has always been a sort of institution at Sarajevo to keep on good terms with your neighbours. Anyone who has a neighbour has a family and that's another reason why nobody believed that this could happen to us. July and August 1992 was a very hard time. People no longer trusted each other. The worst off were the Serbs; nobody trusted them and everybody ignored them. Then people got used to living in these abnormal conditions and started doing things together again – preparing meals for example. Where there was one warm room they all came into it. They got together because they'd had enough of the war.

* * * * * * * *

CHAPTER 2

The Flame beneath the Embers

The *New York Times* of 28 November 1990 foretold the breakup of Yugoslavia,[1] which a United States government official expected to take place halfway through 1991. This opinion was shared at the time by many expert observers of Yugoslavia including Assistant Secretary of State Lawrence S. Eagleburger.

The pessimistic tone of this article was based largely on forecasts by the US Central Intelligence Agency (CIA). Public opinion took little notice of it but it was nevertheless justified. Two months before, there had been serious incidents between Serbs and Croats at Knin and tension was still high there:

> The roads are blocked, there are no more trains from Split to Zagreb via Knin, the communes set up in September in the self-styled 'Serbian autonomous region of Krajina' will not allow Croat police to enter their territory and the Croat police is attempting to set up police stations and affirm the authority of the republic wherever possible.[2]

Prior to this recent episode, and without going back to the dawn of history, the situation in Kosovo had for more than 20 years been a blueprint for the intercommunal clashes that later became the Yugoslav tragedy. The trouble started there with student riots in 1968, when the western universities were also a prey to agitation, and turned into crises of a more political flavour in the 1970s, and into serious disturbances immediately after the death, on 4 May 1980, of Tito. In the spring of 1981 the autonomous province of Kosovo was swept by riots in which according to the authorities 11 people were killed and 57 wounded, and according to local observers there were more than 200 victims.[3]

The situation in the province never again became stable but flared up worse than ever in February 1988, when the Kosovo mineworkers went on strike. On 18 November 1988 tens of thousands of the people of Kosovo of Albanian stock took to the streets of the capital, Pristina, in protest against the expulsion of two of their compatriots from the regional party leadership. This was the first 'Albanian' demonstration on such a scale since the disturbances of 1981. Twenty-four hours later, in Belgrade, more than a million

9

Serbs called upon their leaders to deal more firmly with the independence movements in their two autonomous provinces.

Since then there has been an uninterrupted series of incidents.
In March 1989 the Serbian parliament reformed the constitution
so as to reduce the autonomy of the two provinces of Kosovo and
Vojvodina. On 28 June, at an enormous nationalist demonstration,
a million Serbs commemorated the 600th anniversary of the Battle
of Kosovo Polje, the birthplace of modern Serbia, at the 'Field of
Blackbirds'. This demonstration was what Paul Garde calls 'the
crowning point of the Serbian reconquest of Kosovo'.[4] The break
between Belgrade and Pristina was completed on 2 July 1990 by
the proclamation of the separation of Kosovo from Serbia. The
Serbian authorities reacted immediately by suspending the
parliament and government of Kosovo.

Division, confrontation and arrests

Amid growing bitterness on both sides, the press was muzzled. The
only alternative to the tutelage practised by one party would
henceforth be the secessionist policies advocated by the other.

Since 1988 the International Committee of the Red Cross (ICRC)
had been seeking information on conditions in the province of
Kosovo. Little detailed trustworthy information was available. The
ICRC tried to cross-check information from various human rights
organizations and statements by the contending leaders. It appealed
to the Red Cross of Yugoslavia, which was invariably reticent and
inclined to play down the gravity of the situation. There were
reports that dissidents were being arrested, but no information as
to the scale of the arrests and the legal safeguards being granted.

It was not clear whether the ICRC could reasonably offer its
services by virtue of its universally recognized right of humanitarian initiative.

The ICRC realized that it had too little information to make a
realistic estimate of the number of political detainees in Yugoslavia.
Its study of the legal provisions in force in the Yugoslav penal federal
code was not reassuring as to the procedure being adopted, for the
legal wording was vague enough to allow widely differing interpretations. Available information on conditions of detention
suggested, to say the least, that they called for close supervision,
and that the situation was continuing to deteriorate.

Nevertheless, from a strictly legal viewpoint, the ICRC was not
in a position to offer its services in a way conforming to all the niceties
of established procedure. But neither could it run the risk of looking
on helplessly at demonstrations that would lead to even more
violent clashes and to loss of life. It therefore attempted to strengthen

its position, and to win the trust of its contacts both in the government and the opposition. It did so cautiously enough to leave any possible door ajar, its number one priority being to get access to the political prisoners. As far back as 1988, Cornelio Sommaruga, President of the ICRC, had had occasion to speak of the phenomenon of political detention, without eliciting any objection to that term from his official contacts in the Belgrade government. The ICRC was not, therefore, making a formal approach, but rather keeping up a dialogue of the greatest urgency on the subject.

Concurrently, the Council of Europe's Parliamentary Commission was conducting an exploratory mission whose agenda included getting into direct touch with the Kosovo dissidents. The Yugoslav authorities' official reception was icy, and the Council was accordingly unable to carry out its plan. When the delegation returned home the bad feeling blew up into a public scandal, leading to an international crisis on the subject of Kosovo that the Yugoslav federal government would willingly have done without. To improve its image it set up a human rights unit whose functions included escorting future missions of this kind.

In this context Francis Amar, the ICRC official responsible for the region, had a series of interviews in Belgrade with officials of the Ministry of Foreign Affairs, members of parliament, politicians, leaders of the Red Cross of Yugoslavia, and above all with the Minister of Justice. This last was a supremely important contact for the ICRC, which was determined to use a combination of favourable circumstances as a lever to exact the grant of permission to visit the prisons. There was soon no need to beat about the bush. Yes, said the authorities, we have about 300 political detainees serving sentences, for whom the Ministry of Justice is responsible. Yes, certainly you can see them. But on the other hand: No, we cannot allow you access to persons for whom the Ministry of the Interior or the Ministry of the Armed Forces is responsible, and who are in police custody for questioning or awaiting trial.

The ICRC delegate seized on this obvious opportunity for ICRC intervention in aid of the political detainees. At several subsequent sessions, he hammered out with his contacts the details of a tacit but firm agreement. In this the ICRC was taking a risk; it might have been preferable to get an even more explicit go-ahead, in writing. Advisable, no doubt, but in the delegate's opinion not essential; he thought the atmosphere was more suited to this informal type of co-operation. He took the risk.

Meanwhile, in the field, the most pessimistic forecasts were coming true; no armed clashes as yet, but constant internal disturbances confirmed by the analyses of early 1990, which were based on reliable information. There was now a permanent crisis. A state of emergency was proclaimed as early as February 1989. A series of strikes, demonstrations and violent clashes claimed many victims. The Serbian community was forming armed self-defence militias and arrests took place daily.

The first prison visits

At the beginning of March 1990 the ICRC delegates were poised for action. Within the next 12 weeks they visited all the places of detention run by the Ministry of Justice – 25 prisons at various locations in the six republics, containing 291 sentenced prisoners. As this was only a first series of visits it was important to get a speedy and overall idea of conditions of detention, so as to be able to make preliminary recommendations for their improvement to the authorities, if necessary.

The delegates got down to work. They split into two teams, each responsible for different destinations. As a matter of practical expediency, the detainees, nearly all of them political dissidents from the province of Kosovo, were distributed over the entire federal penitentiary system, so that many of them were in prison at great distances from their place of origin. Another difficulty was that because of the structure of the federal government the delegates had first to get clearance from the Ministry of Justice of each republic, so as to ensure procedures for the visit were approved. Belgrade having done its part, first contacts between the delegates and the prison authorities were good and the delegates were given a friendly reception. It was clearly in the interests of both parties that this should be so – in the interests of the ICRC to get on with its urgent humanitarian work, and in those of the Yugoslav authorities to give the impression that they were a government that respected human rights, keen to co-operate with a specialized, discreet, and therefore efficient institution.

In the course of their work the delegates became familiar with the geography of their territory. They scoured the country from end to end, discovering every day new problems of organization and logistics linked to the nature of the regions they were crossing. They also had to use interpreters who, to be acceptable both to the prisoners and to the party detaining them, had to be neither natives of Kosovo nor Serbian. Recruiting them was difficult and had to be done partly in Switzerland. These obstacles, once overcome, were a source of valuable information for future use; for the delegates could feel that the federal structure was breaking down; there was ethnic tension in Krajina; the Serbian minorities in Croatia felt unsafe, and Kosovo was permanently on the brink of an explosion.

An internal memorandum by Jean-François Berger, the official in charge of Yugoslav affairs in Geneva, reads:

The year 1990 was a major turning point in the development of the most complicated country in Europe. Politically speaking, the components of Yugoslavia have now all accomplished the first phase of the movement towards democracy by electing their own parliaments; all of them, that is, except Kosovo province, which boycotted the elections because it was refused essential guarantees. The results are decisive; they emphasize the profound differences within the Yugoslav entity.

The gap between north and south widened daily, the more developed north burning for independence and the south (Serbia and Montenegro) wanting the old centralized structure. It could not be long before the nationalism, the clash between the two sides, flared into open war. And it had yet to be seen what the federal army would do when this happened.

New symbols, those of the separate republics, were beginning to appear in the Yugoslav press. Rising politicians harangued their various electorates in frankly nationalist terms. But meanwhile distrust was growing between north and south, Slovenia and Croatia keeping their distance, Bosnia-Herzegovina and Macedonia still fairly quiet. In the words of a delegate: 'The smell of gunpowder grew stronger every day.'

1991: on the brink of war

Following the example of Krajina, which proclaimed itself an independent republic in September 1990, the Serbs of eastern Slavonia, who are numerous but in a minority within the communes, embarked upon an escalating series of disturbances at the beginning of 1991. These culminated on 2 March at Pakrac in clashes so violent that federal troops had to be called in. Both sides exploited the incident for propaganda purposes. As Paul Garde says, 'The Serbian leader Raskovic was talking about a declaration of war on the Serbian people and the beginning of a new genocide, and the Croat president Tudjman about a war of nerves against Croatia.'[5] But there were as yet no deaths. The first victims of this undeclared war were on 31 March at Plitvice.

The national park of Plitvice is situated mainly, as Paul Garde says

> on the territory of Titova Korenica, a commune in Krajina which has a large Serb majority. Part of the park is however in the commune of Slunj, where the majority is Croat. At the end of March an armed detachment of Serbian militiamen arrived at Slunj and took over the hotels and the management of the park in the name of the Government of Krajina. A strong force of Croat police arrived to expel them. The Serbs opened fire,

which was returned. The affray left three dead, two Serbs and one Croat.

Other observers and historians of Yugoslavia situate the turning point of disintegration as early as 9 March, when the Serbian opposition took to the streets to defy Milosevic. Jacques Rupnik holds this opinion. He describes the episode as 'a frantic resort to extremes of nationalism and violence in order to retain power'.[6] He goes on to say, 'the wave of nationalism – nationalism of one kind or another – spread from south to north ... and conversely the logic of war progressed from north to south'.

As a delegate noted in February 1991, 'Make no mistake about it, Belgrade and Zagreb are flexing their muscles, and the future of Yugoslavia will depend on the outcome.' In terms of international humanitarian law, even at the beginning of the year a strict legal assessment lagged far behind the likelihood that the tension between the two capitals would explode into violence. Rather than lose its grip on the situation, the ICRC had therefore to assume that the worst was going to happen, build up a fund of knowledge and trust in this new context as it had previously done for Kosovo, and make good use of the support it might derive from the ability of the Red Cross of Yugoslavia, and its sections in the various republics, to operate in open crisis.

The Red Cross of Yugoslavia, one and divisible

Secretary General Dr Rade Dubajic, of the Red Cross of Yugoslavia, regards 1991 and 1992 as the busiest for half a century, not excepting the Second World War years. 'We were prepared for an attack from outside,' he said, 'but nobody expected this.'

From the spring of 1991 onwards, as tension mounted and press campaigns became increasingly violent, it became clear that the Red Cross of Yugoslavia would have to make far-reaching changes in its outlook and working methods. It had hitherto been more used to playing the leading part at international meetings than to occupying what might be called the operational field. But even before it came round to this new way of thinking, the local Red Cross was in frequent touch with ICRC delegates both at federal level and at that of the various republics. It was indeed in the interests of them all to co-operate closely, except in the programme of visits to political prisoners, which the ICRC, as is customary, conducted alone.

The history of the International Red Cross and Red Crescent Movement will record the failures and successes, the stubbornness and flexibility, the friction and the strokes of good fortune that marked this crucial period for a National Society which found itself the mirror of the altercations between the republics. The ICRC did what it could to help the National Society by encouraging a constructive approach in those willing to think and lend their services. That was not always easy – when the most vital contacts on Kosovo were taking place relations between one institution and another were strained and there was little room for manoeuvre. There was more readiness to talk as the situation got worse and the depressing evidence of this accumulated. Red Cross leaders got together on essentials when they had no other choice.

This indeed was what the President of the ICRC was expecting when on 10 May 1991 he sent his 'message to the Presidency of the Red Cross of Yugoslavia'. By anticipating events in this way the ICRC, knowing that it was going to need the fullest co-operation when war broke out, appealed to the sense of commitment and responsibility of a humanitarian organization faced with a growing danger. What was also at stake was the survival of a Red Cross Society torn between the devil and the deep blue sea by the heart-rending divisions likely to take place in its country. To say so was not to act as a prophet of woe.

The ICRC never ceased to repeat this message, especially at its information seminars in Belgrade in June, so as to strengthen the sense of sharing ideals and belonging to a movement, that came into being through war. A delegate reported that at the beginning of these seminars Red Cross representatives from all the regions and republics of Yugoslavia indulged in some verbal sparring:

> They were all trying just a bit to take the wind out of each other's sails, the atmosphere was strained but it was also intense. They all danced together in the evening and played folk music. The ambience was good, but there was a bit of a feeling that the end of the world was coming, and that this was the end of the Yugoslav dream.

These two seminars took place after a preliminary experiment in co-operation, carried out impromptu between 15 and 18 May, when a joint evaluation mission by the ICRC and representatives of the Yugoslav as well as the local Croat Red Cross Societies entered the two most difficult regions at that time, Krajina and Slavonia. Thierry Germond, the ICRC Delegate General for Europe, took part in the journey. He reported during a phone call on 16 May that

> in Knin (where it is snowing) tension is at its peak and is maintained by the deployment of the various armed forces and militias. It would only need a spark to blow everything sky high … Wherever this delegation goes, it makes important contacts

which show what a good thing it is for the Red Cross to be here, out in the field, at this crucial moment in Yugoslav history.

At that moment, he said, everyone he talked to, whatever his or her loyalties, was extremely anxious for the various communities to become more close-knit. This heralded the subsequent regrouping, voluntary or otherwise, in the ethnic groups. During this mission, there was friction between representatives of local Red Cross Societies which showed more plainly than ever how necessary it was to train a united group of officials who could cope with the unexpected, whilst respecting humanitarian principles and steering clear of political advantage.

These efforts towards reconciliation did much to improve relations between the ICRC and local Red Cross branches in all sectors connected, even remotely, with operations in the field. The seminars revealed a number of principles that might be used to improve Red Cross ability to intervene. Thus it was agreed to form mixed mobile teams, with all the necessary logistic and other equipment, to help any community however composed. At the end of June the Red Cross of Yugoslavia was to make a list in order of priority of the areas most needing its attention. That was the plan of action – only hours before hostilities broke out between Slovenia and the Yugoslav armed forces.

The ten days' war

On 21 May 1991 the ICRC delegates were engaged in the second round of visits to political prisoners. They had managed to get their contacts in the Ministry of Justice to agree that ICRC access to the prisoners, hitherto restricted to those who had been sentenced, should be extended to all categories of persons detained in connection with the events in Kosovo, that is, untried prisoners, including those in police custody. Since the first round of visits in 1990, more than 200 political detainees had been amnestied and others were about to be released. The number of persons seen by ICRC delegates between 21 May and 18 July 1991 in 14 places of detention was accordingly only 64, 58 of whom had been seen in the previous round of visits.

Whilst the delegates were continuing their journeys from one place of detention to another in the various republics, events were coming to a head. On 25 June 1991, Slovenia and Croatia proclaimed their independence, which was to become effective on 26 June. The Yugoslav federal government rejected these proclamations. The federal forces stationed in Slovenia were put on the alert, took up positions along the frontiers with Italy, Austria and Hungary and sealed off Slovene air space. On 27 June 1991, clashes left 40 dead and several dozen wounded. They continued until the following evening, when a cease-fire came into operation. On the same day the European Community 'Troïka' (the Ministers of Foreign Affairs of Luxembourg, Italy and the Netherlands[7]) negotiated a compromise with Croatia and Slovenia whereby both states were to suspend their declaration of independence for three months. It also insisted that the federal troops should return to barracks and then leave Slovene territory, and asked that the Croat Stipe Mesic should take up his duties as President of Yugoslavia. He should have done so in May, and this unfortunate delay had set the war machine racing.

A message from the Slovene Red Cross arrived in Geneva on 28 June 1991, stating that humanitarian work had begun and recording the first steps taken. ICRC delegates at their posts in Yugoslavia were ready to start operations. Having received the green light from headquarters, they organized a journey from Belgrade to Ljubljana for the next day, in liaison with the Red Cross of Yugoslavia, which was to take part in the expedition. There were many checkpoints on the way and the Belgrade number plates on the vehicle belonging to the national Red Cross drew hostile comment when crossing the Slovene lines. At one of the checkpoints, that vehicle was even searched from top to bottom and its passengers were kept covered by firearms, under the interested gaze of many journalists. The incident passed off without further complications.

Once the convoy was met by Slovene Red Cross representatives, both parties together drew up a list of priorities. The ICRC was to concentrate on prisoners and deserters. The local and federal Red Cross organizations undertook to compile lists of the persons arrested and conduct programmes of assistance to hospitals and the needy population.

Some commentators have called this 'little' war in Slovenia, with its ten days of fighting, 40 victims and 2,000 attendant journalists, a musical-comedy war. For all those involved, and for the ICRC, it posed real problems and nobody knew at the time how long it would last. The delegates' approach to it depended on two factors. The first was how to act in what the Slovenes (who claimed to be exercising national sovereignty) regarded as an international war and the federal authorities as an internal armed conflict. The second was how to resist the counter-productive and indeed pernicious effects of the propaganda of all kinds that underlay official decisions and statements on either side of the fence and did not spare the Red Cross, now embroiled in events.

The interest shown by the international press in this conflict was mainly due to the historical fact that this was the first war in this region in the post-communist era. The ethnic question did not arise because the Slovene population was particularly homogeneous. This also explains Belgrade's fairly moderate reaction; it did not feel called upon to rush to the assistance of a threatened Serb minority, because there was practically no such thing on the territory of the republic.

For the local media the situation was different. All the features of daily life in this conflict were potential material for a propaganda campaign. So much so that delegates visiting their official contacts had to insist emphatically that prisoners should be protected from public curiosity and should not be exploited to feed press campaigns. This message was fairly well received until the official Yugoslav news agency TANJUG published, for confidential use, all the names of prisoners transmitted by the Red Cross of Yugoslavia to the authorities in Belgrade. Previously, the otherwise highly efficient Slovene Red Cross had also taken the well-intentioned but unfortunate step of informing the families of prisoners through the press.

Another episode made much of by the media is the so-called 'Mothers' Popular Movement'. From 3 July 1991 onwards (when the first releases of prisoners were being prepared, priority being given to the rank and file) a widespread movement for the defence of the family sprang up in all the republics whose nationals had been captured or belonged to the contingent of the Yugoslav federal army based in Slovenia. There were many such prisoners, reportedly between 2,000 and 3,000, but their exact number never became known because of the short time between their arrest and release. Thousands of people converged on Ljubljana by rail and road. The Red Cross Societies in the republics were under extreme pressure to help organize these highly symbolic journeys by mothers coming to rescue their sons from Slovene barracks. A great deal of passion, emotion and hustle was expended in this spontaneous operation, from which the Red Cross finally emerged in creditable fashion. The press gave ample coverage to the scenes of reunion and there were no disagreeable incidents, only a very typical Balkan confusion. Some commentators even saw this, a mass movement originating in the family unit, as achieving more than its primary objective (to prevent young men from getting killed in a war that the great majority of the population did not want) and becoming a decisive element in settling the conflict.

Throughout the ICRC's prison visits its relations with the detaining authorities were extremely cordial and this made its work much easier. For the ICRC had to be both quick and flexible. Feeling ran high on both sides as to how the conflict, and therefore the prisoners taken in it, should be classified. From the legal point of view, this was undoubtedly an armed conflict between two armed forces, but what sort of conflict? If it were an international conflict as the Slovenes maintained, the members of the armed forces arrested were prisoners of war according to the Third Geneva

Convention (whose main provisions were, as the delegates were able to check, posted up in all places administered by the Slovene authorities). But some members of the federal army, especially officers, felt humiliated at being classed as prisoners of war in their own country, and threatened to go on hunger strike.

But Slovenia had not signed the Geneva Conventions, nor could it sign them, because it was not yet recognized as a state. On the other hand, as a people claiming the right to self-determination it could at least invoke Additional Protocol I, which provides that a population under alien occupation may have recourse to these provisions, but in the case in point it was out of the question to plead that this was an international conflict. The ICRC could not be obliged to express any opinion on the proclamation of independence, which is a political act, and it took care to protect its capacity for humanitarian intervention by maintaining a neutral profile.

Since the Yugoslav federal state was the only body possessing international legal status, everything turned on whether its existence was disputed by one of the parties to the Federation, in which case Protocol II additional to the Geneva Conventions, intended to cover non-international armed conflicts, applied because Yugoslavia had ratified it. Detailed examination of the conditions in which this Protocol was applicable to the Slovene situation showed that all the conditions of the Protocol were fulfilled, including the existence of clashes between armed groups under responsible command, and control over part of the territory.

In the interests of efficiency, the ICRC avoided entering into any arguments as to the kind of conflict that was taking place. It confined itself to a general reference to international humanitarian law and to urging that the parties should agree to allow everything possible to be done for the protection of victims of the conflict. It is true that its public appeal of 2 July 1991 (see below) did not fully state this position, as it talked of clashes without even using the term 'armed conflict'. Here and as usual the ICRC was too cautious in its wording.

The Brioni Declaration negotiated by the European Community's Ministerial Troïka sets out the procedures for the maintenance of the cease-fire and the eventual end of hostilities (see Appendix, Document I). It includes the question of prisoners, stating that they shall be unconditionally released no later than 8 July 1991, and that the parties to the conflict shall co-operate with the ICRC for that purpose. Both conditions were fulfilled.

The steps taken to cope with the humanitarian consequences of the Slovene conflict proved sufficient, partly because of the great help given by local Red Cross Societies. Things were to be very different in the major crises that were already building up further south. The scale of these, and the impossibility of ever reducing them, were all too often to make humanitarian action not only inadequate but irrelevant.

ICRC APPEAL FOR THE RESPECT OF INTERNATIONAL HUMANITARIAN LAW IN YUGOSLAVIA

The International Committee of the Red Cross (ICRC) is deeply concerned about the gravity of the situation in Yugoslavia and its consequences in humanitarian terms.

The ICRC calls on all the parties to respect international humanitarian law and to ensure that it is respected by everyone involved in the fighting.

The civilian population and people must not be attacked and must be protected from any act of violence. Persons captured must be treated humanely and the wounded and sick must be cared for in all circumstances.

The ICRC urges all parties to respect the protective Red Cross emblem so that those displaying it in the course of their humanitarian activities can do their work safely and without constraint of any kind. Misuse of the emblem is prohibited under international humanitarian law.

The ICRC also trusts that the parties concerned will continue to grant its representatives and those of the Red Cross of Yugoslavia and of the Republics the facilities required to enable the Red Cross to bring assistance to all victims of the clashes.

CHAPTER 3

Summits of Disillusion

Make-believe diplomacy

When the time comes for historians to study the role of diplomacy in the conflicts of former Yugoslavia in the 1990s, they will notice that never in the course of recent decades have dialogue and negotiation, with all their attendant formal agreements and undertakings, been so intense over so short a time. UN bodies, European political institutions, regional organizations, humanitarian agencies and *ad hoc* commissions debated, drew up by consensus, commented on and explained resolutions and recommendations containing constructive, or supposedly constructive, proposals. Enemy met enemy, and belligerents who had been placed outside the pale of world society sat in the highest assemblies. Never was the dialogue interrupted. This perfect harmony seemed almost miraculous. After more than two years of uninterrupted fighting the miracle had still not taken place.

'How much longer are we going to go on talking whilst the massacre goes on?' asked Jan Krauze in *Le Monde*.[1] He is echoed by the authoritative voice of Mr Kozyrev, Russian Minister of Foreign Affairs, who said 'We have been discussing a settlement in the Near East for the last 45 years. Resolution 242 is not a girl any more, but a woman in her prime.' This suggests a mixture of patience and resignation at the difficulty of settling the major crises of our time. For example, nearly 20 years on, the Cypriot conflict and its so-called solutions showed that the agreement painfully concluded after the battle was by no means equivalent to a legal settlement of the crisis that led two communities to go to war with little hope of reconciliation.

Everything happened as if, whilst diplomacy took its course, all the parties (including the Europeans, who are the people most concerned) were bent on leaving for posterity indelible traces of their stubborn fight for peace – like the shining trace of silvery slime left by a snail on a stone after a stormy night.

Cries of 'Agreed!' – two harsh and peremptory syllables – were to punctuate the entire conflict. Already way back in 1991, the belligerents promptly accepted the negotiators' proposals. They 'Agreed' to raise the blockade of the barracks, 'Agreed' to release the prisoners, 'Agreed' that displaced persons should return to their regions of origin, 'Agreed' on convoys to besieged towns – without anything very much ever happening. Everyone played for time by exchanging memoranda and protocols, whilst the humanitarian workers whom the politicians were urging to go to the front were trying to put a brake on the horrors there.

As Véronique Soulé wrote in *Libération* on 27 April 1993, 'the two great weaknesses of international action have been improvisation and an extraordinary lack of imagination. From the very beginning the West seems to have had no political plan, no idea what to suggest on the breakup of Yugoslavia.' However deeply involved the negotiators were, their hesitation waltz[2] was a foretaste of the drift that later led governments to adopt the makeshift solution of humanitarian convoys rather than risk the dreaded break-off of negotiations.

Jacques Freymond, an historian of contemporary international relations and former Director of the Graduate Institute of International Studies of Geneva, is also an expert, for he was Vice-President of the International Committee of the Red Cross (ICRC) at the time of the Nigeria/Biafra civil war and the Black September crisis of 1970, which came within an inch of setting all the Near East aflame. He was one of the first to point out the danger of allowing politicians to devote their energies to humanitarian work instead of to politics. On this he commented: 'When Mitterand leaves Lisbon for Sarajevo [on 28 June 1992] he is doing the ICRC's work, whereas his proper job should have been to bring about conditions in which the ICRC could do its work. It is impossible to run a humanitarian policy in conditions of anarchy.'[3]

Looking at the various stages of international involvement in the Yugoslav crisis, one wonders how much of it was due to confusion and how much to abandoning responsibilities freely undertaken. The western world had effective machinery to protect it from the Cold War. It was left alone and naked when dogmatic communism collapsed, and that finely tuned machinery gradually seized up through individual indifference and collective neglect, leaving the field open to warlords practising banditry on a grand scale rather than the art of war as Clausewitz describes it. The gap between the statements of politicians and diplomats and conditions in the field widened as the value of humanitarian action depreciated. Thierry Germond, the ICRC's Delegate General for Europe, is convinced that the ICRC retained the initiative in its own field of action throughout the first conflict and until the summer of 1992, and then suffered an extremely paralysing and frustrating loss of autonomy due to the growing interference of politicians who first appropriated and then misused humanitarian vocabulary and methods.

Advantage Europe

The epilogue of the Slovene war was recited at Brioni, an island town in the south of Istria province. At the invitation of the Yugoslav government, the European Troïka, then composed of the Ministers of Foreign Affairs of the Netherlands (whose turn it had been since 1 July 1991 to fill the Presidency of the European Community), Luxembourg and Portugal, bent all its efforts to preparing a declaration fixing the conditions for a peaceful settlement. Apart from the implementation of a cease-fire, this text gave the European mediators greater powers regarding the future of the Yugoslav Federation by providing that a mission of between 30 and 50 European observers should be deployed to ensure the application of the Brioni Agreement of·7 July 1991 (see Appendix, Document I). It coincided with the suspension for three months of the declarations of independence of the Croat and Slovene republics, a proposal that undeniably provoked further tension by imposing a deadline and was a wait-and-see political gesture likely to postpone settlement of the conflict to a later date.

Concurrently, the European mediators proposed to set up several technical committees including the arbitration commission (the Badinter Commission) composed of five presidents of constitutional courts, which would be concerned mainly with Yugoslavia's internal and international frontiers and the protection of minorities.

The ICRC regarded the Brioni Agreement as the final stage of its direct involvement in the Slovene conflict, since it stipulated that all prisoners were to be released without delay and with its co-operation. This is what happened for the great majority of the persons still detained, but with difficulties on either side and mutual accusations that the agreement was not being respected, especially as regards the release of officers. The ICRC kept up its presence in Ljubljana until August 1992, which it used as a rear base and to support its work caused by the fighting, which had meanwhile spread to Croatia and then to Bosnia-Herzegovina.

Whilst the European observers were confined to Slovene territory, events were moving fast in Croatia. At their meeting on 29 July 1991, the ministers of the twelve states composing the European Community discussed the question of internal frontiers and declared them to be 'as inviolable as international frontiers'.[4] This was a useful precaution, as Cornelio Sommaruga confirmed in these words:

> Anybody acquainted with the old Yugoslavia knew exactly that the frontiers between the republics were an absolute reality. When you were talking to a federal representative, the first question that you had to have in your mind was whether he was a Slovene, a Serb, a Croat, a Bosnian or a Macedonian, and to vary your

conversation accordingly. Those national distinctions were already there.

Until the conference on Yugoslavia chaired by Lord Carrington, the ICRC found difficulty in establishing liaison with the European Community. As President Sommaruga said with regret:

> The dialogue we should have liked to have at the political level of the Presidency of the Community never took place. I don't know how many times I tried to see the Netherlands Minister for Foreign Affairs but was never able to! But Germond managed to meet Lord Carrington, which was important at the time.

The twelve ministers held many meetings. They sent many missions into the field and made many declarations such as that of 27 August (mentioned by Henry Wynaendts[5]), which proclaimed that

> it could no longer be denied that elements (the ministers went no farther than 'elements') of the Yugoslav national army were actively intervening on the side of the Serbs, but that the European Community and its member States would never accept a policy based on the *fait accompli*. They were, so they declared, determined not to recognize changes in frontiers brought about by force.

They took infinite pains, through negotiators, to find a compromise for the deployment of observers in Croatia, where the situation continued to get worse. Regular artillery bombardments began on Vukovar in Slavonia, and only ended three months later, on 18 November 1991, when that town fell. The people of Osijek spent their nights in shelters, and the future was uncertain for the Hungarian minority in Vojvodina. In regions where there was fighting every day, tens of thousands, and later hundreds of thousands, of the inhabitants were fleeing to safer areas. Fighting had also flared up in Krajina. War, even though undeclared because it was still an internal war, was no longer merely a threat but a reality. Prisoners were taken who, as was usual in this conflict, were often released, exchanged or bartered only a few days after capture, rather than at the end of hostilities and in the presence of the ICRC, as current practice requires.

On 1 September 1991, the European negotiators, led by Hans Van den Broek, Netherlands Minister of Foreign Affairs, succeeded in getting the Yugoslav Federal Presidency and the representatives of the six republics to initial an agreement, mainly for a cease-fire, which, if it proved to hold, would open the door to the introduction of European observers into Croat territory. The failure of the 14 cease-fire agreements concluded under Community auspices makes it easier to understand the difficulties that had to be overcome before observers could be sent into the territory, but this was finally and arduously achieved during September.

Like the ICRC delegates, the European observers soon had to look to their own safety. One incident after another took place, some of them serious, varying from crude threats to anti-aircraft fire against a helicopter used by European Commission observers (on 6 September). Already in July and August 1991, the ICRC, co-operating closely with local Red Cross Societies and the Red Cross of Yugoslavia, was faced with dangerous working conditions in regions where cease-fire agreements were not respected, armed elements were making improper use of the Red Cross emblem, and ICRC principles were in general unknown. This is what decided the delegates to launch a large-scale information campaign in the national media jointly with the Red Cross of Yugoslavia. This began on 17 August 1991 with articles, discussions, posters and videos illustrating humanitarian methods and aims. At the same time, Geneva's appeals that international humanitarian law should be respected became more and more pressing, especially as ICRC delegates were increasingly present and active in the republics (see map). On 22 August a first appeal for funds (still a modest one, only 7.8 million Swiss francs) was made to finance programmes of assistance to displaced persons (of whom there were already 100,000 by mid-August), supplies to hospitals, visits to prisoners and material support for the local Red Cross, which was coming under increasing strain.

Before leaving for Ljubljana, Belgrade and Zagreb, where he stayed from 1–5 September, Jean de Courten, Director of Operations, informed the Executive Council of the ICRC that he was extremely worried about the volatile situation in the field. He quoted delegates' reports that all the belligerents were attempting to politicize and take the credit for Red Cross activities, as well as publicly casting unjustified aspersions on ICRC impartiality. This attitude, already serious in itself and considered as unacceptable, was all the more dangerous since it sowed doubt and questioning in people's minds, especially in the minds of the combatants delegates were meeting every day in their travels. It was making it more difficult for them to cross the firing lines, and delegates reported a general worsening of safety conditions.

To emphasize the importance of this mission by the Director of Operations, on 30 August President Sommaruga wrote an identical letter to President Franjo Tudjman of Croatia, President Milan Kucan of Slovenia, President Slobodan Milosevic of Serbia, and President Mesic for the Yugoslav Federation. It invited them to shoulder their responsibilities and observe their international under-takings to respect international humanitarian law and cause it to

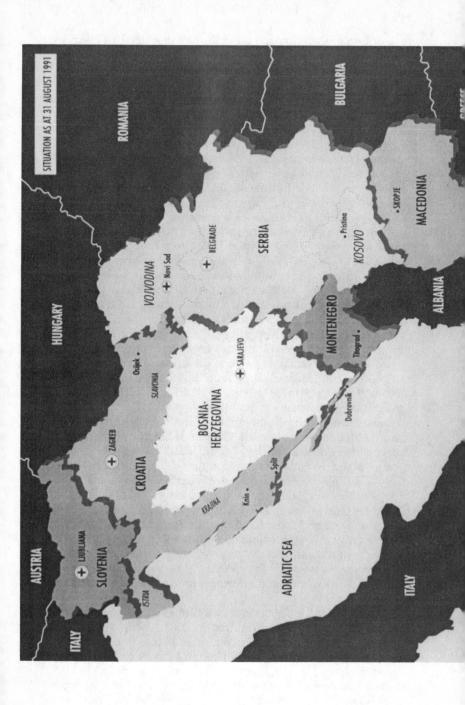

SITUATION AS AT 31 AUGUST 1991

be respected (see Appendix, Document II). Jean de Courten and Thierry Germond, who was accompanying him, had no difficulty in seeing Presidents Kucan, Mesic and Tudjman, but President Milosevic of Serbia would not himself see them and deputed his Prime Minister to do so. In this way, Milosevic maintained the official position that Serbia was not a party to the conflict and did not feel obliged to hear what the ICRC wanted to tell him. The interview with his minister 'in charge of Serbians abroad' nevertheless shows that even if not formally involved, Serbia was not unaffected by events. At their meetings with the Yugoslav and republican Red Cross Societies, the two ICRC officials had to listen to statements of policy much like those of official circles, but all these Red Cross Societies, whatever their ideological differences, were well motivated for emergency action.

The steadily worsening situation in the field convinced the European negotiators that they could not go on chalking up breaches of cease-fire agreements and that it was high time for more effective diplomatic action. In this atmosphere the peace conference on Yugoslavia opened at The Hague on 7 September 1991, the first session lasting five days. It was chaired by Lord Carrington, who thereby became responsible for European mediation and chaired its subsequent meetings until the London Conference took over in a different form. At its first meeting the European Arbitration Commission was formally constituted and its chairman, Robert Badinter, was admitted to serve as such in the Conference. All the parties to the conflict were present at the establishment of a dialogue which was to be a permanent one.

Enter the United Nations

At its 3009th session, held in New York on 25 September 1991, the United Nations Security Council adopted Resolution 713 supporting the European Community's past and future efforts and deciding, under Chapter VII of the Charter of the United Nations, to impose an embargo on deliveries of weapons and military equipment to Yugoslavia.

This was the first of a long series of resolutions adopted at intervals throughout the conflict in former Yugoslavia, in which the small, medium and great world powers, hiding behind the screen of the 'international community', 'condemned', 'reproved', 'reaffirmed', 'strongly urged', 'called upon', 'demanded' and 'decided'.

Opposite Situation as at 31 August 1991

It was also Europe's first admission that it was powerless to get results. Until then it had merely kept the United Nations Secretary General informed of its endeavours and their outcome, as on 7 August after an inconclusive mission by the Troïka, whose hopes of a negotiated peace were fast fading.

Meanwhile in Belgrade, Thierry Meyrat, the ICRC's head of mission, had become convinced that there was room for humanitarian initiative and that they should seize the opportunity of stepping up action in the field. He was all the more sure of this because his regular contacts with government ministries had convinced him that this was what the political and military leaders were expecting. There was one particularly urgent case, that of the federal army's barracks, surrounded in what had become enemy territory, and the thorny question of deserters from that army, of whom there were many because of the gloomy prospects opened by intercommunity clashes. The federal defence minister even suggested that a tripartite forum should be set up to discuss humanitarian work as a whole with the Croat authorities and in the presence of the ICRC. Pierre-André Conod, Meyrat's colleague in Zagreb, was instructed to transmit this proposal to his contacts among the Croat authorities. Dialogue of this kind was a foretaste of the Tripartite Commission formed in the following month to deal with the matter of prisoners and make agreements for their release. It also paved the way for a later development, the 'meetings of plenipotentiaries' which from November 1991 onwards punctuated the ICRC's diplomatic and humanitarian efforts with varying success.

In spite of Resolution 713, the United Nations was slow to commit itself. It did so to some extent in November 1991, when the Secretary-General mandated the office of the United Nations High Commissioner for Refugees (UNHCR) to assist displaced persons. José-Maria Mendiluce was appointed special representative for humanitarian action in Yugoslavia in December. The United Nations also prepared itself through the frequent missions of Cyrus Vance between 8 October 1991, when he was appointed the Secretary-General's personal envoy, and 10 December, when Javier Perez de Cuellar submitted the resulting report to the Security Council. But the United Nations (especially the UNHCR which was responsible for UN co-ordination in the field) never really got going until April 1992, even though the UNHCR first appealed for funds in November 1991. There were several causes for this prudent approach by the United Nations: it had to respect its own cumbrous procedure; it wanted to leave the Europeans to take the initiative on their own continent, and it needed to observe the nature and extent of the changes then taking place in Belgrade where, according to an ICRC delegate on mission there, 'the federal government is breaking up, and in the corridors of power here you get the feeling that it is holding its own farewell party in confusion and distress'.

The EC and the ICRC go it together

Despite incomplete information and political uncertainty, priorities in the field were being conditioned by major events. Dubrovnik had been besieged since 1 October. The federal barracks were still being blockaded by the Croat forces who, since the proclamation of the UN embargo on weapons and military equipment bound for Yugoslavia, were keen on getting hold of the heavy weapons there.

And the expiry on 7 October of the moratorium on the reaffirmation of the independence of the Slovene and Croat republics created not only tension among their enemies and in the federal army, but also strained relations between European partners who were either for or against speedy recognition of these future states.

On the spot, ICRC and European Community representatives were trying, with some difficulty, to harmonize their activities, which sometimes overlapped on identical terrains of intervention and had different aims and working methods. On a mission to Brussels on 8 and 9 October 1991, the President of the ICRC, who was accompanied by Paul Grossrieder, Deputy Director of Operations, was given an assurance that the embargo on Yugoslavia imposed by Security Council Resolution 713 of 25 September would not affect humanitarian aid. That assurance was backed by a gift of one million ECUs (the second of such gifts since the action started). But this demonstration of the European Community's generosity left a slightly bitter taste behind it. Was this not using humanitarian assistance to make up for the most crying needs caused by the embargo, a political decision that would inevitably harm civilian standards of living more than the military performance it was intended to weaken? This doubt persisted and grew as the months went by, although it has to be admitted that the embargo on arms and equipment for Yugoslavia was at least an attempt to contain the conflict. Nevertheless, lacking sufficiently coercive measures to ensure that the embargo was effective, things went from bad to worse. The misgivings of humanitarian aid workers steadily grew as they saw that the international community was washing its hands of the whole matter, but salving its conscience by offering a reassuring umbrella of humanitarian assistance to camouflage its utter inability to stop the war.

European observers in white uniforms appeared on the field and on the media. There was an unwelcome climax on 18 October, when they were escorting a convoy organized by *Médecins sans*

Frontières (MSF, known in English as 'Doctors without Borders') which was evacuating sick and wounded persons from Vukovar. An anti-tank mine, deliberately planted on the road which by negotiated agreement the humanitarian convoy was to use, exploded under one vehicle, seriously wounding two nurses. This was a dramatic pointer to the ambiguous character of humanitarian convoys under military escort. Furthermore, access to the besieged town was part of a package deal negotiated by the European Community, which included the simultaneous opening of the federal barracks in Zagreb and free exit of its garrison. This complicated approach, combining purely humanitarian objectives (assistance to the people of Vukovar) with political-cum-military objectives (evacuating the barracks in Zagreb) inevitably led to mistrust between the belligerents and to these terrible consequences. This precedent seriously alarmed ICRC delegates and top officials. It showed that humanitarian principles were weakening and that properly contracted agreements were not worth the paper they were written on. MSF agreed. They were furious and ruled out any possibility of undertaking similar action in the near future. As for the EC observers, they were sent a reminder from Brussels that their instructions were to monitor observance of the cease-fire, but to avoid becoming involved in prison visits or assistance activities.

A few days later, the delegates stationed in Zagreb submitted to the federal army and the Croat Ministry of Defence a memorandum setting out the conditions for the simultaneous release of all prisoners on either side and the role that the ICRC could play in this operation. This text (see below), dated 24 October, was in deference to the wishes expressed by the parties to the conflict, both of whom were anxious to set free large numbers of prisoners as soon as possible. Two days earlier, the Tripartite Commission on the prisoners held its first meeting with representatives of the Croat Ministry of Defence, representatives of the federal army, and European observers.

On 28 October, from Vienna – the seat of the commission for migration, refugees and demography of the Parliamentary Assembly of the Council of Europe – an appeal was launched that the work of humanitarian organizations in aid of displaced persons should not be hindered in any way. Population movements away from the fighting had greatly increased (they numbered 370,000 at the end of October) and the commission expressed its 'consternation at the powerlessness of the European countries to prevent a war that should have been avoided'.

The plight of displaced persons and prisoners was high on the agenda of the meetings between the European Community and the ICRC which took place on 31 October and 1 November in The

MEMORANDUM

The ICRC has been informed by representatives of the JNA and of the Ministry of Defence of the Republic of Croatia of their common willingness to release and return all the prisoners captured during the present armed conflict, regardless of the number each party is holding.

The ICRC welcomes this initiative and is pleased to note that both parties have requested its help in implementing the process, in conformity with international humanitarian law.

In reply to this request, the ICRC confirms its readiness to act as a neutral intermediary for the release and return of the prisoners, within the framework of its mandate.

The ICRC hereby wishes to submit to both parties the basic principles which govern its participation in such operations.

The principles are the following:

(a)   the ICRC must be given lists of all prisoners held by both parties, including their places of detention;

(b) the prisoners must be registered and visited by the ICRC in accordance with its specific criteria;

(c) the list of the prisoners registered by the ICRC must be regarded as authoritative;

(d) no prisoner must be returned against his will, and each prisoner must be free to express his wishes to the ICRC;

(e) no pressure may be brought to bear on prisoners with a view to persuading them to refuse or agree to their return;

(f) no reprisals shall be taken by the parties against prisoners refusing to return, or against their families;

(g) the ICRC reserves the right to withdraw its services at any stage should it appear that the process is no longer serving the interests of the prisoners to be released and returned.

Furthermore, the ICRC would like to state that it is ready to gather information from official sources concerning missing persons and to arrange for the return of the mortal remains of those killed in action.

Hague, and were attended by Thierry Germond, the ICRC's Delegate General for Europe. There was an urgent need to redefine respective responsibilities in the field, and improve the quality of dialogue with the bodies established since the opening of the Conference on Yugoslavia. A highly interesting conversation between Germond and Lord Carrington, the president in office of the conference, emphasized their preoccupations. It took place in London at Christie's, the art auctioneers, of which Lord Carrington is director. It was concerned mainly with the ability of humanitarian organizations to work and have access to victims, and with ensuring

---

STATEMENT
ON RESPECT OF HUMANITARIAN PRINCIPLES

We, the undersigned,

undertake to respect and ensure respect of international humanitarian law and remind all fighting units of their obligation to apply the following fundamental principles:

- wounded and ill persons must be helped and protected in all circumstances,

- all arrested persons, and notably combatants who have surrendered, must be treated with humanity,

- all detaining authorities must ensure the protection of the prisoners,

- the civilian population and civilian property must not be attacked,

- the Red Cross emblem must be respected. It may be used only to designate sanitary troops or buildings as well as persons and vehicles belonging to this service,

- all Red Cross personnel and medical personnel assisting civilian populations and persons *hors de combat* must be granted the necessary freedom of movement to achieve their tasks,

- unconditional support for the action of the ICRC in favour of the victims;

support unreservedly the humanitarian action of the Red Cross and in particular of the International Committee of the Red Cross (ICRC).

---

respect for formal undertakings entered into by the belligerents. There was already a yawning gulf between the content of the cease-fire and other agreements signed, and conditions in the field. Lord Carrington did not try to hide his disillusionment which, although couched in terms of understatement, was plain to Thierry Germond, who was well aware of all the difficulties and frustrations experienced by his delegates.

Three days later, as an echo to Lord Carrington's disenchanted remarks, encouraging though they were for the ICRC, the Yugoslav leaders of the six republics signed a declaration on the respect of humanitarian principles (see opposite) as the ICRC had long hoped they would. Unfortunately little or nothing came of this 'Beginner's Guide to Humanitarian Behaviour'.

When the declaration was issued, the ICRC obtained a previously negotiated agreement on the exchange of prisoners from Ivan Milas, Croat Vice-Minister for Defence, and General Andrija Raseta, for the armed forces of the Socialist Federal Republic of Yugoslavia. This was initialled by Ambassador Dirk-Jan Van Houten for the European Community (see Appendix, Document III). Under this agreement, signed on 6 November, a first series of releases took place on 9 November at Bosanski Samac, where 700 prisoners were set free. This was only a small percentage of the persons covered by the agreement (the ICRC delegates had visited approximately 1,800 prisoners since the beginning of the conflict, but a certain number of releases had already been made without their taking part).

The ICRC keeps the initiative

At this stage in the conflict, all was going well for the humanitarian negotiators. They were convinced that, unless everything was rotten in the state of the Balkans, something could be done for the non-combatants and ex-combatants. At the end of 1991, the ICRC delegates' greater source of frustration was that the expected reinforcements from Geneva were not arriving quickly enough. For needs had grown tremendously and new offices had been or were scheduled to be opened all over the republics (see map). The Belgrade and Zagreb heads of mission were grabbing the new arrivals, trying hard to remember that the ICRC had commitments in every continent with more than 50 delegations, and that there was keen competition between colleagues for the best staff.

Jean-François Berger, who went through all the stages of the war in 1991 and until mid-1992, both in Geneva and in the field, recalls:

> Between August and January was when we suffered most from the shocking lack of resources. At first, delegates were appointed

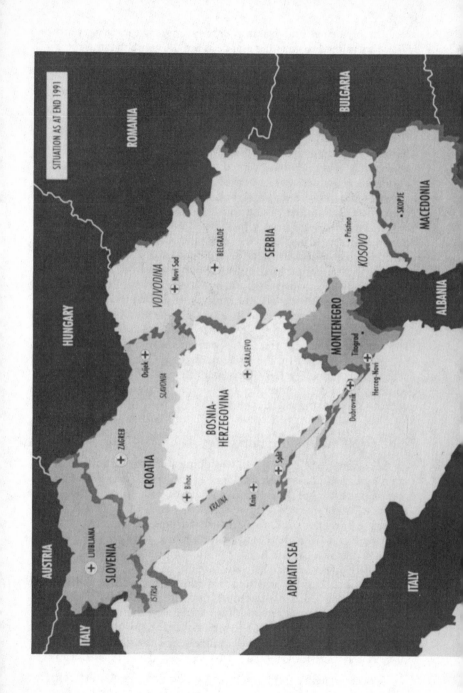

SITUATION AS AT END 1991

ITALY

AUSTRIA

HUNGARY

ROMANIA

BULGARIA

SLOVENIA

+ LJUBLJANA

ISTRIA

CROATIA

+ ZAGREB

+ Bihac

KRAJINA

Knin +

Split +

ADRIATIC SEA

ITALY

Osijek +

SLAVONIA

VOJVODINA

+ Novi Sad

+ BELGRADE

BOSNIA-
HERZEGOVINA

+ SARAJEVO

SERBIA

Dubrovnik +

Herceg Novi

MONTENEGRO

Titograd +

KOSOVO

• Pristina

• SKOPJE

MACEDONIA

ALBANIA

from permanent headquarters staff and came for only a few weeks
at a time. Teams were changing all the time. Internal mobilization
was suffering from slow-downs. In some sectors it was hard for
delegates to realize the dimensions of what was to become a major
crisis. For historical reasons, the 'Europe zone', which was
responsible for the Yugoslav file, was less well prepared than
others such as the African or Asian sections to plunge straight
into the escalating operations, as its recent past had prepared
it more for diplomatic action. And then, we were culturally
unprepared for the brutal reality of war on European soil.

The tragedy intensified from September onwards and, perhaps
because of media coverage, the conflict seemed to be on television
screens rather than in the field. People were not dying of hunger,
this was not Somalia. There were not yet any pictures of
Vukovar, and nobody in the international community really knew
what was going on. Things were not being taken seriously. We
were pretty well alone in the field. The UNHCR was not yet
there, and *Médecins sans Frontières* (MSF) was working in its own
field. So we were the only relief organization for a displaced
population that was growing at an alarming rate.

Fitting in the increased staff turned out to be a more complicated
business than providing a mere presence. The geographical dividing
line of responsibilities was still undefined. Operational efficiency
and political susceptibilities made it no easy matter to decide what
regions were to come under Zagreb rather than Belgrade. Even the
President of the ICRC, in spite of his reputation as a stickler for
punctilious management, had to admit that 'We have worked
miracles in spite of everything.'

Then there was the 'plenipotentiaries affair', as Berger calls it, and
its driving force, the Delegate General. On 8 November, taking
advantage of the belligerents' unwonted concern for the humanitarian cause as defined in The Hague Declaration on Respect for
the Principles of International Humanitarian Law, a letter on similar
lines was sent to Belgrade and Zagreb,[6] proposing a high-level
meeting to discuss that subject (for the text see below). This was
the beginning of a diplomatic–humanitarian spiral, a relatively new
approach for the ICRC about which it later had reservations because
of the treachery encountered in the field in spite of all the firm
promises made on both sides.[7] The first meeting of the protagonists was just after Vukovar was captured on 18 November, which
marked a crucial point in the rising curve of hostilities and showed
that the parties present were letting the situation get out of hand.
One of the ICRC's proclaimed objectives was therefore to halt this

Opposite Situation as at end 1991

drift by urging the belligerents to take a tighter grip on events and agree on what had to be done to respect the law applicable.

As is plain to everyone, the conflict in Yugoslavia is worsening daily, with dramatic humanitarian consequences that the ICRC is unfortunately obliged to observe directly.

In these deteriorating circumstances and in accordance with its mandate, the International Committee of the Red Cross endeavours to bring necessary aid and protection to a growing number of victims. For the last four months our regular assessments of the situation have urged us to step up our activities in the field and seek effective ways of improving the plight of the civilian population, and of members of armed forces who are *hors de combat*.

More than ever, the ICRC considers it essential to promote respect for international humanitarian law in the spirit of the declaration signed by the highest republican authorities of Yugoslavia on 5 November at the plenary session of The Hague Conference. The ICRC accordingly desires to organize a meeting in Geneva to consider all aspects of humanitarian law and its application, in the presence of plenipotentiary representatives of the Federal Executive Council, the Republic of Croatia, the Republic of Serbia and the Yugoslav Federal Army. At the present stage, discussions could cover the following principal subjects:

- assistance to the civilian population
- the plight of prisoners
- the fate of persons listed as having disappeared, and identification of the dead
- the fate of the wounded, the sick and vulnerable persons in the regions affected by the conflict
- the possibility of establishing hospital zones and localities in accordance with Article 23 of the First Geneva Convention
- the supply of medical material and equipment to hospitals and clinics.

Needless to say, these proposals are not exhaustive and could be extended to other humanitarian subjects of mutual interest.

In the hope that you will give your approval to an initiative of this kind, I invite you to appoint a personal representative to attend such a meeting at the headquarters of the International Committee of the Red Cross in Geneva, at a date to be fixed by mutual agreement.

One of the basic principles of the meetings of plenipotentiaries was that they should be held in Geneva, well away from the conflict and press acrobatics, so that enemies should meet in an atmosphere favourable to conciliation. The result at this level quickly exceeded all hopes. Personal relations were established, the greatest courtesy was observed, delegates from opposite sides sat down together to chat or take refreshment, and meanwhile the tragedy continued to run its course in the field. The ICRC representatives regularly taking part in these meetings (those based in Geneva and responsible for protection, aid, medical activities, family reunions, and so on, as well as the heads of mission who had come specially from Belgrade and Zagreb) studied this strange rapprochement carefully lest it should lull them into a feeling of false security, for fighting and nego- tiating at the same time is a curiosity of this Yugoslav war. A delegate summed it up like this: 'They bombard each other, they sign, they bombard each other again and sign again, and so on.' Another describes matters no less bluntly:

> It was a stroke of genius to hold these meetings. Unfortunately it's cancelled out by the lack of respect for the agreements arrived at. I'm absolutely flabbergasted by their way of saying yes and doing just the contrary, as they do in this conflict. I can't understand it and I'm not the only one. And I wonder whether this is just a local phenomenon or a foretaste of what is going to happen in other wars in Europe.

The 'Memorandum of Understanding', signed by the plenipoten- tiaries at the end of the first meeting on 27 November 1991, is a model of its kind (see Appendix, Document IV). It is a sort of pocket Geneva Convention covering practically the whole of humanitar- ian law in less than three pages. It enumerates the essential rules for behaviour in battle and manages, without entering into a legal debate, to introduce a reference to Additional Protocol I, which grants extra protection and assistance to the civilian population in an international conflict. In another paragraph, this text mentions the possibility of setting up protected zones, which it places (somewhat imprudently, considering what was going to happen as the conflict wore on) under ICRC responsibility. It even goes so far as to add an annex containing a standard draft agreement in the event that any such zones are opened. Moreover, the final communiqué issued after these two days announces the formation of a 'joint commission' to trace missing persons. This had become an especially sensitive issue since the fall of Vukovar and the still- remaining doubts as to the fate of hundreds of missing persons.

That the parties to the conflict were able to agree on a memorandum of this kind plainly showed that they wanted to overcome their basic differences as to the law applicable. For, as in the war in Slovenia, the Federal Republic of Yugoslavia, being anxious to maintain the unity of the federal state, described its conflict with Croatia as an internal one and accordingly accepted recourse to Article 3 of the Geneva Conventions and to their Additional Protocol II, applicable to non-international armed conflicts. The Republic of Croatia, however, which was fighting for independence, regarded the conflict as an international one between two sovereign independent states to which the whole of humanitarian law should be applied. It was therefore important not to state these irreconcilable legal positions too openly, for fear of stopping the dialogue that had only just begun. Rather than trying to remove the dangers that lay ahead, they had to be prudently circumvented.

Whilst containing their exhilaration within reasonable bounds, the ICRC leaders were openly pleased at getting the envoys of Federal Yugoslavia, including a lieutenant-general of the armed forces, and those of the Republic of Croatia to sit down together at one and the same table, in the historic room where the meetings of the International Committee have been held since the end of the Second World War. This, it seemed to them, was a step forward that augured well for the discussions that were to take place 48 hours later in Budapest, where the President of the ICRC had already arrived to attend preparations for the International Conference of the Red Cross and Red Crescent.[8] Vice-President Claudio Caratsch was speaking on behalf of the President to the plenipotentiaries at the opening session when he expressed

> the profound conviction that your presence here is a sign of hope for the victims of the tragic Yugoslav conflict. The efforts of all of us in the next few hours will certainly raise great hopes. The risks of disappointment are real, but let us set ourselves the goal of overcoming them. Let us separate humanitarian and political issues.

His reference to the Geneva Conventions and their Additional Protocols, supposedly an obstacle to total war and to the dangers of general annihilation, was accompanied by a reminder of the obligations that the presidents of the six republics had undertaken to respect and enforce in The Hague on 5 November. Mr Caratsch ended his speech thus: 'The international community expects concrete results from this meeting. And the victims of the conflict await a sign of hope.'

The beginning of the end of hope

While Vice-President Caratsch was speaking in Geneva, he could not know that in Budapest, late the same evening and after extremely stormy debates, the Standing Commission[9] decided once and for all that there would be no International Conference in Budapest, and to postpone any such conference indefinitely until the advent of better days. In the words of the ICRC's Annual Report[10] 'the Standing Commission took this decision after noting that, despite intensive diplomatic efforts, agreement could not be reached as to the form that Palestinian participation in the Conference should take'. This had no connection with the nearby Yugoslav war, but it was nevertheless a severe blow for all those, particularly in the ICRC, who had hoped that the International Conference (uniting representatives of the International Red Cross and Red Crescent Movement and those of states signatory to the Geneva Conventions) would strengthen humanitarian activities, which were already exposed to obstacles of the worst kind in the field. The only remaining trace in the records of the Budapest meeting relating to former Yugoslavia is an appeal for international understanding subtitled 'Peace in people's hearts', made by the Council of Delegates.[11]

Disappointment was all the keener because the Red Cross Societies of the six republics and the Yugoslav Red Cross had carefully prepared their case on 15 November at ICRC head-quarters in Geneva, in concert with representatives of the Federation and the Secretary General of the Hungarian Red Cross. They were all there: the representatives of Bosnia-Herzegovina, Croatia, Macedonia, Montenegro, Serbia and Slovenia, and the Belgrade federals, all determined to remain united in action and to do everything possible to prevent humanitarian issues from becoming politicized. Beyond these excellent resolutions still lay the question whether the Yugoslav Red Cross would take part in the Budapest conference. Its legitimacy was not questioned at international level, but the Red Cross Societies of certain republics, especially those of the regions in open conflict with Federal Yugoslavia (Slovenia and Croatia) and those jealous for their autonomy (Bosnia-Herzegovina and Macedonia) disputed its suitability as a representative and sought a solution that would at least enable them to be present at the discussions as observers. A long and rather difficult discussion followed, ending in a humanitarian truce and a flexible agreement noting the full participation of the Yugoslav Red Cross and inviting the leaders of the Croat and Slovene Red Cross Societies *ad personam*, provided the Standing Commission would accept this procedure, for which prior provision had not been made. The Yugoslav participants in the preparatory meeting together drew up a joint declaration to be read on their behalf by the chairman of the International Conference. In the end these laudable efforts came to nothing, since the Conference was cancelled, but at least they showed that, despite all that lay at stake in the conflict, it was still possible within the Red Cross to concentrate on essentials, namely aid to victims about to suffer their first wartime winter.

The Red Cross and Red Crescent Movement had no time for self-pity; the International Conference was dead until further notice and in the field needs remained and were growing. Material aid to fugitives from battle areas was being organized and was on the increase. The 'Family Parcels' scheme was reaching its cruising speed. Its aim was to provide needy families and those sheltering them with an essential supplementary ration of food and vitally necessary goods so as to lessen their privations.

Throughout the month of December, diplomatic activity moved into high gear. It was stimulated by a major initiative from the then Secretary-General, Javier Perez de Cuellar, who reported to the Security Council on 11 December 1991 on the situation in Yugoslavia as observed by his Personal Envoy, Cyrus Vance, in the course of four missions in the region (11–18 October, 3–9 November, 17–24 November and 1–9 December 1991). He pointed out that in all sectors of public life, conditions were worsening. The plight of persons living in battle areas was aggravated by their loss of livelihood, economic restrictions and shortages of all kinds.

More than half a million people had already been obliged to take to the roads in internal exile, an exile made hardly less bitter by the sympathy and generosity of families who took them in at the price of additional hardship to themselves. More and more people were seeking refuge abroad, primarily in nearby Hungary, which had taken in more than 40,000 of them. Meanwhile, UN aid was getting under way. The UNHCR, responsible for co-ordinating UN humanitarian assistance, made its first appeal for funds to cover the cost of a six-month programme. The $24.3 million for which the appeal called were to be apportioned within the three agencies involved, namely the UNHCR, UNICEF and WHO.

In the course of his missions and during his stop-overs in Geneva, Cyrus Vance acquainted himself with the work of the ICRC in conversations with its leaders and delegates, who told him of their principal concerns. These, and the efforts made by some 50 ICRC delegates in the field at that time, are enumerated in the report made by the UN Secretary-General. This gives special prominence to the growing number of incidents in which civilian members of minority communities were forced to leave their homes with little hope of an early return. The report also notes the operations for the release of prisoners carried out by either side under ICRC supervision, and mentions the first meeting of plenipotentiary representatives of Croatia, Serbia and the federal army on 26 and 27 November. Submitted to the Security Council, the detailed account of the ICRC's humanitarian operations clearly shows how extensive these had become in the eight months since the ICRC arrived, and the obvious necessity for the United Nations to take this into account when planning their own assistance programmes. And although the main purpose of Perez de Cuellar's speech of 11 December was to decide whether deployment of UN forces would be fully justified, Cyrus Vance's reports on the subject of humanitarian issues and their immediate requirements provoked much thought and discussion in UN circles.

As field conditions worsened, multilateral diplomacy quickened its pace. The ICRC, although primarily concerned with action, nevertheless took a series of diplomatic initiatives that required from its leaders the physical fitness of a marathon long-distance runner. From the end of 1991 and throughout 1992, meetings, committees, conferences and extraordinary sessions followed each other at a frantic pace. On top of all its own meetings, the ICRC had to attend all those fixed by the international community, which was staring into the bottomless pit of Yugoslav suffering. The ICRC delegation, accredited with observer status to the United Nations in New York, was present without interruption at the Security Council's meetings on Yugoslavia, and followed the work of all the UN bodies involved. Its Geneva-based specialists on Yugoslavia frequently visited European capitals, especially Brussels and Strasbourg, headquarters of the European Community's administrative bodies. They went to Pècs in Hungary to set up the joint Commission for Tracing Missing Persons and Mortal Remains, and in December 1991 to negotiate the neutralization of Osijek Hospital with the belligerents. In May 1992, in Vienna, they attended an international meeting on refugees from Bosnia-Herzegovina. They also attended the meetings of plenipotentiaries convened for 20 December 1991 and 31 January, 27 March and 24 May 1992. At the meeting in May (which coincided with the admission to the United Nations of the republics of Slovenia, Croatia and Bosnia-Herzegovina) the Croat and federal plenipotentiaries undertook to respect the agreements previously concluded and, going even further, recognized that the Geneva Conventions were applicable in their entirety.

The delegates also followed the proceedings of various commissions which met frequently to discuss missing persons and prisoners and were in constant touch with the other organs of the International Red Cross and Red Crescent Movement, especially the Societies involved in the field and their Geneva-based Federation.

This was the position until the Bosnia-Herzegovina conflict broke out in May 1992. So serious and complicated was this that it added still further, if this were possible, to the number of international meetings. On to the already crowded scene now entered the Human Rights Commission, the London Conference (later the Geneva Conference), the Organization of the Islamic Conference and others. At this time too the non-governmental organizations (NGOs) appeared. Except for MSF, the NGOs had taken little part in the first conflict, but now they began to deploy in the field.

The profit and loss account

During the initial era of the Yugoslav conflict, humanitarian diplomacy had a certain spontaneity fostered by the relative lack of interest, or even understanding, shown by a western public virtually unaware of the reality of the situation. The heavy artillery of international communications was scarcely mobilized during the first year of the war. Only the printed press, giving the subject regular attention, reached the readers of the quality newspapers, but until August 1992, it did little to penetrate the collective unconscious.

The President of the ICRC was satisfied with the institution's diplomatic activities although well aware that it had often teetered on a tightrope when manoeuvring its way between humanitarian interests and politics. The ICRC negotiators enterprisingly and untiringly opened and kept up business-like discussions with the belligerents, and this single-mindedness led to meetings of plenipotentiaries who, having learned the bitter lesson of Vukovar, were determined above all, recalls Thierry Germond, 'to see that Osijek was spared. Their other and wider objective was to build up a political and legal basis for truly humanitarian initiatives.' Thierry Meyrat, the head of the ICRC delegation in Belgrade, was of a similar opinion. He writes in an internal report:

> I believe that the ICRC initiative in convoking the parties so as to establish a dialogue and 'legal/operational' working rules is essential in handling conflicts as chaotic as this one. The results can never be equal to expectations, but nevertheless exceed what should have been negotiated in other ways.

By starting this dialogue between enemies the ICRC was able to keep an eye on its development – in terms of time, by fixing how often the parties should meet, and geographically, by proposing the agenda. Germond believes that 'this worked fairly well in the conflict between Croatia and Yugoslavia but not in that of Bosnia-Herzegovina, where the roles were distributed differently.' On the Croat side, confidence in the ICRC received a tremendous boost, for it was regarded as the first organization to enable Croatia, not then fully recognized as a sovereign state, to negotiate on equal terms with its Yugoslav counterpart.

One of the reasons enabling the ICRC to play such an active part in the first conflict was that few other humanitarian organizations were then operating. It would be going too far to say that it did so because no one else was available. Situations of this kind are commonplace in the ICRC which, specializing as it does in emergency operations, often acts alone. But this does not always mean that intense diplomatic activity is going on. The procedures provided for in such circumstances nevertheless have precedents in recent ICRC history. 'Veterans' like Germond learned a lot from their experience in Cyprus (1974/75), which was in many respects similar to the Yugoslav crisis. Both were conflicts between two communities entailing displaced persons, dispersed families and missing individuals, where the ICRC had established an ongoing dialogue with and between the parties to the conflict, without neglecting the experience accumulated by the local Red Cross Society, which was at the time one of the ICRC's staunchest partners. This multilateral dialogue brought together in a humanitarian context belligerents who would have greatly hesitated to meet each other had their encounters been of a political nature, with the implied risk of a kind of recognition of the adverse party.

It was in this spirit that the Commission for Tracing Missing Persons and Mortal Remains was set up. It comprised representatives of the belligerents who were to agree on tracing procedures and exchange all the information they held on this subject, and representatives of the Red Cross Societies of the republics involved, basically those of Croatia and Serbia in the first conflict. These Societies were to do the actual work, through a network of investigating offices whose job it was to make inquiries in the field. It has to be admitted that this Commission, which came into being through the wishes of the plenipotentiaries in November 1991, did not fulfil its main purpose, which was to answer the serious questions raised after the fall of Vukovar, where there were hundreds of missing persons. Pierre-André Conod, head of the Zagreb delegation, believes that this was a major challenge. His internal end-of-mission report said that the Commission's evaluation of its work was

> very limited and contrary to the hopes raised when it was formed ... It also saddled the ICRC with some degree of responsibility as far as public opinion was concerned although, officially, the ICRC was only supposed to do notarial work and remind the parties of their humanitarian duty.

For, as often happens to the ICRC, a case at first solely humanitarian slid into the political arena because of its highly emotional context. Under constant pressure from street demonstrations, the Croat leaders were constrained to tell the families concerned what had become of the 13,000 or so people whom they estimated were missing after the Vukovar tragedy. It was hard to come by news of any of them, for organizational reasons – the regional research offices achieved limited results because communications between the regions were complicated and local authorities had more power than the central ones. But the main reasons why it was hard to get replies were objective ones; it was impossible – 'for security reasons', according to the Yugoslav representatives – to produce eye-witnesses because these were the military or paramilitary officials who drew up the plan to evacuate the town. The Commission soldiered on from December 1991 to July 1992, when its work was suspended. Had it to be admitted that the great majority of the missing persons were dead or, as the belief persisted in some quarters, that many of them were in secret places of detention somewhere in Yugoslavia? That was one of the questions pondered by Tadeusz Mazowiecki on his appointment in August 1992, and he too tried to calm Croat impatience.

As for the prisoners taken in the first conflict, the ICRC delegates, who visited them as soon as they were captured, very soon noticed that many detainees were not in their cells at the time of the next visit. They had been released and exchanged in operations organized direct by the parties to the conflict, often in the presence of European Community observers, without the ICRC taking part. This greatly complicated the delegates' work. They had the utmost difficulty in finding out what was happening in the prisons, bringing their lists up to date and being able to pass on correct information to the prisoners' families. Immediately the ICRC learned of these exchanges it considered whether it should become involved in the process in order to exercise some control over it. In August 1991 Jean-François Berger, the desk officer in Geneva, knew that 'either we took no part in it and things would be balkanized still more, or we went into it, dirtied our hands a little and ran the risk of appearing to guarantee the exchange'. The result was that the ICRC gradually became the driving force of the Tripartite Commission, made up of representatives of the federal army, the Croat Ministry of Defence and the European Community. Between its first meeting on 22 October 1991 and August 1992 there were shifts in the Commission's priorities. At first it was the EC observers who were the most active, the ICRC representatives keeping in the background because the main item on the agenda was then the evacuation of the besieged Yugoslav army barracks in Croatia. The ICRC was only marginally associated with this because it dealt with transmitting family messages. But from the day the Commission decided to discuss the exchange of all prisoners, it was the ICRC's contribution that was preponderant, for on this subject its experience was virtually irreplaceable.

Marco Altherr, head of the Zagreb delegation from October 1991 to February 1992, noticed the change at once and moved in to fill the gap by offering the ICRC's services to carry out a complete exchange operation. The parties promptly accepted the terms proposed. On 6 November they signed an agreement for the release of all the prisoners in their hands, in accordance with the principle 'All for all', that is, irrespective of the numbers on either side – all of them without restriction. The agreement provided that the lists of detainees were to be handed to the ICRC and that the delegates were to interview all detainees to make sure that they wanted to return home.

This agreement faithfully followed the procedures described in the 'Memorandum of Understanding' of 24 October (See p. 31). Marco Altherr, formerly head of the ICRC delegation in Peshawar, appears to have drafted this memorandum, for arrangements of this kind had been tried out in the Afghan conflict. Said Altherr:

> The Commission met more than twenty times in two and a half months, and at these long meetings, many of them at night, discussed and decided much of importance. They enabled the ICRC to make some useful points about detention and international humanitarian law, and to extract from the authorities their long-delayed permission to visit the people captured at Vukovar. Above all, they led to the release of more than two thousand prisoners in full compliance with ICRC criteria.

The release operations took two days, 9 November and 10 December 1991. A useful spin-off was that the local media gave them good coverage, thereby adding to ICRC credibility.

'The Commission nevertheless failed in one particular', says Altherr in his end-of-mission report:

> it never succeeded in stopping unofficial locally-organized exchanges. But it did manage to limit their number and effects; for humanitarian reasons, the ICRC has always been against exchanges of this kind, because they encourage local authorities to take hostages.

Releases of prisoners taken in the first conflict continued until August 1992, and even later on a reduced scale. The first two operations in November and December did not clear up all the doubtful cases, especially those of prisoners against whom legal proceedings had been taken, although the agreement implicitly provided that this should not delay their release. The ICRC obstinately maintained its pressure on the belligerents, who were no longer fighting each other – yet another reason for urging them to honour their commitments. Another release operation, a partial one, took place on 26 January, and on 11 February 1992 the Tripartite Commission met after several weeks' interval, this time at Sarajevo, where the participants could more easily gather since the federal army's representatives had completely evacuated Croatia. Croatia, like Slovenia, was by then recognized by a large section of the inter-

national community. Weeks and months went by in a whirl of contra-
dictory figures and data, lack of information on names and places
of detention, and propaganda. The arrival in April 1992 of the United
Nations Protection Force (UNPROFOR) in the areas it had been
ordered to protect made it even more difficult to classify the
detainees. Were they Croat citizens of Serbian origin, born in an
UNPROFOR area, or Croatian Serbs wanting to enter another area?
This tangled skein was tying itself into knots. The ICRC had to
be more insistent in its efforts to get the problem unravelled once
and for all.

The ICRC leaders were very keen to close the file concerning
releases in the first conflict because they knew that the second phase
of the war had begun, and were particularly fearful it might spread.
Everybody, whether the inhabitants of Bosnia-Herzegovina or
observers in the field, agreed that if Bosnia-Herzegovina went up
in flames the world would be on the brink of a disaster worse than
anything the Balkans had gone through in 1991. The ICRC would
have to be prepared to meet emergencies in an extremely difficult
environment, because the various communities were inextricably
mixed. They had so far lived in good relations with each other but
it only needed a spark to set everything ablaze. The ICRC also feared
that the modest progress of humanitarian activities in the previous
few months would disappear in a new conflict. Everything would
have to be renegotiated, ICRC principles of intervention would
probably be largely ignored, and discussions would doubtless have
to start up again from square one, with new contacts who would
be more numerous and less easily identified than the central
characters in the Croat–Yugoslav conflict.

The ICRC plays its trump card

By the end of March 1992 the entire release process had been started
up again with the support of the plenipotentiaries, who at the
ICRC's request had also taken the matter in hand. More than 400
prisoners had gone home, but this did not account for all of those
left, who were believed to number more than a thousand. After
promises, meetings, agreements and cancellations (the ICRC
meanwhile establishing itself firmly in Bosnia-Herzegovina, where
hostilities were spreading) local exchanges went on, although on
a small scale. Civilians were arrested purely and simply to be used
as bartering units, and conditions of detention were deteriorating
in some places. The new Yugoslav Federal Republic having expressly
renewed its undertaking to respect all the obligations contained in
the Memorandum of Understanding, the ICRC became more
pressing. It sent a *note verbale* to both parties demanding the

immediate release of all their prisoners. Because of the war in Bosnia-Herzegovina, it was no longer possible to meet in its capital, and the Tripartite Commission moved to Budapest.

It was in the Hungarian capital that the epilogue to the saga of the prisoners was acted out. The principal roles were played by the Croat and Yugoslav prime ministers, and, for the ICRC, by its President. Cornelio Sommaruga brought ICRC influence to bear on the negotiations of 28 July in Geneva when, outside the meeting convoked by the UNHCR on the situation in former Yugoslavia, he had talks with the vice-prime minister of Croatia, Mr Granic, and, in a separate meeting, with the Yugoslav prime minister, Mr Panic. He impressed on both of them that under Article 118 of the Third Geneva Convention, their states were under an obligation to release all prisoners at the end of hostilities. The following day, he managed to get both parties to sign a declaration of intent to proceed to a final exchange without delay. In one extraordinarily hectic episode, ICRC officials pursued Mr Panic on his way to Geneva airport, and besieged Mr Granic, who was still in the UNHCR conference hall, in order to get their signatures.

But this mere declaration of intent was not specific enough to do away with the residual problems which had prevented any agreement until then. The ICRC therefore proposed that these two statesmen should meet a week later on neutral ground. The meeting took place on 7 August 1992 in Budapest. It was preceded by a conversation with Jozsef Antall, the Hungarian prime minister, who at their request granted separate interviews to Mr Gregoric, the Croat prime minister, and Mr Panic, the Yugoslav prime minister. These interviews took place in the presence of Cornelio Sommaruga, who was the neutral humanitarian guarantor of the event. It was he too who, as President of the ICRC, opened and directed the meeting, which began in a very strained atmosphere. He said later

> I had an extremely difficult time at first, for after all, I was talking to two prime ministers. This was not a mere quarrel between civil servants or diplomats, and I had to try to control a very delicate situation. The first miracle was that, when the meeting was suspended for procedural reasons, the prime ministers left the hall by the same door and shut themselves up together without us. I've no idea what they did for the next two hours, but in any case they talked to each other.

Another minor miracle took place in the presence of the journalists who had been called in to witness the agreement concluded by the two heads of government; that is, once they had signed the agreement, Panic held out his hand to the Croat prime minister. As President Sommaruga relates,

I was standing between the two prime ministers, so I stepped out of their way and they were photographed congratulating each other under the Red Cross emblem. [There was a big Red Cross flag on the podium.] The photograph was widely circulated in Budapest and the surrounding area.

A week later, on 14 August at Nemetin, 1,131 prisoners were released, leaving behind them about 60 cases complicated by the situation in Bosnia-Herzegovina and which the ICRC continued to follow. The tortuous negotiations before the release at Nemetin were at least successful, not always the case with the ICRC's efforts in this region or elsewhere. One only need remember the fate of the prisoners of war taken in the Iran–Iraq conflict. This ended in 1988 but thousands of prisoners are still waiting to be released and go home.

The share-out between ICRC and UNHCR

'The UNHCR has always been in Yugoslavia,' as François Fouinat, co-ordinator of the UNHCR special operation in former Yugoslavia, rightly says, referring to the long years spent by his organization in dealing with the issue of Balkan refugees. He adds that it was in the autumn of 1991 that his organization considered becoming involved in the Yugoslav tragedy, or to be more precise, in November after a joint evaluation mission with UNICEF that showed the growing difficulties of persons displaced by the conflict. The findings of that mission led to an appeal on 3 December 1991 for $24.3 million to finance the assistance operations contemplated by the UNHCR, WHO and UNICEF. At the same time the UNHCR opened an office in Zagreb (it already had one in Belgrade), but did not yet contemplate large-scale field operations. These did not come until later, progressively, as war spread in Bosnia-Herzegovina.

Meanwhile, on 6 December 1991, United Nations Secretary-General Javier Perez de Cuellar asked the UNHCR to add to its usual function of aiding refugees that of investigating the living conditions of displaced persons, in consultation with the ICRC. President Sommaruga recalls that he received a telephone call a few days previously from the United Nations Secretary-General, followed immediately by another call from Sadako Ogata. Both assured him that the United Nations wanted to 'do something in Yugoslavia'. This was good news for the ICRC, which had been involved since the beginning in a conflict that was making life unbearable for the civilian population. The ICRC therefore welcomed the arrival of partners with whom it could share out the work.

In Geneva and in the field, ICRC and UN officials discussed how best to redistribute the work. In the six months of war between Croatia and Yugoslavia, material and medical supplies to the civilian population had steadily increased. By the end of 1991, the Red Cross of Yugoslavia and the Red Cross Societies in the various republics were regularly assisting 600,000 displaced persons and running a support programme for the medical system that covered dozens of hospitals and medical centres whose stocks were running out. Since the coming into force of the cease-fire of 4 January negotiated by Cyrus Vance, which was being respected, the ICRC could consider withdrawing progressively from regions that were again calm, such as Croatia and Vojvodina, and from Slovenia, to concentrate on areas where the fighting was fiercer, such as the Krajina, where the UNPROFOR forces were not yet in action. The ICRC therefore intended transferring to the UNHCR the greater part of the relief operation consisting of monthly distributions of parcels to displaced persons and to the families sheltering them, until they could return to their native towns and villages.

The handover between the two organizations was not achieved without a few hitches. The hope of a settlement of the conflict between Croatia and federal Yugoslavia was mixed with growing fears that a devastating war was about to break out in Bosnia-Herzegovina. Without being prophets of doom, the officials directing humanitarian aid could not pretend to be unaware that the region was heading not for calmer days but for a new kind of conflagration that no political or military force seemed able to prevent. Between February and April 1992, the centre of gravity of the conflict shifted inexorably, and the humanitarian institutions were preparing for radical reorganization, if not a complete break with their working methods.

Although it was in February 1992 that the UNHCR officially took over the operation for assistance to the persons displaced by the Croat–Yugoslav conflict, the ICRC and its natural partners, the local Red Cross Societies, had to fill the gap for a few weeks longer, until the United Nations was really operational. In any event the UNHCR continued to draw on Red Cross experience to install its relief distribution network, especially in Croatia, where volunteers worked miracles. It also benefited indirectly from the operations of the German and Austrian Red Cross Societies, which did much to help the persons displaced in the first conflict, and from the substantial achievements of the International Federation of Red Cross and Red Crescent Societies in co-ordinating emergency relief outside areas of conflict.

The UNHCR – and its special envoy José-Maria Mendiluce, who was made responsible for co-ordinating the whole United Nations system in former Yugoslavia – prepared to resume the assistance

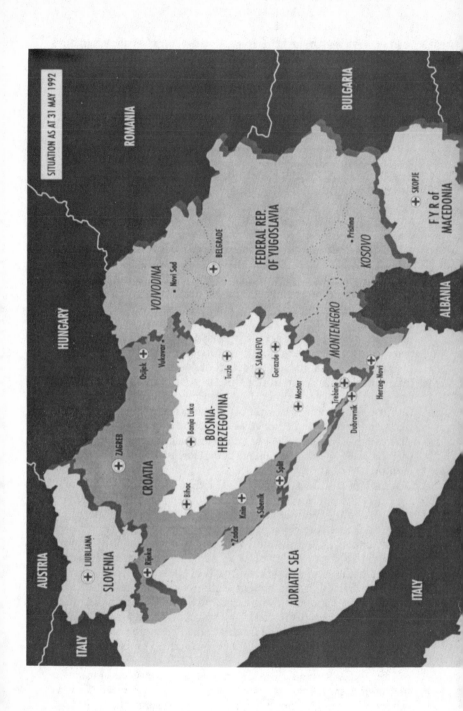

SITUATION AS AT 31 MAY 1992

programmes involved in the first conflict, but was more concerned by developments in Bosnia-Herzegovina. Its number one objective in that region was to use every means of inducing the civilian population to stay where they were instead of swelling the numbers of refugees; that is, to promote survival conditions so that inhabitants who felt threatened because they belonged to a minority group in one part or another of the republic should no longer consider flight as the only possible solution. The ICRC delegates supported that policy, for they were well placed to observe the alarming movements occurring all over the republic (see map). In April 1992, when UNPROFOR Director of Civilian Affairs Cedric Thornberry[12] visited the ICRC delegation in Belgrade, he made no secret of his misgivings at the deployment of UNPROFOR, the choice of Sarajevo as headquarters, the difficulties caused by blocking Croat and Slovene air space, and his inadequate staff (he had at first only three colleagues).

On 11 April, Mendiluce persuaded the three presidents of the parties comprising the Bosnia-Herzegovina government coalition[13] to sign a declaration on the 'humanitarian treatment of displaced persons' within the republic. This declaration emphasized that such persons should be treated without discrimination or political preference, and that 'the drama of displacement [of populations] is not misused for political or sectarian ends'.

This is doubtless the first example of a solemn public engagement undertaken by the warring brothers of this unhappy republic to respect the civilian population and humanitarian activities. It also marks the exact point at which the UNHCR departed from its usual role and resolutely entered a situation of armed conflict. Encouraged by Mendiluce, it did so with panache, after a few false starts quickly erased by the need to make an impression and demonstrate its efficiency. In so doing it implemented the main recommendation made by High Commissioner Sadako Ogata, who particularly asked that everything should be done on the spot to prevent excessive population movements or the formation of new groups of refugees. As she never tired of repeating, 'we must help people where they are'. Also, the UNHCR's need to raise large quantities of funds from the international community is not unconnected with the shift of UNHCR action priorities from Croatia to Bosnia.

The ICRC, observing this change of policy, kept in close touch with the UNHCR in Geneva, Belgrade and Zagreb. The ICRC knew that it had no monopoly of humanitarian intervention in a conflict, and claimed none. It was aware that the new war would raise urgent and serious problems for everyone operating in the field, who

Opposite Situation as at 31 May 1992

would have to rely on numerous informants who were still unfamiliar to them. It was therefore anxious that aid programmes should meet real needs as observed on the spot. For there were still ambiguities: at the co-ordination sessions early in May 1992, the share-out of tasks still assumed that the ICRC would be foremost in Bosnia-Herzegovina and the UNPAs,[14] the UNHCR being expected to concentrate on the neighbouring republics. At the end of May the delegates observed that, in spite of the agreement signed in February, family parcels were being distributed only intermittently, even though large numbers of refugees from Bosnia-Herzegovina were beginning to arrive in Croatia, where a quarter of a million people uprooted by the first conflict had already taken refuge.

Meanwhile, Sarajevo, subject to incessant bombardment, had become the symbol of a tragedy for the ICRC too, for an ICRC delegate was killed when one of its convoys was attacked on 18 May. As a result the ICRC withdrew from the capital, to which its delegates returned officially only seven months later, after countless attempts to obtain guarantees of safety that remained a dead letter. Like Nature which abhors a vacuum, the UNHCR occupied the empty space, awaiting the reopening of the airport and the start of the humanitarian airlift for which UNPROFOR reinforcements had been voted (by the Security Council's Resolution 761 of 29 June 1992). That airlift was to mark the real take-off of a military-cum-humanitarian operation on a scale without precedent in UNHCR annals.

The ICRC revolts

Whilst Sadako Ogata was making her first visit to the field between 6 and 9 July the ICRC delegates, now back in Bosnia-Herzegovina after a six-week absence caused by the Sarajevo murder, began to resume a large-scale programme of prison visits, reactivated the network for the distribution of food and medical supplies, and reoccupied their bases at Bihac, Banja Luka, Mostar and Trebinje. They planned to open new offices at Tuzla, Zenica and Jablanica so as to cover the whole of the republic, but were never able to do this completely, for eastern Bosnia (about 20 per cent of the territory) remained hermetically closed to them until the spring of 1993.

From eye-witness accounts gathered during their journeys to towns and villages and, above all, by listening to the first prisoners they met once prison visits were resumed, the delegates realized that the worst had happened during the period in which no neutral independent observer was on the spot, except in Sarajevo where an international presence was maintained. Appalled by their discovery, they passed the information to Geneva via the ICRC delegations in Zagreb and Belgrade. The delegate responsible for detention activities in Bosnia-Herzegovina then came to Geneva for urgent consultation.

For there was every need for urgency and the impending 'International Meeting on humanitarian aid for victims of the conflict in former Yugoslavia', convened by Mrs Ogata on her return from Sarajevo gave the ICRC an opportunity to make known its revulsion to the world. Information coming from the field left no doubt as to the terrible acts of violence committed against the inhabitants of Bosnia-Herzegovina.

On 29 July 1992, the ICRC decided to make its voice heard. From the tribune of the United Nations in Geneva, President Sommaruga addressed the entire international community, his partners in humanitarian effort and the media. He said he was horrified by the intolerable situation which already bears

> the mark of the greatest human disaster in Europe since the Second World War ... Behind this nightmare situation, nourished by revenge and hate, there is a deliberate plan based on the exclusion of others. For a man of the Red Cross like myself, this is quite abhorrent ... I am referring, of course, to the terrible ravages of 'ethnic cleansing', in whose name whole populations are being terrorized, minorities intimidated and harassed, civilians interned on a massive scale, hostages taken, and torture, deportation and summary executions are rife. Such methods, which we thought had been consigned to the museums showing the horrors of the Second World War, have become almost common practice in the war-torn territory of what was Yugoslavia.
> — (see Appendix, Document V)

This speech should be read and re-read. For the ICRC it is not a routine speech cast in the mould of international usage. Its cry of alarm that day echoed in public the shock felt even by war-seasoned delegates at the terrifying realization that a civilian population, subjected to the most appalling acts of violence, was actually what was at stake in a war that was no mere civil war but a war *against* civilians. And it denounced 'ethnic cleansing', that criminal concept of creating ethnically homogeneous regions by forcibly uprooting minority populations, the brutal implementation of a policy that deliberately and openly violates humanitarian law.

But, at that moment, the ICRC protest went unheeded. Admittedly the audience understood it, but it did not provoke the expected shock wave. This is a stark example of how ineffectual words can be when addressed to an ill-informed public disinclined at the height of summer to put aside other interests that make fewer demands on their conscience. It was also a bitter disappointment for the ICRC, which had hoped that a speech delivered from so illustrious a tribune would have had more effect. And the ICRC delegates who, since mid-July 1992, had been visiting Manjaca camp and other places of detention with sinister reputations were left very much alone to bear the weight of such knowledge. World conscience was not awakened until the British television channel ITN showed the emaciated bodies of prisoners, just as in 1985 it had been awakened by a disturbing BBC documentary on the plight of the Ethiopian civilian population after long months of famine. Even then, the international community took an incredibly long time to react to the tragedy in Somalia. On all these occasions, and others besides, the humanitarian organizations, especially the ICRC, had set the ball rolling by describing the extent of the disaster, pestering embassies and urging journalists to interest themselves in lost causes with no immediate success.

The conclusions of the International Conference of 29 July, as submitted by the UNHCR, urged a general increase in protection and assistance to civilians, and that population movements should be slowed down in all possible ways so as not to overwhelm countries of asylum (there were already two million refugees in internal or external exile at that time). The Conference also pointed out the difficulty of access to victims, as many regions and towns were still suffering military blockade which was preventing humanitarian aid workers from doing their job. There was however no specific reference to the grave breaches of international humanitarian law denounced by the ICRC, although the first priority in the conclusions of the Conference refers to 'respect for human rights and humanitarian law by all parties'. The Conference dodged the question of 'ethnic cleansing' and showed the utmost discretion regarding the violence committed against persons duly protected by law. In short, despite the praise bestowed officially on the humanitarian institutions, and an awareness of the situation that began to show during the meeting, it must be admitted that the crescendo for which President Cornelio Sommaruga and the ICRC delegates had hoped became a diminuendo in the consensual phraseology typical of most international conferences.

This semi-setback did not damp the combative ardour of the ICRC, which continued to elbow its way into all the circles devoted to former Yugoslavia. Unlike other leading lights of charitable work such as Rony Brauman, President of MSF, who publicly urged withdrawal when confronted by political appropriation of humanitarian aims, it would not take no for an answer. It believed that the statement of 29 July was in reality a change of strategy decided on by its directors after long and careful thought. As Paul Grossrieder, the ICRC's Deputy Director of Operations, said at the meeting of the ICRC's Executive Board held to prepare the part the ICRC would take in the UNHCR Conference, what we now need is to stir up public opinion, politicians and those actively involved in the conflict. This is no longer the time to negotiate as we have done in the past; if we want to slow down the spiral we must use other arguments than persuasion, give prominence to words and symbols and change the nature of our inability to intervene.

This approach gives moral discourse preference over traditional negotiation. It was to inspire the ICRC's major declarations in the following months.

The emotion caused some days later by Roy Gutman's article on the 'Death Camps' in New York *Newsday*, 2 August 1992, and later by televised documentaries, justified the decision of the ICRC's Executive Board and encouraged it to rethink its usual practice of confidentiality. It had decided to speak out loud and clear; but without moving towards a reversal of its internal doctrine that requires it to be extremely careful about making public declarations on breaches of international humanitarian law. This is still valid. If in this case the ICRC chose to relinquish its usual reserve, it was because the acts of brutality reported by its delegates were so serious and so frequent, and because it became convinced that by speaking out publicly it would not be endangering its objective, which was to protect victims.

During the meeting of the European Parliament, at which Paul Grossrieder spoke on 10 August 1992, the ICRC's policy of confidentiality was unexpectedly and deliberately attacked in the strongest terms by the leader of the Liberal group, Simone Veil, who accused it of cowardice and likened its present behaviour to that which she said had been typical of it in the Second World War. Her reproach was particularly unjustified under the circumstances, in view of the courage displayed by delegates in the field and the ICRC's outspoken attitude ever since the conflict began. It stemmed from a misunderstanding over a passage in Paul Grossrieder's speech in which he 'wondered how much longer the ICRC would have to confine itself to these confidential approaches and from what point it should speak up and say publicly where it stood'. The passage ended with the words 'The ICRC will always be careful not to overstep what I would call the moral threshold beyond which it could no longer keep silence without itself becoming guilty.' That silence had, needless to say, been relegated to the background by President Sommaruga's highly explicit statement of 29 July. But what public opinion expected in August was proof by example, denunciation of the guilty and description of forbidden practices, and the ICRC had given none of these. It is not its business to do so, and it left it up to such courts of enquiry as might be appointed to reveal, for example, the truth about prison conditions since public interest was now focused on the detention camps.

Camp diplomacy

From August 1992 to January 1993, there was a change of direction in political and diplomatic activity, until then concerned mainly with providing shelter for displaced persons and refugees in former Yugoslavia and abroad. In the corridors of the crystal palace of UN headquarters in New York and in European circles, as well as among humanitarian experts, there was much talk of places where terrible things had happened – Omarska, Keraterm, Brcko, Trnopolje and Manjaca. The Hague Conference was nearing an unremarkable end without having been able to outline a settlement of the Bosnia-Herzegovina conflict. The London Conference loomed on the horizon, but nobody yet knew its aims nor who would take part in it. Imperceptibly, the international community, having run out of political ideas, decided to tackle the affair of the camps.

A day particularly prolific in statements of position and decisions on this subject was 13 August, the date fixed by the Commission on Human Rights to meet at the request of the United States government, and for the first time in its history in extraordinary session. The only item on the agenda was to examine the situation in former Yugoslavia. After two days' discussion the Commission made its position known. It demanded the release of all persons arbitrarily detained, and unimpeded, immediate access by the ICRC to places of detention. And it appointed a special rapporteur, Tadeusz Mazowiecki, the former prime minister of Poland, whose many missions in the field were to produce extremely detailed reports on breaches of human rights and international humanitarian law.

Again on 13 August, the Security Council adopted two resolutions directly connected with humanitarian action,[15] in which the ICRC was mentioned. In Resolution 770, the Council demanded that access to victims should be guaranteed and the sending of humanitarian aid assured, and in Resolution 771 that the ICRC should be granted immediate, unimpeded and permanent access to all places of detention.

Yet again on 13 August, the ICRC issued a particularly firm and explicit press release[16] in the form of an appeal to the parties to the conflict (see below). An appeal to the belligerents' responsibility for controlling all the combatants claiming to serve under their banners, and to all states signatory to the Geneva Conventions, who bear 'a collective responsibility in this regard, having undertaken not only to respect but also to ensure respect for those Conventions in all circumstances'.

This press release especially denounced the practice of mass detention, which the ICRC delegates considered as the tip of the iceberg known as 'ethnic cleansing'. They were well aware that the civilians they saw in the camps were only a small percentage of those subjected to the ravages of that practice, and already realized the flagrant inadequacy of humanitarian aid in a country completely putrefied by a policy that although avowed and practised without dissimulation, was a gross and permanent transgression of the laws of war.

BOSNIA-HERZEGOVINA: ICRC ISSUES SOLEMN APPEAL TO ALL PARTIES TO CONFLICT

Geneva (ICRC). – Following the visits its delegates have conducted during the last few days to places of detention in Bosnia-Herzegovina, it is evident to the International Committee of the Red Cross (ICRC) that innocent civilians are being arrested and subjected to inhumane treatment. Moreover, the detention of such persons is part of a policy of forced population transfers carried out on a massive scale and marked by the systematic use of brutality. Among the long list of methods used are harassment, murder, confiscation of property, deportation and the taking of hostages – which reduce individuals to the level of bargaining counters – all in violation of international humanitarian law.

With regard to living conditions in these places of detention, it is imperative that urgent measures be taken to guarantee the physical and moral integrity of the detainees in accordance with the provisions of the Third and Fourth Geneva Conventions, which must be observed in their entirety.

ICRC delegates have had only limited access to the republic's various regions and, despite repeated approaches made in this respect, they have still not received comprehensive lists of places of detention controlled by the various parties to the conflict or been notified of persons captured, and are thus unable to bring help to all the victims. The ICRC has had access to only a very limited number of prisoners of war, while the places of detention are crowded with innocent and terrified civilians.

The ICRC wishes to draw attention once again to the fact that the parties to the conflict in Bosnia-Herzegovina bear full responsibility for all acts committed by their respective combatants.

After several weeks of intense activity in the field and in the places of detention in an attempt to protect and come to the aid of the victims of this conflict, the ICRC notes that the parties to the conflict are not complying with the provisions of the Geneva Conventions, despite their commitment in this respect.

In these circumstances, and especially in view of the pressing need to clarify the situation in all places of detention in Bosnia-Herzegovina, the ICRC hereby solemnly appeals to all parties concerned to:

(a) put into effect their commitment to comply with international humanitarian law, in particular the Third and Fourth Geneva Conventions;
(b) instruct all combatants in the field to respect captured persons, civilians, medical establishments, private and public places, and the Red Cross emblem;
(c) refrain from carrying out forced transfers and taking other illegal measures against the civilian population;
(d) take immediate steps to improve living conditions in all places of detention in Bosnia-Herzegovina, in accordance with the recommendations made in respect of places already visited by the ICRC;
(e) notify the ICRC immediately of all places of detention in Bosnia-Herzegovina, and supply accurate lists of all persons held in such places;
(f) take the action necessary to ensure that ICRC delegates can work effectively and rapidly in adequate conditions of security.

The ICRC earnestly hopes that implementation of the above measures by all parties to the conflict in Bosnia-Herzegovina will at last enable it to bring protection and assistance to all victims of the conflict, in line with its humanitarian mandate.

The entire community of States party to the Geneva Conventions bears a collective responsibility in this regard, having undertaken not only to respect but also to ensure respect for those Conventions in all circumstances.

In the period before and after the London Conference (26–28 August 1992) and until the beginning of the process of release from the camps, organizations and personalities of all kinds, special envoys and other correspondents, decided to capitalize on the issue of the prisoners, made impromptu visits to places of detention, and reported the brutalities observed in a lightning tour of one camp or another. On some days there were so many visitors that the ICRC delegates, whose vocation and business it is to make such visits, had to retreat from the prison gates because of the excessive number of visitors and cameramen. This led to some confusion in the minds of the military responsible for the camps, who had to choose which visitors they preferred: the quiet but demanding delegates of the ICRC or the heralds of popular opinion, a neutral independent organization or a political figure who might be able to bring them some immediate advantage. In time the humanitarian workers won the day – they came oftener and were more insistent – but it was a close shave.

On 17 August, during an official visit to the Polish government, the President of the ICRC met Tadeusz Mazowiecki in Warsaw. The former prime minister was about to leave for his first mission in the field, in order to observe and catalogue the grave breaches of humanitarian law committed by the belligerents. The ICRC foresaw that the work done by Mr Mazowiecki as special rapporteur would complement that of its delegates in the field and the ongoing efforts to put a stop to the most flagrant acts of violence. The President remained in close contact with Tadeusz Mazowiecki and his team throughout his mandate, sharing his growing frustration at the lack of progress made, and worse, the persistent deterioration in the living conditions of the persons subjected to the combatants' despotic, despicable and apparently unstoppable behaviour.[17]

At about the same time, Thierry Germond, the ICRC Delegate General for Europe, in a whistle-stop tour to prepare for the London Conference, visited the heads of the three parties to the Bosnia-Herzegovina conflict in order to check with them what had been done to apply the recommendations made public by the ICRC on 13 August. Here too, he saw the alarming extent to which the gap was widening between the encouraging official declarations and undertakings of Messrs Boban, Izetbegovic and Karadzic and the behaviour of the combatants in the field, who did not hesitate to attack the delegates and property of humanitarian institutions. The argument – often used by the belligerents – that the various military commands were not in control of all the armed bands operating was refuted by many observers with expert knowledge of the field, who knew that the communication networks between the general staffs and combatant forces were efficient.

Strategic orders got through, and any attempt to suggest that there was chaos in their transmission was a fabrication intended for foreign consumption.

These were the circumstances in which the ICRC went to London to take part in the Conference on former Yugoslavia, where it enjoyed the specific status of observer with the right to speak. President Cornelio Sommaruga, seated between Mr Eliasson, Under-Secretary General for Humanitarian Affairs of the United Nations (who kept a low profile), and the very vocal Mr Eagleburger, then United States Secretary of State, attended the three days' debate in which the fate of the populations of this dismembered country was to be decided by the European Community, the permanent members of the UN Security Council, all the countries bordering on former Yugoslavia, a group of *ad hoc* countries (Canada, Japan, Turkey and Saudi Arabia), the Organization of the Islamic Conference, the Conference on European Security and Co-operation, and naturally by the representatives of the various states into which former Yugoslavia had broken up. The leaders of the Serb and Croat communities of Bosnia-Herzegovina were not admitted to the plenary hall, but followed the proceedings from an adjoining room.

The ICRC President and his delegation were at first optimistic. They saw before them a full agenda and hoped for real progress. But soon came disillusion at the emptiness of some of the orators' statements, consternation at the failure of the principal participants to enter into any commitment, grave concern when they remembered the emotionally charged remarks of Mazowiecki who returned on 27 August from his first mission, when the Conference was in full swing, and disappointment to see that the humanitarian effort was being used as a smokescreen to veil political indecision. Of course, miracles could not be expected and the procedures introduced in these last days of August contained all the expectations of the international community. Led by Cyrus Vance for the United Nations, and David Owen (who had taken over from Lord Carrington) for the European Community, the Geneva Conference, as it was now called, took over responsibility for supervising affairs in former Yugoslavia on a permanent basis. The ICRC would closely follow the progress of its humanitarian proposals, which were covered in one of the sub-groups of the Conference, headed by Sadako Ogata.

Meanwhile, the ICRC was all the more disappointed because it was conscious of the gap between the real priorities observed in the field and the main lines of political debate; the interest in humanitarian work was exhibited by the Conference to cloak its political inadequacies. Admittedly, world diplomacy was buckling down to solving the problems of closing the camps, a cause it was championing, and the delegates knew that the prisoners would then benefit from a minimum of protection whilst awaiting release. But they were extremely worried about the harassed villagers, despoiled of their elementary rights and expelled from their homes empty-handed, if indeed they managed to escape execution. This was the crux of President Sommaruga's speech to the Conference on 26 August, when he declared emphatically that things could not go on in this way, that the humanitarian organizations had done all in their power to mitigate suffering but found that their efforts were not enough, and that it was time for the international community to shoulder its responsibilities. Civilians in Bosnia-Herzegovina were then living in such terrible conditions that he regarded their return to normal life in the near future as altogether impossible. He called for acceptable stop-gap remedies, including the orderly transfer in complete safety of sectors of the population to temporary safe areas or internationally protected zones. And he repeated that the ICRC could no longer assume such vast responsibilities on its own.

Thierry Germond thought that the safety of individuals was what mattered above all else. He realized that to say so meant that the ICRC would be dragged into 'the vicious circle of "ethnic cleansing", but in the present state of affairs no other solution is possible'. The ICRC's contacts in international organizations, diplomatic circles and the media did not altogether understand, sometimes even rejected this view based on the painful everyday experience of delegates facing human tragedies that beggared description. Accepting the obligation to transfer people, even on the conditions laid down by the ICRC, was to demonstrate *a contrario* the failure of political reasoning and the inability of governments to impose their will to obtain what they most insistently demanded, namely that frontiers should not be changed and that populations should stay in their places of origin. By adopting this attitude, justified on humanitarian grounds since its aim was to save life, the ICRC went against majority opinion (only Austria agreed with the ICRC), but it persisted in believing that the first need was to protect, and finding durable solutions came later. It took months, and the tragedies of the Muslim minorities confined to pockets of eastern Bosnia at the beginning of 1993, for the international community to come round to this view, which was a matter more of ethics than of reasoning.

Saving life

On 3 September 1992, the United Nations operation in Bosnia-Herzegovina met with its first serious incident entailing loss of life. An Italian plane placed at the disposal of the airlift was shot down on approaching Sarajevo. The crew of four was killed and the airlift was suspended. With this news Sadako Ogata opened the second meeting of the 'Follow-up Committee on Global Humanitarian Response', held the next day at the Palais des Nations in Geneva. This abstract title conceals the body appointed to implement the recommendations of the International Conference of 29 July under the aegis of the UNHCR. The High Commissioner therefore headed two kinds of committees working in parallel, namely the follow-up committee of 29 July and the humanitarian affairs sub-committee initiated by the London Conference. It was for her to bridge the gap between them and avoid unproductive overlapping. The ICRC took part, both to help co-ordinate the work between institutions, then concerned mainly with organizing the forthcoming release of prisoners and their reception in a safe place.

In this rapprochement and the now daily contacts between the UNHCR and the ICRC in Geneva and in the field, Sadako Ogata and Cornelio Sommaruga came to the conclusion that a new language, and an even closer form of co-operation, had to be found to bring home to the world at large the depths of the tragedy in former Yugoslavia. They decided to address the international community together on this subject at a joint press conference on Saturday, 3 October at ICRC headquarters in Geneva.

The aims of the UNHCR and the ICRC, although not identical, were complementary. The UNHCR – which announced on the same day that its airlift would be resumed after having been suspended for exactly one month – wanted to impress on world opinion the vast scale of humanitarian needs which were still growing, and the consequent vital necessity to reinforce UN deployment on the spot. The ICRC drew up a cutting catalogue of the inaction of the parties to the conflict, completely disregarding undertakings to enforce international humanitarian law, and of the many grave breaches of that law which therefore took place in the field. It expressed its anger at the difficulties it was having in reaching the victims; it repeated that now that the first operation for the evacuation of prisoners from Trnopolje had been achieved, there was an urgent need to release all the inmates of all the detention camps unconditionally as the London Conference demanded; and it noted with concern how insignificant were all its efforts in comparison with the scale of the tragedy, and especially its pow-erlessness to put a stop to the criminal acts of 'ethnic cleansing'.[18]

Previously, on the morning of 3 October, the President of the ICRC had convened a meeting of the ambassadors accredited to the UN in Geneva to impress them with his concerns and ask for their immediate effective aid in putting a stop to the most serious violations of international humanitarian law, and to save lives in Bosnia-Herzegovina. For its part, the Security Council, being anxious to put into practice Resolution 771 on the respect of international humanitarian law, decided to appoint a Commission of Experts to enquire into the breaches that had been perpetrated, and to report thereon to the Secretary-General.[19]

The intense diplomatic activity of October 1992 raised the question whether the enthusiasm generated by the London Conference would collapse so quickly. Many delegates were embittered by the feeling that they were becoming administrators of political failure. The efforts of the international negotiators were hampered by the decision at the opening session of the General Assembly of the United Nations to exclude the new Yugoslavia from its 47th session,[20] contrary to the wish for multilateral discussions on the Balkans imbroglio. And the sanctions imposed on Serbia and Montenegro only made the parties even more unwilling to compromise.

The second winter: things hot up

But apart from these considerations, the calendar was a constant reminder that winter was on the way, and that it was therefore essential to find solutions regardless of differences of opinion. The greatest concerns of ICRC delegations were the down-to-earth ones of how to get relief convoys over mountain roads blocked by snow, so as to avoid the main roads reserved for military use, or dangerously mined, or rendered impassable because the bridges on them had been destroyed. Logistics specialists had to find answers to these questions every day, which shows how little the belligerents cared about emergency humanitarian aid. Other pieces from the same jigsaw puzzle were how to arrange the travels of ICRC delegates who had to visit prisons and camps and organize release operations, and how to ensure that the tens of thousands of family messages transiting monthly between members of families separated by the war were forwarded regularly. This was not only a matter of logistics, but also of obtaining the authorization to move from one zone to another from the officials controlling the various regions, and of safety, for all the combatant forces had to be notified of movements of lorry convoys and personnel.

These matters, urgent though they were, were hardly touched on by the plenipotentiaries representing Bosnia-Herzegovina, who met three times in 1992 in Geneva under ICRC auspices (22–23 May, 6 June, 30 September–1 October 1992). The first two sessions were stymied by an unfavourable working environment. The political positions of the parties were not only complex and antagonistic but often hard to understand. The Bosnian government, for example, claimed to be a victim of aggression by the Yugoslav Federal Republic, whilst insisting that its own conflict with the Bosnian Serb party was an internal matter. The same Serb party considered that it should be recognized as the 'Serbian Republic of Bosnia'. Furthermore, the level of representation at the meeting of 22–23 May was unequal.

The Bosnian representative had been sent from Zagreb because it was impossible for logistic reasons for the designated representative in Sarajevo to leave the town. The Croat party appointed *in extremis* the representative of the Croat community in Switzerland. Only the Bosnian Serbs managed to get themselves represented by their intended plenipotentiary. Right from the start, the Serbian party's insistence that the inhabitants of the various communities had to be regrouped in homogeneous areas made discussion difficult. The ICRC did its best to focus attention on the two priority aims of the meeting. The first of these was to agree on the law applicable; on the conduct of hostilities, and on the behaviour which the belligerents undertook to adopt towards the wounded, captured combatants and the civilian population. The second was to create conditions in which humanitarian work could be resumed after being suspended at Sarajevo, and later throughout Bosnia-Herzegovina, following the attack of 18 May on the ICRC. The first two meetings of the plenipotentiaries concentrated on these points. The third, at the end of September, was almost entirely concerned with implementing the decision of the London Conference on the global release of all prisoners.

Like Bosnia-Herzegovina itself, whose breakup was far advanced, this group of plenipotentiaries suffered from a lack of homogeneity which made negotiations difficult. Although the ICRC could congratulate itself at having persuaded the representatives of the three parties to the conflict to sit down together at the same table, it nevertheless regretted the complications which constantly cropped up and gave little promise that the agreements so laboriously arrived at would really be put into effect. Following the example set in higher quarters of broken promises unpunished except by universal reprobation, the plenipotentiaries officially undertook to assume all obligations to respect international humanitarian law. They promised to notify the ICRC of all places of detention and to take steps to ensure that ICRC delegates should have access to them without delay. They also agreed to appoint liaison officers to facilitate humanitarian work. Ten months later, the ICRC was still awaiting notifications and liaison officers and its delegates became increasingly convinced that many prisoners were escaping their attention.

The agreements signed by the belligerents on 1 October are clear on one point, namely that all civilians detained by all three parties should be unilaterally and unconditionally released by 31 October. The ICRC accordingly took steps to carry out a plan in two stages.

The first, scheduled for 26 October, was to cover nearly 5,000 people. The second would deal with the release, at the earliest possible date in each case, of detainees whose legal status was more complicated. It proved impossible to adhere to this very optimistic timetable, mainly because the host countries of the released prisoners had given no guarantees. Those countries had been slow to act in spite of the decisions of the London Conference to which in their enthusiasm they had subscribed. The transit centre appointed by the Republic of Croatia at Karlovac was still crowded with the first group of 1,560 persons evacuated on 1 October from Trnopolje, and there was no other similar centre to supplement it.

Pierre Gassmann, then responsible for operational co-ordination on the spot, admits that in fixing such an exact date the ICRC was bluffing. It had no other choice:

> We soon realized that these simultaneous releases could not take place because reception facilities in the transit camp and the countries of asylum were insufficient. Knowing that things were not going to turn out as planned, we made all the noise we could to encourage the mediators and the United Nations to put pressure on the relevant states to increase their capacity for asylum.

These tactics, conducted openly, were two-edged, for had any countries immediately complied with that appeal, the gaolers would still have had to be persuaded to release all the detainees on the same day. And this was by no means certain.

The date of 26 October was not honoured, any more than the deadline of the end of the month to complete the release operation, in spite of an information campaign ending with a particularly vigorous speech by President Sommaruga to the ambassadors of the states represented in Geneva, who were invited to attend a meeting at the ICRC headquarters on 30 October. In this speech the president urgently asked that their countries should admit the released prisoners and their families. 'Mrs Ogata and I await your announcement,' said the President, who again emphasized the extreme urgency of also finding ways of safeguarding the lives of the threatened civilian populations, for example by setting up protected areas. 'At this very moment,' he said, 'more than one hundred thousand Muslims are living in fear of their lives in northern Bosnia. Their only wish is to be transferred to a safe place.' The Security Council began to listen to him, for on 16 November it again condemned breaches of international humanitarian law and urged the Commission of Experts to continue its efforts to collect evidence of such breaches and 'invite the Secretary-General to study the possibility of and the requirements for the promotion of safe areas for humanitarian purposes' (Resolution 787 of 16 November

1992, paragraph 19). Nevertheless the question was still hotly disputed, the ICRC fervently advocating the safe areas, the UNHCR adopting an extremely reserved attitude and many government delegations unsure of the line they should take.[21]

Not before 18 December 1992 did the great majority of the civilians detained by the Bosnian Serbs recover their freedom, leaving behind them some hundreds of persons spirited away at the last moment unknown to the ICRC, whose delegates later caught up with them again and followed them for several months. On 23 December, the Serbian detainees held by the government of Bosnia-Herzegovina were also released. But as an ICRC press release, issued the same day,[22] noted with regret, the Croat forces did not respect the agreement signed by their representatives on 1 October, and released nobody in their power, on the pretext of certain legal provisions to which persons held by them would be subjected.

Pierre-André Conod, the ICRC's head of delegation in Zagreb, believes that although this large-scale release operation was in general a good thing, it nevertheless had disadvantages. The first of these was the immediate one that delays by the countries of asylum encouraged the resumption of shady exchange practices in a conflict where prisoners were regarded only as units of barter. The other lasted longer. It was that the ICRC was fully engaged in this release operation for several months and no longer had the resources necessary to tighten the screw on those who were hiding the places of detention from it. Time after time, the delegates had the impression of being hounded from one emergency to another, and they wasted a lot of energy in trying to do their humanitarian work in a rational way while having to follow the whims of an international community at its wits' end.

Meeting after meeting took place. The Vance–Owen peace plan, on the stocks since September 1992, appeared to be nearing completion. Besides the regular meetings of the leading figures in the Geneva Conference and all its sub-groups, the UNHCR's follow-up meetings and the meetings for co-ordinating the work of the organizations active in the field, the diplomatic marathon of late 1992 was enriched by two extraordinary sessions. On 30 November, that of the Commission on Human Rights examined the three reports made by Tadeusz Mazowiecki after many missions in the field. In these he and his team observed how horrendous were the violations of human rights committed, and especially the ravages caused by 'ethnic cleansing'. On 1 December, the Commission adopted a resolution that declared the Serbian party guilty of these outrages. The other meeting was that of the Organization of the Islamic Conference[23] which, in the presence of Cyrus Vance, Lord Owen and Sadako Ogata, adopted a more vigorous stance and pressed for a republic possessing defensive weapons, the establishment of protected areas, the creation of an international tribunal for the trial of war criminals, and the final closure of the detention camps, in which connection it mentioned the role of the ICRC.

The fruit of the palaver tree

'Throughout the summer and autumn of 1992, humanitarian definition and inter-cultural diagnosis blunted political awareness ... Barring a belated burst of energy, the political abasement of Europe was sealed by humanitarianizing war in Bosnia.' So said Alain Joxe.[24] Although many countries subscribed to the thesis of the aggressor and the aggressee, its logic was scarcely observed. Rather than react in the direct natural way of coming to the help of the oppressed party, the international community preferred to negotiate. The corollary was impunity for all those guilty of breaches. During 1992, one international tribune after another was set up, so giving the illusion that the politicians had decided to make an all-out attack on the problems and on solving them. But the discussions very soon centred on the only subject that really meant anything. The media had already fastened on to it; it was humanitarian aid.

Since the outbreak of the Bosnian conflict, the ICRC, impressed by the encouraging results of the previous year's negotiations, had tried to enter upon a similar dialogue with the new belligerents. This did not take into account the fact that political morality was disintegrating nor that the humanitarian aid workers were dealing with people prodigal in verbal promises, ready to sign anything officially, but whose commitments were repudiated in the twinkling of an eye by conditions in the field, where nothing was or would be respected.

The purpose of the diplomatic manoeuvres directed from Geneva by the ICRC's Executive Board, its President, the Directorate of Operations, specialists in humanitarian law, and the Delegate General for Europe and his team was to be present and make themselves heard everywhere and without respite, and to keep the dialogue going at any price in the hope of getting tangible advantages for humanitarian action. In playing this game, the ICRC ran out of steam; its convictions were as strong as ever but it made no major gains. Cynicism, indifference and the scattering of centres of decision over the international scene had sapped its penetrating power. The excellence of individual performances was powerless to change this. The message did not get through, or only very imperfectly, but the humanitarian workers were not to blame.

The ICRC's dialogue with the parties to the conflict nevertheless overcame some of the impediments to the release of prisoners from the camps, once it was realized in August 1992 that the detainees were living in intolerable conditions. If it did not bring more substantial results 'it was not for want of trying', as the officials responsible for humanitarian work said; and indeed they had done everything possible to improve the living conditions of the victims of the conflict. There is much to be said for and against the other international partners on the diplomatic and operational front. The 'man to man' relations established in United Nations and European circles were sound but could not always overcome the obstacles. Results would have fuelled discussion; but since there were no results, discussion became merely theoretical. The ICRC did not give up trying and fought hard to enforce humanitarian law. There were repeated appeals to a sense of responsibility, and cries of alarm rang out in the conference halls of political Europe in Brussels, of parliamentary Europe in Strasbourg, of the UNHCR in Geneva, and, on 12 November 1992, of the Security Council in New York. Even at the General Assembly of the United Nations, before which President Sommaruga made his speech of 20 November 1992 on the subject of co-ordinating humanitarian aid, without referring expressly to former Yugoslavia, he pinpointed the worst difficulties caused by confusing humanitarian affairs with politics or military matters.

In the field, heads of delegation were not at the source of diplomatic initiatives; rather they were acting as conveyor belts between the victims they were assisting and the headquarters that was striving to obtain acceptable working conditions for them. They were working in close contact with United Nations, European and non-governmental organizations. There too, results were not always consonant with the quality of individual relations, because of institutional policy differences. Dialogue was easier with UNPROFOR representatives in the UNPAs, because it was extremely concrete, than with the European observers, whose mission sometimes overlapped the ICRC delegates' work of protection. François Fouinat believes that one of the things the UNHCR would regret was that

> the ICRC does not like to be associated with other agencies. That is a pity. We should have been more effective had we done more things in common. Would it be possible even to imagine fighting side by side? Perhaps it would, although the UNHCR and the ICRC have very different philosophies and mandates and move in very different circles. Saving lives does not mean the same to everybody.

To which André Collomb the ICRC's Deputy Delegate General for Europe replies realistically: 'Since the end of 1992 a united front has hardly been possible any more, because of differences in terms of reference and different interpretations of the concept of protected areas.' That concept was proposed by the ICRC, sent for examination to the United Nations and then put on ice until the spring of 1993. It then emerged in the form of safe areas for a number of minority pockets in eastern Bosnia, leaving UNPROFOR, which had to put it into effect, to overcome almost insurmountable difficulties.

In the words of Cornelio Sommaruga,

> As regards bilateral intervention, and also our declarations to the press and our statements in the various conferences, I think I can say that we have changed our methods of approach. We have called upon governments to shoulder their responsibilities, perhaps we have done so more bravely than in the past, but at the risk of making them feel that they have had about enough of our warnings. This is a difficult balance to maintain, for we need those governments, if only to finance us. But what was going on in former Yugoslavia made any more diplomatic language impossible.

The ICRC was of course disappointed to see that everything it had tried to say and do had produced so little result, but this was the price of politicizing humanitarian work. Nevertheless, President Sommaruga believes that it is important to remember that

> things of this kind could happen in other countries that had federal structures and authoritarian regimes when they fell apart, and where ethnic conflicts can again emerge. In such cases, diplomacy and negotiation are still important, although it is not easy to avoid mixing politics with humanitarian work.

As a negotiator, the ICRC will always have at least one strength and one weakness. Its strength is knowing that it will not deviate from its course and will not abandon victims unless compelled to do so by force of arms; its weakness is that it cannot use the threat of leaving the field as an ultimatum to belligerents who care not a fig for humanitarian principles.

CHAPTER 4

Sarajevo 1992: pandemonium

In camera

'We were not there when things were at their worst.' Thinking of what happened to Bosnia-Herzegovina, those few words come to mind, endlessly repeated by humanitarian workers like a leitmotiv. And the survivors say, with a fatalistic shrug, 'You were not there when things were at their worst.'

The most evil and appalling practices – mass deportations, round-ups and imprisonment, massacres, rape, plundering and looting – took place between April and July 1992, on a scale out of all proportion with what happened afterwards.

A year later, perspective became distorted. The tragedies of eastern Bosnia – of its martyred towns Cerska, Zepa, Srebrenica and Gorazde, of Mostar and devastated central Bosnia – blunted the memory of the conflict's most dreadful and dramatic moments, which had taken place out of sight, without witnesses, without journalists. Without help. Behind closed doors. For humanitarians it was indeed one of the unchanging factors of this war that they were never there when they were needed to prevent or correct the worst. It was not a question of incompetence but rather impotence at the inexorability of a plan of destruction that no political or military force could stop – and powerlessness to make the regular soldiers and paramilitary groups who systematically obstructed humanitarian action see reason.

At the beginning of 1992, emerging from the war between Croatia and federal Yugoslavia, and at a time when the cease-fire agreed upon on 4 January with Cyrus Vance as mediator appeared to be holding better than the others, ICRC delegates turned their attention to Bosnia-Herzegovina, a republic apparently calm until its progress towards independence made it the centre of world attention.

The referendum took place on 29 February. It was the first chapter of the tragedy that began quite quietly when the Bosnian Serbs boycotted the referendum and threw up barricades in reprisal. The people of Sarajevo were not too worried about this. They thought it was only a bit of Balkan folklore, a logistic complication (the town being cut in two) rather than a danger they had to protect themselves against. Life went on as normal, the only difference being that many people did not go to work for those few days. People were sure that nothing serious could happen, and the barricades were a curiosity that crowds turned out to see. It was less dangerous than venturing into the Latin Quarter in Paris in May 1968. Indeed, Zlatko Dizdarevic's *Journal de guerre* (*War Diary*)[1] only begins a couple of months later, on 25 April, just after the first cease-fire negotiated by Lord Carrington.

The ICRC's first contacts with the authorities of Bosnia-Herzegovina, with a view to opening an office in its capital, date from October 1991. The plan took shape in December, when the three political parties composing the government coalition showed that they were interested. The delegate responsible for the office opened it in January 1992. She recruited local staff and began work on the humanitarian concerns of the time, which arose mainly from the conflict between Croatia and federal Yugoslavia. The office was a centre for the family messages exchanged between Belgrade and Zagreb, direct communication between the two cities having been broken off. At that time Sarajevo was an ideal transit point, for its telephone network made it possible to contact any place on earth.

The European Community observers were present in Sarajevo, as was *Médecins sans Frontières (MSF)*, which had been there since May 1991. The UNHCR was not due to arrive until March 1992. There were few international journalists around.

The ball had started rolling. The situation in Sarajevo was appreciably different from that of the first conflict of 1991. Bosnia-Herzegovina was fatally heading for a breakup because of the intricate mix of Muslim, Serbian and Croat communities, and the potential danger was therefore much greater than in more homogeneous regions. Belgrade was Serbian, Zagreb Croat; but here was multicultural, universal, convivial Sarajevo, where different communities lived together in harmony. The coexisting official militias or territorial forces were polishing their weapons, and at home every man was cleaning his rifle. Even before the referendum, people were getting out their weapons and yet, for the people of Sarajevo, war was still something that happened in distant towns like Dubrovnik and Vukovar. They could not believe what was going on in front of their eyes. For the ICRC employees native to Sarajevo, these first barricades seemed like a hoax.

And then the second lot of barricades was thrown up on 4 April, accompanied by a wave of demonstrations in front of the parliament building. There was violence, and the first shots were fired against the demonstrators. On 6 April Bosnia-Herzegovina became a full member of the United Nations. This international recognition, welcomed by some and cursed by others, increased the intercommunal rivalry. Federal army and police contingents sent out mixed patrols in an effort to pacify public opinion. Rumour was rife and propaganda intense. According to the inhabitants of Sarajevo, it was from that time on that people began to fear their neighbours, a fear which little by little turned to hate.

The humanitarian aid workers stationed in Bosnia-Herzegovina viewed the tragedy with a mixture of ambiguity, realism, blindness and delusion. The delegates thought that 'if the balloon goes up in Bosnia, things are going to be very nasty'. But at the same time, they were all telling themselves that there must be some way out. Humanitarian operations were planned in an atmosphere of some mental confusion. The ICRC was preparing to draft new forces to Bosnian territory, which had become the number one priority. It opened offices in various regions of the republic, including Banja Luka and Mostar. The assistance operation in Croatia was no longer classed as an emergency, and was progressively handed over to the UNHCR. UNPROFOR began deploying in the Krajina and opened its base in Sarajevo.

At the end of April, delegates from all over Bosnia-Herzegovina assembled in Sarajevo to take stock of the situation. The atmosphere there was already very heated and left its mark on the meeting, which started on 30 April. The outlook of the delegate stationed in Sarajevo seemed alarmist at the time, but her forebodings were amply confirmed by the events of 1 May, when Sarajevo went up in flames both literally and figuratively. The post office was set on fire and burned all night. The delegates could not meet because clashes went on for hours. Three delegates lost contact with their base, being unable to leave a café since the middle of the previous day. Most of the ICRC's 17 vehicles parked in front of the Hotel Zagreb were damaged. This was 2 May 1992. The war had started.

The convoy of 18 May

The delegates went back to their posts, those stationed in Mostar with great difficulty, for this town too was in peril. The Sarajevo team, numbering half a dozen, went back to its quarters and got on with its work. In the next few days, one after another, the great majority of the UN representatives, including the UNHCR, withdrew. So did the European observers. The ICRC was the only institution apart from MSF to stay behind and again found itself with a humanitarian monopoly in a city whose every building had its checkpoint and where it often took an hour and a half to cover two kilometres. The atmosphere was unstable, like the war there, where idyllic spots suddenly went up in flames for no apparent reason. In this first fortnight of May, the humanitarian workers were very popular although their activities were rather limited. People were grateful to them for staying behind. At roadblocks they were more often treated to a cup of coffee than abuse.

But Sarajevo was already a town under siege and latent tension was making the atmosphere more menacing. It was becoming a matter of urgency to relieve the personnel on the spot and top up stocks of material needed for assistance, especially medical supplies. The Belgrade office organized a convoy. A first attempt failed because of fighting along the route chosen, and the expedition finally set out on 17 May towards Pale via Zvornik. This itinerary was not the one at first fixed. It was imposed by the Bosnian Serb forces, who were very keen on the ICRC convoy going through the capital of the self-proclaimed Serbian Republic of Bosnia.

At Pale, discussions were held on neutralizing a hospital, the position of Serbian doctors and other matters. The delegates included the future head of the Sarajevo office, the very experienced Frédéric Maurice who had been lent by Geneva headquarters. These improvised interviews were regarded as a favourable opportunity to strengthen ties with one of the parties to the conflict at a time when the ICRC was seeking to extend its operational network.

By the end of the next morning all the necessary permissions had been confirmed. The convoy set off and arrived without incident at the agreed meeting place with the delegate from Sarajevo. An exchange of prisoners had just been concluded there. The vehicles continued on their way, guided by that of the Sarajevo delegate. They passed the first Muslim checkpoint, and two bends further on, before arriving under the walls of the old city, they were attacked.

Jean-Claude Mulli, the ICRC doctor with the convoy, recalled:

> The first shell exploded between the first and second cars. In the second car were Frédéric, Ivan [Lalic] the interpreter and Roland [Sidler], a delegate. Immediately afterwards, a second shell fell, this time at the rear of the same vehicle. The drivers of the two lorries that followed, and I at the end of the convoy, could go no further. We did not know at that time that we were so near the town. Shells continued to rain down on us. We left the vehicles and ran back as quickly as we could. It was the only thing to do, for we could not turn round with the vehicles. We were trapped but under cover, about thirty metres from where the shells were landing. The firing lasted an hour and finished with an incendiary rocket hitting the biggest lorry, which caught fire. It was out of the question to proceed. Everything was in flames in this short stretch of narrow road between a rocky slope and houses. Then Muslim militiamen came out of the forest opposite and beckoned to us. It was then we saw Frédéric's car riddled with holes, its tyres punctured. We came upon Roland,

who was slightly wounded and given medical attention on the spot. Together we went to the hospital, where we were told that Frédéric was in the operating theatre, as was Ivan, who appeared to be the more seriously wounded. We arranged for a place to stay the night.

Throughout the attack and until nightfall the fugitives from the convoy maintained radio contact with the Sarajevo office. Their reports were extremely confused, but the local employee understood the main drift and tried to work out who was wounded and in hospital, and where the other members of the mission were. She was more or less reassured, but had a bad night. The next day at 6.30 a.m., she made radio contact with the Belgrade delegation to report. The line was bad and she was preparing to postpone the call when she heard a deep voice say to her 'Let's pass on AMTOR.'[2] 'Then', she said,

> I knew something had gone wrong. It would never have occurred to anybody the night before that Frédéric was going to die. He didn't seem to be all that badly wounded. We were much more worried about Ivan. Then my colleagues arrived in the office one after another, in the usual way. How was I to tell them? Instead of saying 'Good morning', I said 'This is not a good morning.' I shall never forget how they looked at me.

In Geneva, and in The Hague where the ICRC President was on the evening of 18 May, 'we went to bed in a fairly optimistic frame of mind, given the available news,' said Francis Amar. He said he had never before been as depressed, and had never seen 'the office' in such a state, in the whole of his career. Everybody was almost ready to break down.

There was plenty to do on the spot. A return convoy to Belgrade had to be organized. Frédéric's body had to be sent home, and his wounded colleague had to be looked after as well as possible. Francis Amar went to Belgrade to support the delegation. The journey from Sarajevo to Belgrade was chaotic. As Dr Mulli said: 'We suddenly realized that the situation had completely changed and that we could no longer follow the most direct routes as we had done before. We expected this but it nevertheless surprised us when it happened. It was war!' Seven hours and 150 kilometres farther on, the convoy met Francis Amar's team which had come to meet them halfway, at Zvornik, on the bridge between Bosnia and Serbia. 'I shall never forget seeing this convoy approach at twenty kilometres an hour,' said Amar,

> They were in the state they had been caught in when they were ambushed two days before. They were unshaven, unwashed and completely haggard. There was blood everywhere. Frédéric's

car was still running, but it was shot to pieces. We set off again, back towards Belgrade. The next day we landed at Geneva. Frédéric's family was there. A very simple and very moving ceremony took place on the tarmac.

Vacuum sets in

When they hurriedly left Sarajevo the delegates told the local employees they were leaving behind that they would not be away for long. They said so in good faith, but it was seven months before they were back. What happened meanwhile?

The outrage of 18 May left the ICRC shocked and incredulous, and compelled it to reflect on its own limitations. Two days later in Geneva, the representatives of the warring parties in Bosnia-Herzegovina met for the first time. They were asked to agree among themselves on what rules were applicable to the conduct of hostilities, to undertake to respect them, and to give guarantees that would make humanitarian work possible. This last request referred particularly to the situation in the Bosnian capital, but also to the entire territory, where the delegates were exposed to major obstructions and their work was sometimes brought to a complete standstill. They could never be sure of the slightest degree of safety, so that their humanitarian activities were much less effective than they would normally have been. The ICRC also expected the parties to conduct an inquiry to identify those responsible for the attack on its convoy.

In internal discussions, the office of the Director of Operations, and later the ICRC's Executive Board, examined all the factors relevant to its continued activities in Bosnia. This led to its formal decision of 27 May 1992 to withdraw temporarily all delegates based in Bosnia-Herzegovina, largely because of a lack of confidence in the ability of the parties to the conflict to ensure that the commitments they had entered into in Geneva four days previously would be respected in the field. The attack on the maternity wing of Kosevo Hospital and, later, on a bread queue in Sarajevo, also on 27 May, were shocking evidence that the doubts assailing the ICRC leaders were justified. It had been hard for them to reach this decision, and it was unpopular in regions where the delegates did not feel personally threatened. The risk of danger was extremely variable and people living in constantly bombarded Sarajevo were in a very different position to those in a besieged city such as Mostar, and others based in Banja Luka, where life was much less dangerous at the time. Both the ICRC and its delegates were unwilling to abandon people needing their help, to whom they had made firm promises; for example, civilians imprisoned in intolerable conditions, or inmates of psychiatric hospitals relying wholly on their assistance. Furthermore, they had a presentiment of the excesses later committed against the civilian population, without yet knowing their scale.

All these factors led to feelings of restlessness, sadness and emotions of varying kinds. Some delegates were found a temporary niche in the ICRC's Belgrade or Zagreb offices, where they made themselves useful until they could get back to their previous work. Others took the opportunity to go on leave. But all of them fully intended to return to where they were awaited.

In Geneva, the office of the Director of Operations prepared a plan for the resumption of work in Bosnia-Herzegovina. This was submitted to the plenipotentiary representatives when they met again in Geneva on 6 June. They accepted it. Agreement is one thing, intent to ensure application quite another, and the parties to the conflict were therefore asked to confirm formally their undertaking to abide by the terms of the agreement, and especially to do everything necessary to improve the safety of ICRC officials, such as appointing political and military authorities to act as guarantors in the field. The plan did not, however, make any mention of an airlift to Sarajevo, for which the parties to the conflict had asked the ICRC as far back as May. The ICRC had not fully studied this request. Meanwhile, the United Nations began discussions on the same subject and the ICRC concluded that it was no longer within its province. The investigation into the attack of 18 May was making next to no progress, so that it was doubtful whether humanitarian activities would be resumed in Sarajevo, which was still being constantly bombarded.

For much of the month of June, the ICRC leaders were torn between two demands: that of institutional responsibility, which required them to make rapid decisions to alleviate urgent needs in the field, and which involved their return; and that of responsibility to individuals, which made the safety of humanitarian workers the main consideration, with all its unknown factors, especially in Sarajevo.

This period of uncertainty and peak frustration coincided with that of the worst abominations, as the delegates were to discover later. It is impossible to say that these would not have occurred if the humanitarian workers had been there. Some observers have pointed out that there were fewer outrages after August 1992, by which time the international presence and journalistic coverage were greater. True, the sinister 'job' was then nearly over in the region of, for example, Prijedor, Kozarac and Sanski Most, as escaped prisoners from Omarska were later to testify. Other observers have said that the combined presence of large UN forces and the media did not prevent the atrocities at Gorazde, Mostar and Srebrenica later on.

The ICRC returns to Bosnia

The ICRC delegates were not good at taking things as they came without being able to do anything about them. They had to get going again. As from 24 June, small teams were scouring the area to decide on what conditions they could return, to get permission to visit detention centres, and to evaluate the most urgent needs. On 1 and 2 July, all the ICRC officials responsible for operations in Bosnia-Herzegovina met in Zagreb with the ICRC Director of Operations and studied the information gathered by delegates on exploratory missions. Those delegates concluded that, in the circumstances, safety standards were sufficient to start work again except around Bjelijna, where they had been subjected to serious intimidation, and in eastern Bosnia, a still inaccessible territory representing about 20 per cent of the republic. They also confirmed that, wherever they had been, there was a crying need for humanitarian aid. On his return to Geneva, the Director of Operations made a detailed report of the conclusions arrived at by the Zagreb meeting, and on 7 July it was decided to resume activities in Bosnia-Herzegovina … except at Sarajevo.

Offices were opened or reopened at Velika Kladusa (in the Bihac pocket), and at Mostar, Banja Luka, Zenica, and Bileca (in the Trebinje region). Warehouses and vehicle parks were reorganized and contacts were made with the authorities to arrange prison visits which were resumed on 7 July at Mostar, Bileca/Trebinje and Morinj. On that date and over the next few days, relief convoys set out for Banja Luka, Mostar, Bihac and Livno. Less than a week later, on 13 July, the Delegate General for Europe used the UN airlift to go to Sarajevo (the first visit since 19 May). There he met the Bosnian authorities (and then the Bosnian Serbs at Pale), and the UNPROFOR leaders, who facilitated the ICRC's stay in Sarajevo by means of their logistic arrangements. Without these it was impossible to move from one part of the town to another. The United Nations badly wanted the ICRC to return, being unable to do all the humanitarian work itself, especially those tasks usually falling to the ICRC such as prison visits, the exchange of family messages and support to hospitals.

The UNPROFOR official responsible for civilian affairs, who was stationed in Sarajevo from May 1992 to January 1993, admitted several months later in Zagreb that he was disappointed that the ICRC had so long postponed its return to Sarajevo. While fully understanding its profound shock at the loss of one of its colleagues, he wondered why the ICRC had not taken advantage of the start of the airlift to resume its work. He remembered how the people who stayed behind were devastated at the departure of everyone representing the 'international community'. He would have preferred to see the Red Cross flag flying, a symbol of cheer in the midst of the destruction.

ICRC delegates carried out several short-term missions to Sarajevo between July and November. On 3 December 1992, the ICRC Executive Board was ready to decide about going back to Sarajevo. Not that the conditions stipulated for the delegates' return had been fulfilled – far from it; the murderers of Frédéric Maurice had not been identified and it was still hardly possible to work without armed protection. Director of Operations Jean de Courten was nevertheless convinced that the situation had improved sufficiently for the ICRC to resume its activities, notably because of the work done locally by UNPROFOR. However, he ruled out any military protection, even by the United Nations, because if the ICRC relied on UN logistics it would seem, in the eyes of one of the parties to the conflict, to be an instrument of the 'anti-Serb plot'. Moreover, it was not possible for a neutral independent institution such as the ICRC to contemplate any close and lasting association with a political organization such as the United Nations. It would even be contrary to its doctrine. This was President Sommaruga's position, as he explained it to the Executive Board; he affirmed that the ICRC must look after its own safety, using means of passive protection such as armoured vehicles and flak-jackets. The resumption of ICRC activities would indeed depend on when this equipment was delivered. On the basis of information coming from the field and the opinion of those directing the operations, the Executive Board approved the proposals for progressive re-deployment of ICRC delegates in Sarajevo, where they were to return for an indefinite period in February 1993.

Throughout the period from June to December 1992, the Red Cross flag had nevertheless been kept flying, albeit discreetly, thanks to the devotion, courage and imagination of four employees (three women and a man) recruited in Sarajevo. Their story alone would merit a chapter, and perhaps a whole book which they may write one day. Marjolaine Martin, the deputy head of the Zagreb delegation, said of them:

> They were expecting us to come back to visit the prisoners, in July or August, as we had promised. And they stayed there on the spot, alone. They had been given very little training and were working in impossible conditions, yet they built up a network of family messages that worked uninterruptedly. They managed to get the satellite telephone going again and learned to use a

computer 'by correspondence', by consulting ICRC specialists
over the radio. In short, they worked wonderfully well, although
we had never been very explicit with them and had let them hope
that we were coming back soon whereas, in fact, we returned
only seven months later.

On their own initiative, and without a penny for nearly two months
(until 13 July, when the Delegate General brought them their
salaries) and with infinite resourcefulness, these four people 'got
on with the humanitarian work' as best they could, helped by the
MSF employees, who were in the same situation as themselves and
had an office in the compound of the Kosevo Hospital. Refusing
to be idle in a city where having nothing to do was the shortest of
all short cuts to mental instability, they determined to be efficient
and persuaded the United Nations to help them transport, either
by land or air, the mail exchanged between the besieged population
and their families outside. They reported to the ICRC delegations
in Belgrade and Zagreb as little as possible, rather than worry
them by their unorthodox methods. They made every effort to keep
busy although they were isolated, hoping that their work would
enable the ICRC delegates to pick up the threads more easily
when they came back. But they had to wait patiently still longer,
for meanwhile visits had started to the detention camps that had
been given the most press coverage – those which the American
journalist Roy Gutman, in *Newsday* on 2 August 1992, called 'the
Death Camps'. These had to be given unceasing attention until
the mass releases in the last quarter of 1992.

Lessons from a nightmare

'That day, we learned everything all at once. We realized that we
could not keep on playing this game, that the context was too rotten
for us to hope to make any moral impression. Humanitarian work
was completely taken hostage.' With these cogent words Françoise
Saulnier of MSF recalls what she went through on 18 October 1991
at the very gates of Vukovar. Her MSF convoy was returning after
loading the most seriously wounded onto lorries, when three federal
army tanks trained their guns on it. All the surrounding hills were
mined. Nobody stirred. Nobody fired. The convoy was trapped and
could only turn round and retrace the itinerary it had followed on
the outward journey, on a route that had been free of obstacles only
two hours before. An anti-tank mine exploded under the fourth
lorry. Only one explosion. It wounded three MSF personnel. The
convoy, with its load of wounded from a town that had been under
siege for the last two months, then made a chaotic 17-hour return
journey over muddy tracks without assistance. 'Fortunately,'

Françoise Saulnier added, 'the press was there and this protected us.' MSF did not withdraw from former Yugoslavia, because one of its rules was not to shut down its delegation unless human life had been lost. Since then, the MSF has been living with the memory of this nightmare experience, which has profoundly affected its staff.

The parallel between the MSF experience at Vukovar and that of the ICRC in Sarajevo, seven months later to the day, is disturbing because of its absolute similarity. MSF dropped what it called its 'swaggering cowboy' style, and the ICRC co-ordinator of operations Urs Boegli declared:

> After Sarajevo the time for adventure was over. We lost our virginity, so to speak. Everybody has become very cautious. Everybody is much more safety-conscious. Our eyes have been opened to the real dangers, not only being fired at like anybody else but perhaps being one of the stakes in this war.

With this loss of spontaneity has come a tendency to practise 'armoured humanitarian aid' using special vehicles, flak-jackets and steel helmets. These have been made essential by the circumstances ICRC delegates have to face every day:

> It's not easy for us to take on all this paraphernalia, even though it's part of standard equipment in other organizations. But for too long, we have been working on the assumption that we were protected by the 'ICRC miracle', namely the belief that the Red Cross emblem would be respected.

The ICRC's temporary and short withdrawal from Bosnia-Herzegovina was fairly well accepted inside and outside the ICRC, but its failure to return to Sarajevo earned it the criticism and even resentment of the UN community, its Bosnian Muslim contacts and some of its own colleagues. Within the ICRC it was hotly and heatedly discussed. As with MSF, reactions varied from perplexity to refusal to understand, from rejection to utter amazement. There were irrational outbursts that were difficult to contain. Deep-buried taboos rose to the surface, consciences squirmed.

The questions the ICRC asked the belligerents in order to clarify the circumstances of the attack on the convoy of 18 May, and to identify those responsible, were never clearly or convincingly answered. It would, no doubt, be naive to expect ever to be given an explanation.

More realistically, and in spite of this enduring doubt, the ICRC had to weigh the advantages and disadvantages of setting up in a town whose appearance had completely changed. Since UN forces arrived at the airport and a regular airlift began in July after François Mitterand's masterly and surprise visit to the city, the international community concentrated all its attention on Sarajevo. The United Nations was represented there by large bodies of officials, both civilian and military, and by the UNHCR – and in their wake came the unending capers of the media. Travelling to Sarajevo, moving about and living in Sarajevo inevitably meant entering the UN orbit, using their airlift and armoured vehicles, and even their residences. The ICRC could not easily accept this, for it would have undermined its necessary independence.

Sarajevo, the scene of so much suffering, was the city receiving aid most regularly, whilst other regions of Bosnia-Herzegovina, far from the limelight, were struggling with the daily difficulties of mere survival without any NGO rushing to the rescue. The ICRC presence in Sarajevo was therefore not absolutely necessary as regards material assistance, but was needed more for its usual priorities of protecting prisoners and maintaining family ties. The United Nations, through its mouthpiece General McKenzie, the officer commanding UNPROFOR in Sarajevo, the Bosnian Muslim authorities and Bosnian Serbs were all of the opinion that the ICRC had been away far too long.

It would in fact have been simpler for the ICRC to resume its activities in Sarajevo without this long delay, thus nipping in the bud any controversial inclinations. The institution would have kept a relatively clean slate and any kind of guilt complex would have been erased. All the soul-searching and delays typical of this episode show plainly that the ICRC is human rather than rational, and that it had not realized, somewhat naively, that its absence from a martyred city, a world-wide symbol of tolerance crushed by bombs, seemed nothing less than absurd.

CHAPTER 5

Crimes Without Punishment

The misconduct of hostilities[1]

Thierry Meyrat is a shrewd observer of humanitarian affairs who has benefited from eleven months' service in the conflicts of former Yugoslavia. He experienced from the inside much of the first war and then the preliminaries and outbreak of the war that was to lead to the breakup of Bosnia-Herzegovina. He was particularly struck by

> the inequality of the belligerents' resources, a conduct of hostilities that totally disregards all laws of war, and the groups of irregulars who are there to inspire terror and to do things even more horrible than those for which law does not provide. The massacres of which these bands are guilty are one of the most powerful ways of justifying the continuance of the war to public opinion; and public opinion is not always sure that it wants the war to go on.[2]

The daily routine of the International Committee of the Red Cross (ICRC) delegates, and of all those in the field confronted by the uncontrollable lurches of the juggernaut of war, is sufficiently eventful and corroborated to deserve attention. Their experiences differ, for they worked in different theatres of war at different times. Their account of these experiences – quite apart from the facts, which are indisputable – is tinged with red or grey or black according to individual personality. But anyone who, at the end of the war, tries to patch up the damage done to humanitarian law by the protagonists in the tragedy would learn a great deal from gathering together these fragments of human experience.

The laws of war were born on the field of battle. At first made by soldiers and later by diplomats, they were enriched and expanded by humanitarian witnesses. They can therefore develop in the right direction only if they integrate the interests of all parties, relying on a *realpolitik* that does not forget the victims, who are, nine times out of ten, civilians.

Civilian casualties in the First World War have been estimated at 14 per cent and those of members of the armed forces at 86 per cent. In the Second World War, 33 per cent of the victims were members of the armed forces and 67 per cent civilians.[3]

The spread of guerrilla warfare and the many wars of liberation since the 1960s tend to abolish the distinction between combatants and civilians by involving civilians in the armed struggle, and have made for vastly increased civilian casualties. These are now at a level that is in humane terms intolerable. Intolerable because it indicates that the grossly perverted logic of war – aided by the conflicts in the Gulf and in former Yugoslavia – is reaching that stage of mathematical perfection in which purely military losses are little more than nil whilst civilian casualties go up and up.

As for loss of human life, international humanitarian law, the delegate's vade-mecum with its Geneva Conventions and Protocols intended to ensure a minimum of protection for non-combatants and ex-combatants, has suffered great harm. Breaches of this law over the months have become so common that it is now old-fashioned even to refer to them. This would be absurd if it were not tragic. It is unfortunately necessary to quote a few episodes that show how modern rules of international law, approved by nearly all the nations of the world, have become debased.

The state of belligerency

In the federal Belgrade of mid-1991, political power continued to weaken and economic and social collapse reached abysmal depths. The federal army too was in difficulties when it returned from the Slovene campaign, which had earned it few laurels. As arbitrator between Serbs and Croats of the tension in Croatia, it was not finding it easy to hit the right note or to stay credible, because its ethnic composition at general staff level rather tended to class it with the advocates of Greater Serbia. As its role of natural intermediary declined, militias and all sorts of armed groups sprang into being, leaping into the breach beside the legally constituted republican territorial forces. To make things worse, the Yugoslav media never ceased to spread simplistic ethnic propaganda from which it was becoming more and more difficult to escape.

In an internal memorandum of 15 July 1991, Jean-François Berger, the ICRC desk officer for former Yugoslavia in Geneva, observed that

> In the light of this escalation, the efforts made to apply the Brioni Agreements are in great danger of coming to nothing because the political background is now so different, having been irresistibly handed over to the unpredictable influence of a power that has ceased to exist.

The Brioni Agreements were intended to settle the Slovene conflict, but also aspired to monitor the situation and even to appease the tension in Croatia. Their reference to the ICRC in paragraph VI of their Annex I on the release of Slovene and Yugoslav prisoners confirmed the ICRC's mandate. The ICRC welcomed this recognition of its role, having until then taken some small advantage of the general indecision to get its views and its humanitarian activities endorsed.

Alleged breaches of international humanitarian law by both sides in the Slovene war steadily increased, and eye-witness accounts began to come in of threats, intimidation and persecution suffered in Vojvodina and in Baranja. ICRC delegates and jurists were being asked how best to ensure a stronger presence in the field.

The ICRC has at its disposal a legal basis, not completely vague but much disputed and hitherto regarded as a necessary evil. Both Slovenia and Croatia confronted the same problem as to how their conflict should be classified; in each case, a seceding state had declared itself independent of a central state which rejected the claim to independence, and the seceding and central states were in armed conflict. As proof of its existence, the seceding state quite naturally invoked the law applicable to international armed conflicts whereas the central state maintained that these armed clashes were, at most, part of an internal armed conflict. To safeguard its freedom of action, the ICRC refused to enter the legal controversy and took its stand on Article 3 common to all four of the Geneva Conventions of 12 August 1949. This Article is in itself a pocket Geneva Convention which offers the ICRC some margin of manoeuvre (see below). The ICRC awaited a more generous agreement, which was signed on 27 November 1991.

Meanwhile, the effects of the crisis in Croatia had to be countered, and the Red Cross – the ICRC, as well as the Yugoslav and the republican Red Cross Societies – was the only organization of any size present in the disturbed areas. In August, nearly 100,000 people had to leave their homes under pressure that might be as extreme as expulsion. Most of them found temporary shelter with host families, whose generosity had to be given material support lest it dry up. This was the start of an assistance programme of family parcels containing basic foodstuffs and toilet articles, that in time became a large one. Then there were the hospital establishments. These suffered from two handicaps. The first was that the conflict itself produced larger numbers of sick and wounded and upset supply lines. The second was that the disastrous economic situation was preventing proper treatment of the chronic illnesses affecting the population. Dr Jean-Claude Mulli, who made a preliminary evaluation tour in August 1991, found conditions very different from those in tropical countries. He reported as follows:

> There was a lack of sophisticated medicines that had to be imported at great cost, such as those for the treatment of

ARTICLE 3

In the case of armed conflict not of an international character occurring in the territory of one of the High Contracting Parties, each Party to the conflict shall be bound to apply, as a minimum, the following provisions:

(1) Persons taking no active part in the hostilities, including members of armed forces who have laid down their arms and those placed *hors de combat* by sickness, wounds, detention, or any other cause, shall in all circumstances be treated humanely, without any adverse distinction founded on race, colour, religion or faith, sex, birth or wealth, or any other similar criteria.

To this end, the following acts are and shall remain prohibited at any time and in any place whatsoever with respect to the above-mentioned persons:

    (a) violence to life and person, in particular murder of all kinds, mutilation, cruel treatment and torture;

    (b) taking of hostages;

    (c) outrages upon personal dignity, in particular humiliating and degrading treatment;

    (d) the passing of sentences and the carrying out of executions without previous judgment pronounced by a regularly constituted court, affording all the judicial guarantees which are recognized as indispensable by civilized peoples.

(2) The wounded and sick shall be collected and cared for.

An impartial humanitarian body, such as the International Committee of the Red Cross, may offer its services to the Parties to the conflict.

The Parties to the conflict should further endeavour to bring into force, by means of special agreements, all or part of the other provisions of the present Convention.

The application of the preceding provisions shall not affect the legal status of the Parties to the conflict.

leukaemia, and of expensive consumable equipment. These were beyond the means of the ICRC, and it had to look for other partners for this type of assistance, which was in constant demand. For lack of a dialysis filter, a patient could die in one to two weeks, just as it is urgent to care for cancer patients, but the urgency is of another kind.

The people then in danger, said Dr Mulli, were 'those who had not been able to take refuge elsewhere, or dependent people like inmates of psychiatric centres or prisoners' and everyone who later suffered the devastating effects of blockade in towns.

On 25 August Vukovar, without realizing it, took its place in history, for thereafter it was under virtually uninterrupted bombardment until its exhausted inhabitants left the town at the end of a three-month siege. In many places in Slavonia the delegates observed that civilian objectives, far from being spared as the elementary rules of humanitarian law require, had become priority targets for military action, and safety conditions worsened so much that it was dangerous for relief teams to move about the field. The Red Cross emblem no longer gave sufficient protection, and the President of the ICRC had to remind the belligerents that it was their duty to respect their obligations in waging war.[4]

During September a steady stream of mortar bombs fell upon Valpovo, Vinkovci and also on Osijek, where the civilian population went to ground. Other regions in Croatia had become dangerous and at times inaccessible to Red Cross convoys, as in the region of Lipik/Pakrac, 125 kilometres east of Zagreb, where delegates had not yet been since hostilities commenced.

It was decided to mount an operation to evacuate the 270 inmates of a psychiatric hospital in Pakrac, in an especially critical area heavily bombarded on 25 September. The patients were sheltering in the basement and supplies of water and electricity had been cut off. The Croat ministers of health and the interior, the commanding officer of the territorial defence forces (the MUP) of the Bjelovar area, and General Raseta, commanding the 5th (federal) Army were given detailed information of the purpose of the mission and the programme it was to follow. After due investigation, both parties confirmed that safety was sufficient and that the operation could go ahead on 27 September in accordance with the very precise plan approved by all. Here is the account of what happened, given by the ICRC delegate responsible for the convoy:[5]

The plan provided for the MUP escort to stop just outside the village of Lipik. We – that is, a land-cruiser and the seven buses – were then to cross the village alone and make for Okucani. After crossing two bridges we would see a group of houses near which we were to await an escort of 'people in the know' who would take us to Pakrac. I asked for two hours to take the patients on board the convoy and the Yugoslav general agreed. The convoy was then to follow the same route, re-crossing the two bridges, and from there to continue alone through the village of Lipik, outside which we were to link up again with the MUP, who would be waiting for us. The meeting at Lipik was scheduled to take place at 3.30 p.m.

That was the plan. What happened was different:

Noon: we informed the officer commanding the MUP of all these details, to which he agreed. We then set off. The MUP commander said he had contacted his forces throughout the region about the convoy and that messages would again be sent when we arrived at Gaj.

1.45 p.m.: we arrived without incident at Gaj, where we waited an hour so as not to arrive too soon at Lipik. Several civilian motorcars coming from Lipik told the MUP that the situation had been calm there for several hours and that there was no fighting. The convoy was made up in accordance with the information given to General Raseta. It was not easy to see the Red Cross flag on our vehicle and we therefore attached it to a long piece of wood which we fixed to the exhaust pipe at the right-hand front side of the vehicle. The flag then floated easily and was completely above the roof of the land-cruiser.

2.50 p.m.: the convoy set off again. After a few kilometres we went through the village of Kukunjevac, where more than a dozen houses had been torn open by shells. It looked like a ghost village.

3 p.m.: we entered the hamlet of Dobrovac. The road went straight ahead over a wide plain with, here and there, a few little houses. At that moment the order of vehicles in the convoy was as follows: the MUP scout car, followed by the minibus (these two vehicles being our escort), was about 200 metres in front of our vehicle, and the first bus about 150 metres behind us.

Two shells exploded, one in front of the land-cruiser and the other just behind. I stopped the vehicle and opened the rear door to let the nurse get out. Shells continued to fall plentifully and the interpreter and I took cover in the ditch at the left-hand side of the road. The nurse fractured her foot in jumping from the vehicle and dragged herself painfully along the ground to the ditch on the right-hand side of the road.

The scout car, still followed by the minibus, backed towards us and tried to respond to the shooting. Shells continued to fall and a house about 30 metres behind us was hit and set on fire.

The officer commanding the escort shouted to us to go off towards Gaj and, once this instruction had been translated to me, I saw that we should have to manoeuvre the land-cruiser, which was there in the middle of the road, and turn it round to face the other direction. I did this, not because I was feeling particularly brave, for shells kept falling, but as a reflex action to an order given by the commanding officer, who was taking the situation in hand ... We were ordered into the other ditch and ten to fifteen minutes after the first two shells were fired I was ordered to take the wheel with the interpreter sitting next to me, whilst two members of the MUP hauled the nurse into the back of the car. We set off like a whirlwind, still fired upon, and the shelling, instead of dying down, appeared to be following my vehicle's exact line of progress. We went through the village of Kukunjevac again at about 90 kilometres an hour. I lost control of the vehicle, and it crashed into the ditch on the left-hand side of the road to Gaj. There was intense machine-gun fire. We were told later that the car was hit on its left side and that a tyre had probably burst, which would explain the accident. But perhaps I simply lost control through my own fault, it's hard to say. When the accident happened the nurse suffered a blow on the ribcage and a slight whiplash injury. Fortunately, the other passengers only had multiple external bruises, none of them serious.

Again we spent ten to fifteen minutes cowering in the ditches, whilst firing continued on both sides ... At Gaj, a safe place, we rejoined the seven buses and their passengers, all of them safe and well ... Finally, at about 4 p.m., the scout car caught up with the rest of the convoy in Gaj. A shell had taken off its roof and it had a number of bullet holes in it. By a miracle, nobody had been killed, there were only a few sprained wrists and suchlike, and in fact the most seriously injured person was the nurse.

This episode ended fairly happily. Compare it with the more dramatic one, described below, undergone by *Médecins sans Frontières* (MSF) and their European escort, on their way to Vukovar three weeks later. Their convoy too was to evacuate sick and wounded from the besieged town and all the necessary green lights had been given.

An article in the Belgian daily newspaper *Le Soir*, on 15 October 1991, had not dampened the rescuers' ardour nor reminded them of their earlier setback. In this article, Edouard van Velthem wrote:

Vukovar must resign itself to its fate. This heroic martyred Slav town, an important strategic target both for the Croat guard and for the Yugoslav army, has yet to come to the end of its Calvary. It has been under siege for weeks, and deprived of its food supplies and medical care. Its sanitary conditions are execrable and it is cut off from the outside world. This 'bastion town' will not even be allowed the comfort of the humanitarian convoy freighted by *Médecins sans Frontières* and 'protected' by European mediators forbidden to carry arms. For days beforehand, there were strict orders from Belgrade forbidding the mission to approach this vital objective, which the General Staff is bombarding incessantly without ever managing to capture it. Moreover, the uncontrollable Serbian militias were implacably hostile to the convoy. And when that obstacle was at last removed, it was Zagreb's turn to send an outright refusal, the exhausted Croat forces being unwilling to weaken their positions by allowing vehicles even briefly through their roadblocks, and by that refusal transforming the proud image of a Croat Stalingrad into a pitiful straggle of toy soldiers. The disappointment was all the greater because a happy issue seemed within reach. Everyone on both sides undertook to observe an ephemeral cease-fire. The thirty or so lorries, bearers of salvation, entered the suburbs and reached a point hardly two kilometres from the centre of the town. And, once again, the world heaved a sigh of relief, believing in yet another lie, yet another step towards the disinformation each of the belligerents pinned its faith to as if it were the key to a ludicrous victory; and forgetting for the time it took to entertain and reject a hope, that reason and humanity have temporarily deserted a country bled white, where the twilight of civilization is followed, more and more every day, by a dawn of ravening wolves.

Françoise Saulnier, in charge of legal affairs at MSF, writes as follows about the attack of 18 October:

We had little experience of the environment, so we decided to be discreet and go about things quietly, relying mainly on negotiation. This was done under the auspices of the European Community. The agreement made included crossing four front lines and two areas of no man's land. It was madness. It seemed to us that we had no control over anything. It was not for us to ask for mines to be removed. That was the belligerents' business, and so were the cease-fires, corridors and so on. The convoy had one European Community car in front and one at the rear to observe the extent to which the cease-fire was being respected. And there were the parties' military escorts, except for the areas of no man's land. The convoy was to enter the town empty, without even light equipment and without blankets. On the way, we changed our itinerary at the request of the Croat party. The convoy crossed a maize field. On arrival at Vukovar we looked after the wounded, having no permission to see anybody else. We were allowed one hour to sort and load the wounded. On the return journey we set out again in the same order, when three federal army tanks trained their guns on us. All the passengers in the convoy threw themselves on the ground. The adjacent

fields were mined. No shots were fired and the incident seemed
to us more like a case of taking hostages. We were compelled
to return by the route we had taken on the outward journey.
The fourth lorry in the convoy blew up on an anti-tank mine.
Only one mine exploded. There was panic, nobody dared to
move, and three wounded were taken away. We all went back
the way we had come and the convoy reached safety 17 hours
later, over dirt tracks where the wounded, lying without protection
in the lorries, were jolted unmercifully.

These were searing experiences for humanitarian workers used to
a modicum of respect for the agreements concluded. Even for
seasoned delegates, it was dangerous adapting to Yugoslav
conditions. The ICRC's heads of delegation met their colleagues
from Geneva at Ljubljana on 14 and 15 October to agree upon their
objectives for the first winter of the war, and their interim assessment
announced even worse difficulties. They knew that their work was
insufficiently known or recognized, and this discouraged them
from deploying in dangerous areas. They had already survived too
many dangers in which the Red Cross emblem had not protected
them to ignore the possibility of future similar incidents. Their
assessment had shown that the conflict had become much worse
and that the number of displaced persons had risen from under
100,000 in August to over 300,000 in October. They had to adapt
relief programmes accordingly, lay in stocks of material and medical
supplies, get family parcels distributed more quickly, improve
logistics, and do more than ever to teach the authorities and the
general public the ideals and aims of humanitarian missions. They
also had to continue visiting detained persons – a priority for ICRC
delegates – and decide how to put into effect the desire expressed
both by the Croats and the federal army to exchange all their
prisoners.

   This injection of energy led to the preparation on 24 October of
a Memorandum of Understanding setting out the rules for the release
of all prisoners taken in the conflict between Croatia and Yugoslavia,
and of another memorandum, that of 27 November, which the
plenipotentiary representatives signed when they first met in
Geneva. Marco Sassoli, an ICRC legal adviser, was one of the chief
architects of this agreement, which his own experience led him to
believe was a model of its kind:

   The agreement of 24 October at once gave us permission to work
   on a very wide definition of prisoners likely to benefit from the
   visits of ICRC delegates, and, in addition, an arrangement for
   the release of 'all persons detained in relation with the conflict'.
   When we were negotiating the agreement of 27 November,
   several alternatives were open to us. One of these was to make

no formal reference to the law, but to restate a number of basic rules such as 'Women must not be raped' and 'The wounded must not be finished off'; in other words, to freely adapt Article 3 common to all the Geneva Conventions of 1949. Another was to restate the rules applicable to an internal armed conflict, adding extracts from Protocol II, which applies to protection of the civilian population in non-international armed conflicts. We also prepared a maximalist version which was the one the parties accepted. We did not expect them to do so. We had instead prepared ourselves for scenes about national sovereignty and for endless arguments as to whether the persons sitting at the table were legitimately entitled to be there. This didn't happen. I found this a fascinating exercise. We wanted to shout 'Hooray!'; in circumstances like these we were so used to getting at most an agreement to apply Article 3. Everybody signed on the dotted line. Later on, thinking it over, we said to ourselves that had there been any jurists in the plenipotentiary delegations we should not have got so far as we did.

The only point not specifically covered by the ICRC draft was the protection of persons in occupied territories. At that time, it was thought that the federal government would not have accepted this concept because it believed itself justified in maintaining peace and safety in one of its republics and would not have agreed that its soldiers should be treated as an occupying army. On the other hand, for the Croats, Slavonia and the regions called by the Serbs 'Krajina' were obviously Croat territories occupied by a foreign power, namely the Federal Republic of Yugoslavia. Agreement on this point was therefore out of the question. But this was not a legal lacuna, since the agreement covered the treatment of civilians in the hands of the adverse party, protection of the civilian population against the consequences of hostilities, and behaviour in battle.

As the guardian of humanitarian law, the ICRC was being less legalistic than it usually seems in such circumstances. Nevertheless it was, without admitting it, drawing on legal rules that are solidly established, even though they date from the *ancien régime*. Rebels and insurgents can thank their lucky stars for Emer de Vattel, a diplomat from Neuchâtel in Switzerland and one of the forerunners of international law. Although he did not invent the phrase 'recognition of belligerency', he made the concept popular and opened the door to some protection for combatants rebelling against a central government. His *Principles of Natural Law* affirms that

whenever a large party believes itself entitled to resist the sovereign, and believes itself able to take up arms, war between them must be waged in the same way as between two different nations, and they must use the same means of preventing excesses in the war and of re-establishing peace.[6]

This was a revolutionary statement at the end of the eighteenth century, for until Article 3 of the Geneva Conventions of 1949, and still more clearly until the adoption of the Additional Protocols of 1977, civil war did not appear in any regulations of the laws of war. As Charles Zorgbibe says of Vattel, 'This was the reflex of an angry politician.' Vattel had realized that because nobody else had any consideration for their armed struggle, rebels could be driven to dreadful lengths in waging war. The new legal situation resulting from recognition of belligerency was not to the taste of twentieth-century governments, who looked upon its acceptance as an admission of failure. This did not prevent General Gowon later on – on 12 August 1967 – from sending a formal 'declaration of war' to the seceding state of Biafra, where the federal forces had hitherto conducted what they called a 'police operation'.[7]

The ICRC's 'recognition of belligerency' approach was therefore as much political as legal. It was in any case a humanitarian choice, since its purpose was to enable humanitarian law to come to the aid of civilian and military victims of the conflict with maximum effect. The delegates regarded the belligerents' agreement to follow these rules as an encouraging step forward.

A hail of fire on Vukovar and Dubrovnik

In October and November, while the rules for combatants' behaviour were recalled and set out on paper, living conditions for the civilian population in blockaded towns were getting worse. The inhabitants of 27 Serbian villages near Pakrac were forcibly evacuated by Croat soldiers. The bombardment of Vukovar continued and it was increasingly isolated. A hail of shells fell on Dubrovnik and its cultural treasures. In answer to an appeal from the Dubrovnik Red Cross, the first team of ICRC delegates entered the city at 6 a.m. on 1 November 1991 to note the damage and determine its most urgent needs. The first radio message stated, 'The town is a shambles, for although well equipped to handle tourist traffic, it has no social infrastructure left.' There was no electricity, there was a shortage of water and essential foodstuffs, but the hospitals had recently received supplies and still had adequate stocks. The town was completely surrounded and displaced persons accounted for one-third of its estimated population of 35,000. Twenty EC observers and about 20 journalists were there. No vessels other than Yugoslav were allowed to berth. The ICRC had to freight its own ships to come to the aid of the besieged population.

The world-wide repute of Dubrovnik saved it from the worst excesses, but it was besieged for several weeks and the hardships of the civilian population were not alleviated until the beginning of 1992. The existence of Vukovar, however, became generally known only because of the stir caused by the attack on the MSF convoy, and until the last hours of its evacuation it suffered outrages unprecedented in the Croat–Yugoslav conflict.

Concurrently with the efforts of MSF, the ICRC delegation in Belgrade was negotiating unceasingly, and as though obsessed, for a convoy to be allowed into Vukovar. Why Belgrade? Because the approach from the Croat side had fallen through and the delegates believed that an operation organized from Belgrade, the Serbian and federal capital, had some chance of succeeding. On 27 October 1991, one week after the attack on the MSF convoy, the ICRC delegates received their first permission to take a medical convoy to Vukovar. The 'go-ahead' signal was soon replaced by the 'wait' signal. The plan was postponed several times for safety reasons. Counter-proposals for the itinerary – the last, across the Danube, discussed on 16 November with the Croat, federal army and EC representatives – were no better received although Vukovar Hospital reported that the medical situation in the town was getting worse.

Two days later, on 18 November, Vukovar was captured and its evacuation began at its southern districts. In retrospect, the opinions expressed by the heads of delegation in Belgrade and Zagreb concurred. Thierry Meyrat of Belgrade wrote that 'Vukovar has every characteristic of a politico-humanitarian case in which the ICRC was driven to the utmost limits of its capacity', while for Marco Altherr of Zagreb 'Vukovar was a profound shock'. Jane Howard, the BBC's permanent correspondent in Belgrade, used the same term, shock, in recalling her impressions of the town. It was at Vukovar, too, that she experienced fear for the first time and saw her first war casualty and her first Red Cross man, Nicolas Borsinger.

Borsinger, the only neutral and impartial witness present when the town fell, describes his experience as the most difficult incident in his ICRC career, 'I was at Pècs in nearby Hungary, the island of sanity nearest the fury of the bombardments, when the ICRC in Belgrade told me to go to Vukovar immediately.'

Feeling that matters were extremely urgent, he rushed off alone, without an interpreter, and reached a military area without the papers he needed to pass the checkpoint. He tried bluff – 'I've got an appointment with the General.' They let him through. At the last village before Vukovar, Negoslavci, he met a number of journalists including Jane Howard. At the entrance to Vukovar waited three Croats representing the southern districts of the town. Together, they went to a spot about two kilometres outside to begin negotiating either raising the siege or the surrender, according to which side you were on. Those taking part in these last moments of the tragedy on Monday 18 November were the three Croats, in a state of nervous collapse after three months of bombardment, two Yugoslavs from the federal army, the ICRC delegate and the press. Before negotiations could begin, two preliminaries had to be settled: whether the ICRC was to act as a notary or an intermediary, and whether or not the press should be present. The press was obliged to withdraw, and on doing so rendered Borsinger, who was very active in the discussion, the highly appreciated service of lending him one of its interpreters.

The negotiations lasted two hours. The Yugoslavs were in a hurry to finish. The agreement provided that bombardment of the southern districts of the town was to cease at noon that day. The population (about one-third of the inhabitants of the town) was to be informed and would be given three hours to prepare to leave. The evacuation itself was to start at 3 p.m.

From then on, columns of people quickly gathered from the southern districts of the town, the rest of which was still being bombarded. A convoy of lorries nearly a kilometre long awaited them. Night was falling. Borsinger used his car radio to call ICRC colleagues to his help. They were held up at a checkpoint. He was alone for 24 hours with this motley procession of young and old, sick and well. The mere fact of him being there helped to lower the tension, but one man alone could do little to calm such a crowd. All he could do was to bring them a little human comfort by going up and down the column uninterruptedly until 2 a.m., with occasional loud-speaker announcements to reassure them and, now and then, training headlights on the Red Cross flag. He got the weakest of them on to the lorries and located those who had the greatest difficulty in reaching the convoy because they could not walk. Simultaneously, the combatants left the town, bearing their arms proudly, and surrendered. The ICRC delegate stated that, throughout the evening, the federal troops' behaviour towards the evacuees was as exemplary as conditions allowed.

> Tuesday 19 November was for us an All Fools' Day. Our contacts from the army, who had hitherto been very coopera-tive, were nowhere to be seen. It was still impossible to go to other parts of the town, including the northern district where the hospital was situated. The European Community observers arrived and began negotiating with the federal army and the ICRC on the rest of the operations. But no important decision was reached, and in the middle of the session a captain I had met during the night of 18–19 November called me away from the meeting and offered to take me to the hospital. This was

something I had been stubbornly refusing until then, and indeed was the main purpose of the negotiations then going on. The lorry containing medical supplies had arrived meanwhile and we set off. The captain gave me half an hour to inspect the premises. The hospital was full to bursting point. Every square yard was occupied, and sick people were being given shelter in the basement, in such numbers that many of them had to stand between the beds.

Borsinger walked through the rooms in a deathly silence, saying who he was and asking for requests and comments on their experiences, but getting no more than pathetic mutters of 'We're all right'. He said later: 'It was as if I was looking at an encephalogram of the whole population and seeing nothing but a straight line at the bottom of the chart.' He met the woman director of the hospital and the medical staff, all of whom were close to collapse.

The half-hour granted by the captain elapsed, then one, then two hours. Relations were getting strained between him and Borsinger who had to choose between staying on at the risk of starting a scene or leaving for the time being. The director of the hospital said she did not feel threatened and urged him to come back the next morning. Borsinger left the hospital. What he could not possibly know was that in Zagreb at that very moment, Marco Altherr's negotiations with the Croats and the federal army for neutralizing the hospital were nearing success. Neutralization was to start at 8 p.m. that same day, and there was no longer a single ICRC representative on the spot to put this into effect. The break in communications that prevented this important information from being transmitted was to weigh heavily on the delegates' minds. They are still wondering today what they could have prevented had they been able to ensure that an ICRC representative was permanently in the hospital.

'The victors were carousing in conquered Vukovar. Blind drunk militiamen were firing bursts at random. Things were out of control.' The civilians in a sorting centre at the edge of the town, already suffering from the effects of the siege, were in a state of terror. Borsinger and the ICRC colleagues who had come to support him did their best to calm them down. Shots nearby were followed by screams. A man in a group of prisoners being transferred was wounded and taken into a neighbouring room. ICRC delegates wanted to investigate, but guns were trained on them and they were expelled from the centre by force.

'Everything pointed to an imminent massacre. There was total chaos everywhere. The federal army was no longer taking any part in the proceedings. We were witnessing a complete breakdown in the arrangements, whether intentional or not it is hard to say.'

Moreover, the ICRC delegates had not failed to notice that, apart from the elderly, there were no men among the evacuated population.

On Wednesday 20 November, the delegates set out for the hospital, which was supposed to be the subject of a neutralization agreement. A tank on the bridge leading to the hospital prevented them from crossing. Borsinger left a delegate on the spot and tried to get through over a neighbouring bridge, but he found that this too was sealed off. Meanwhile a large convoy escorted by the European observers arrived at the first bridge to evacuate the hospital. Nicolas Borsinger had an argument with the responsible officer, who insisted that the ICRC produce evidence that an agreement for neutralizing the hospital had been concluded. A completely ridiculous argument followed, which the federal army officer ended by declaring that it was too dangerous to go to the hospital just then, although things were dead calm and not a single shot had been heard since dawn.

At that moment, a convoy of at least three buses coming from the hospital appeared on the road from which the tank had just withdrawn. Borsinger sent a radio message to his colleague nearby, asking him to follow it. Whilst his colleague was with great difficulty turning his vehicle on a narrow path encumbered by all kinds of rubble, the three lorries vanished into the distance and the delegate lost track of them. Then, miraculously, the situation cleared, the humanitarian convoys were allowed through, and the ICRC delegates hastened in with them.

All round the hospital there was total confusion. It was soon obvious that it could not possibly be neutralized in such chaotic circumstances, nor whilst the army officers with whom the ICRC delegates were dealing showed no intention of respecting the agreement concluded in Zagreb. The main provisions of this agreement were that the neutral zone should be clearly marked off and identified by the Red Cross emblem, and that access to it should be strictly controlled. Only protected persons, namely the sick and wounded and the personnel appointed to care for them, were to be allowed to reside there and the presence of weapons in the hospital was strictly forbidden. The belligerents were to refrain from attacking the zone, and were to allow entry of all the supplies it needed to function, such as foodstuffs, water and electricity. The ICRC was to supervise the zone thus neutralized. Borsinger's hands were tied. At an impromptu press conference, he told the journalists present of the situation and said that it was impossible for him and his colleagues to put the neutralization agreement into effect.

Inside the hospital, people were silent. Nobody knew what had happened during the night, nor what these buses were, nor who was on board. They were obsessed with the desire to get out of this hell. The director of the hospital had disappeared. The delegates later learned that she had been arrested, exchanged in December 1991, and had given a full account of her experiences on Zagreb television. The deputy director was arrested under the eyes of the delegates, whilst all day long the evacuation of the premises continued under European Community protection. The ICRC team stayed on the spot for another three days and nights until 22 November, trying to take down the names of as many wounded as they could, whilst all around the situation was still extremely volatile, with hidden snipers and countless mines and booby traps all over the town.

Blaine Harden of the *Washington Post* gathered eye-witness accounts of the three days, 18, 19 and 20 November, in which the hospital was evacuated.[8] According to one of these accounts, patients were taken out by the back door of the hospital on 20 November, the officer responsible telling the ICRC delegates that safety conditions in the building were inadequate. The *Tribune*'s article was published more than a year later, after a mass grave was discovered near Ovcara. It was in this village that the experts charged by the United Nations Commission to investigate war crimes began their work, using a list of 210 patients and staff of Vukovar Hospital who had gone missing.

On 23 November 1991, the head of the Belgrade delegation made an interim report on the work of the ICRC which states:

> The civilian population of Vukovar has been entirely evacuated. There is now practically nobody left there (the town having been razed to the ground, it is anyway no longer habitable). In organizing this population displacement, the JNA (Federal Army) divided the population into two categories: women, children and old people of either sex being the first, and men aged between 20 and 50 being the second.

Generally speaking, the delegates reported that the conquerors were careful to treat persons in the first category correctly. They gave the ICRC and the local Red Cross section permission to help such persons, and allowed them to choose their destination freely. Their choice was however limited from a personal standpoint; families had been separated and did not dare leave before they had news of their relatives. For the men still in Vukovar at the end of the siege were considered as combatants by the attackers and arrested. This, however, did not automatically give them the benefit of treatment as prisoners of war, which would have ensured them some protection. Rather, they were regarded as precious bartering counters for use in future bargaining. On leaving the interrogation centre, some of them were accused of war crimes for which they were to stand trial. Others may have been summarily executed when arrested or just afterwards. The United Nations experts appointed to investigate the mass grave at Ovcara have still to report their findings.

The delegates' priority aim was to have access, either in the interrogation centres or the detention camps, to all persons arrested, and in this they were largely successful by virtue of the agreements later negotiated in Geneva with the belligerents' plenipotentiaries. But the missing persons will always be an open wound in the memory of their families and for those who tried to trace them. This torments Marco Altherr, who noted in his end-of-mission report that 'more and more people do not understand why the ICRC has not yet succeeded in tracing the two hundred or so slightly wounded persons arrested at Vukovar Hospital'. For two months, families invaded the offices of the ICRC tracing agency in Zagreb. Altherr notes that they were 'extremely worried' and 'would not leave until they had been seen. Indeed, some of them were extremely aggressive and uttered bloodcurdling threats.'

The fall of Vukovar was a rude awakening for politicians and humanitarian organizations. The use of artillery and tanks on a grand scale to recapture the town plainly showed how completely the Yugoslav Federation had disintegrated. Any idea of confederacy was dead and gone. This military victory was in fact a political disaster for the Federal Republic of Yugoslavia, from which were to emerge an independent Slovenia and Croatia. It was also an opportunity for the international community to bring more pressure on Belgrade to calm down war fever and spare other besieged towns.

It was now clear to the ICRC that if other towns, such as Osijek and Dubrovnik, were to be spared the fate of Vukovar, it would have to act on all fronts at once and set in motion negotiation of an original kind based on strictly concrete issues. The result was the first meetings of plenipotentiaries, intended to render mandatory the agreements they concluded, and the more technical commissions on tracing missing persons and mortal remains, as well as on prisoners. The avowed aim of all these procedures was to apply a brake to the grave breaches of international humanitarian law committed during the first months of the war, and to improve the performance of the people on the ground, who were faced with insuperable problems of security.

The neutralization of Osijek and Dubrovnik

From the end of September 1991 onwards, Osijek was under incessant bombardment. Civilians were obliged to spend most of the time in basement shelters, and the continual pounding by artillery posed major problems to the town hospital serving the entire region. It was unprotected against the bombardment, particularly as it was in the same district of the town as the barracks which, although largely disused, were nevertheless a military objective.

The ICRC had an office in the heart of the town, facing the entrance to the municipal shelter. It saw every day that the intense bombardment was suspended for all too rare intervals in which the inhabitants bought what food they could find. It was therefore urgent to impose humanitarian measures that could spare the people of Osijek the fate of the inhabitants of Vukovar. The ICRC's first objective was to protect the hospital infrastructure, and it was this that the plenipotentiaries discussed at their first meeting in Geneva. They also discussed Dubrovnik, where conditions had been worsening for several weeks, to the undoubted dismay of European governments. There was also an urgent need to protect its hospital installations, especially as a particularly violent attack on 6 December 1991 did major damage to the town and port. This attack was made although the belligerents were nearing a regional cease-fire agreement that had been under negotiation for several days previously at Cavtat on the Dalmatian coast.

The attack on the port was the second, after that of 1 December, which obliged the *Rodos II*, a vessel freighted by the ICRC, to leave the waters of Dubrovnik without discharging its cargo of relief supplies and to seek refuge in the neighbouring port of Zelenica. To endanger in this way a humanitarian mission duly notified to the competent military authorities in the region was contrary to international humanitarian law and to the recent memorandum concluded by the parties to the conflict on 27 November, as the ICRC in Geneva pointed out in an official note to the Permanent Mission of the Federal Socialist Republic of Yugoslavia.[9]

When the ICRC negotiators proposed that Dubrovnik Hospital, and Dubrovnik Monastery (where the delegates were living) and, later, Osijek Hospital, should be neutralized – as they were on 6 December 1991 and 3 January 1992 respectively – the question was far less controversial than it became in the Bosnian conflict. It consisted merely of applying Article 15 of the Fourth Geneva Convention, which reads:

ARTICLE 15

Any Party to the conflict may, either direct or through a neutral State or some humanitarian organization, propose to the adverse Party to establish, in the regions where fighting is taking place, neutralized zones intended to shelter from the effects of war the following persons, without distinction:

(a) wounded and sick combatants or non-combatants;

> (b) civilian persons who take no part in hostilities, and who, while they reside in the zones, perform no work of a military character.

> When the Parties concerned have agreed upon the geographical position, administration, food supply and supervision of the proposed neutralized zone, a written agreement shall be concluded and signed by the representatives of the Parties to the conflict. The agreement shall fix the beginning and the duration of the neutralization of the zone.

The jurist Marco Sassoli confesses that 'I hardly dare say so in public, but the agreement for the neutralization of Osijek Hospital was the first of its kind in the history of international humanitarian law that was expressly and completely based on Article 15.' This did not save the hospital from being bombarded after neutralization, on several occasions between 3 January and 30 June 1992 when its neutralization came to an end because the region was once again calm. In the six months of neutralization, the maintenance of the zone nevertheless passed, in the eyes of the Croat observers, for 'a heroic action on the part of the ICRC'. Marjolaine Martin, one of the five members of the ICRC team monitoring the proper functioning of the zone (against a background of explosions!) and like a Paris *concierge* checking up on anyone entering day and night, says this six-month period was 'surreal'. This sort of monitoring is not necessarily an ICRC prerogative. It can also be done by police forces or local soldiers or any other organized group, if the parties agree. The Dubrovnik Hospital zone was monitored by the local karate club, and in Osijek the ICRC delegates were helped by the Croat police, for as Marco Sassoli points out, Red Cross philosophy maintains that

> the logic of a protected zone is one of confidence not armed defence. If such a zone is established and no longer contains any military force or installation, the adversary will see for himself that it is no longer a military objective, and will cease to attack it.

That is, within the limits of good humanitarian intentions, even if codified; for when Osijek was inspected a year later, it was found that fewer shells had landed on the disused barracks next to the hospital than on the hospital buildings.

Assume a virtue, if you have it not

With hindsight, and remembering all the ignominies of the war in Bosnia-Herzegovina, one can on the whole feel satisfied that international humanitarian law was respected in the hostilities between Croat and federal forces. It is certainly a matter for rejoicing that the ICRC delegates were allowed fairly easy access to the prisons containing all the persons who, in the words of the Memorandum of Understanding of 27 November 1991, were 'deprived of their liberty for reasons related to the armed conflict'. It is important too that nearly all the provisions of that memorandum – the setting up of commissions on prisoners and missing persons, notification of persons arrested, and the establishment of neutralized zones – were put into effect. The head of the Zagreb delegation, Marco Altherr, was foremost in saying how interested he was to have taken part in a real ICRC operation in which ICRC delegates could visit the prisoners, the work of the Central Tracing Agency specialists was both possible and prominent, the relief operation was treated with real urgency, and the ICRC was in its rightful place, 'above the madding crowd'.

For all this exhilaration, Altherr did not lose his grip on reality. Taking each paragraph of the memorandum in turn, and comparing it with what actually happened, he realized that the picture was not such a pretty one.

Had the wounded and sick been treated correctly and without discrimination? Yes, probably, so long as they were in hospital. But it was hard to forget Vukovar, where 200 wounded and sick were removed from the hospital just before it was evacuated by the humanitarian convoys. No trace of them had since been found. Would their bodies be exhumed one day, as rumour has it, from the mass grave in Ovcara?

Were arrested persons detained in decent conditions? The great majority of them said they were. The difficulties started at the time of the mass release, when a number of prisoners were kept in reserve, to be exchanged for some advantage or other. They were victims of the vicious circle of reciprocity.

What happened to the civilians who fell into enemy hands? All those who were trapped by the encirclement and military blockade of their town or region suffered in varying degrees from conditions forbidden by international humanitarian law; either no relief supplies reached them at all, or they came too late, medical care was harder and harder to get, and indiscriminate bombardment compelled them to live in holes like rats. They were hostages caught in a vice, and their one hope was to leave the place in which they had been born and brought up.

The protected and neutralized zones functioned with varying degrees of success. Not at all in the tragic case of Vukovar, imperfectly at Osijek Hospital, and more or less satisfactorily at Dubrovnik Hospital.

The programmes of assistance to displaced persons worked without too many hitches. They attracted little attention from the media, being less popular than those run by bodies making a great show of their political preferences, but they enabled hundreds of thousands of civilians to live at an acceptable subsistence level. More would have been done had the delegates, and their colleagues in the local Red Cross sections, not had to face so many of the ordinary dangers of war, such as roads made impassable by mines or bombardment near front lines, and the much less tangible dangers caused by the behaviour of militiamen and extremist armed groups, which made it impossible to predict whether convoys would be allowed through the lines.

There was some slight disagreement within the ICRC on the subject of respect for the Red Cross emblem. Opinions differed as to whether it would be an improper use of the emblem for any old pharmacist or doctor to embellish his car with a red cross because he thought it would help him to get through military checkpoints. Perhaps it would, but the danger of this type of appropriation is negligible. Moreover, buildings and vehicles in any country at war bear a profusion of red crosses of all shapes and sizes, going from pale pink to the most vibrant vermilion. However regrettable this misuse of the emblem may be, it has never caused an official humanitarian mission any severe trouble. It would be more serious, and punishable, to use the emblem perfidiously to cover the transport of military equipment. Some delegates are sure that excesses of this kind have been committed, but they cannot prove it. Others say that many of their colleagues have something of an 'emblem fixation'; that they consider as an infringement of the rules for respect of the emblem any military mishap in which the red cross was visible. Thus, to attack a hospital is reprehensible in itself, and not because a red cross is painted on the roof of the building. What is certain is that this dispute among specialists in no way hides the brutal reality of ICRC convoys, duly announced beforehand, being knowingly attacked, as in September 1991 near Lipik and at Sarajevo in May 1992.

Apart from an official protest, the only remedy the delegates have if international humanitarian law is breached is to make themselves known and explain tirelessly to all concerned, from a high-ranking officer to a drunken militiaman, why the ICRC is there, and to remind them that it is not all right for them to wage war in any way they please. The states signatory to the Geneva Conventions in general and the parties to the Memorandum of Understanding of 27 November 1991 in particular have moreover undertaken to do all that is necessary to make known the principles of humanitarian law to the rank and file. Little has been done to implement this undertaking. Instruction in humanitarian law is far from being one of the best sellers in military training courses, and the ICRC's appeals for moderation, for example in attacks on civilians, have hardly ever been listened to. But – not that this is an excuse – the combatants in Bosnia-Herzegovina were to commit even worse excesses, numbing the shock of Vukovar in people's memories.

Between the wars

The period from January to April 1992 appears to have been quieter than the previous six months. The 15th and last cease-fire, in force since 4 January, seemed to be holding, although the European Community lost five of its observers when a Yugoslav plane shot down their helicopter on 7 January.[10] The republics of Slovenia and Croatia were beginning to add up the number of states that recognized them on and after 15 January. Nevertheless, certain events carried the germ of the upheavals to come in the Bosnia-Herzegovina war.

The treatment of the civilians inhabiting the Papuk mountains, a mainly Serbian region halfway between Zagreb and Osijek, showed the excesses committed when Croat forces reconquered the territory. On their arrival in the area, the ICRC delegates found that innumerable houses had been burned down because they were occupied by Serbian residents. Marjolaine Martin was there, and remembers the difficulties the ICRC delegates had in getting around, when they were caught between fires lit in several parts of the same village at once. They arrived too late and drove through deserted villages. Obviously the inhabitants had left either individually or following the retreat of the Serbian territorial forces. Was this due to a scorched earth policy or the beginnings of 'ethnic cleansing'? The terminology matters little; in either case the reality was the same. Everything pointed to headlong flight: 'Cows and their calves, and pigs and chickens were running in all directions. Soup was still heating on the stove and washing was drying in the garden.' Here were snapshots of daily life, less their human dimension.

As soon as it was informed, the ICRC delegation in Zagreb pressed officials at all levels, up to the deputy prime minister, to urge the authorities to restrain the misconduct of the armed forces. The Croat government admitted that excesses had been committed, that human rights had been violated, and that private property had been attacked. It therefore published a decree on 4 February 1992 condemning non-respect for minorities, reaffirming its guarantee of constitutional liberties, and undertaking to impose stricter discipline in the use of force by combatant units.

Another example foreshadowing difficulties to come was the Mostar region, where Heidy Huber, the delegate in charge of the

ICRC office in Sarajevo, spent the period 8–11 January 1992 on a preliminary evaluation mission. She realized that the population of this town, which was 35 per cent Muslim, 34 per cent Croat and 19 per cent Serbian (the remainder being of mixed origin known as 'Yugoslav') formed a highly explosive mixture. The strong concentration of troops at this important strategic crossroads increased the risk; many soldiers who had left the federal army's barracks in Croatia had regrouped at the nearby military base of Nevesinje. It was hard to get discussions going with the Yugoslav military authorities, and the delegates' most harmless questions encountered a wall of suspicion that disappeared only after Belgrade had given the green light.

Moreover, the geographical situation of the Mostar region makes it an enclave, in which the Muslim element slightly predominates, encompassed by a large Serbian majority to the west and south (75 to 90 per cent) and an equally strong Croat presence to the east (54 to 99 per cent). At the same time, differences between Serbs and Croats were deepening. In response to the creation in September 1991 of the Serbian autonomous region (RAS) of Krajina, the Croats proclaimed the republic of Herzeg-Bosna, making Mostar its capital.

At the end of this first mission in the region, Heidy Huber, seeing that the needs of the population were covered, did not initially believe that the ICRC would have to maintain a permanent presence in Mostar. But she reported that 'the region is vulnerable, and the humanitarian consequences of a conflict could be very serious'. She recommended that the situation should be closely followed and that regular access to the region by ICRC delegates be maintained.

There was similar or worse tension in the Krajina and in the disputed areas of western and eastern Slavonia, where the UN protection force was to be installed. These Croat territories, whose population was predominantly Serbian, or became so after the departure of Croat inhabitants endangered by the Serbian conquest, were already one of the worst headaches for UN and independent humanitarian institutions, despite the acceptance in principle on 21 February 1992, by Security Council Resolution 743, that a UN protection force should be set up. To this elaborate pattern of people forced to leave their houses and other people 'imported' to occupy them, the international community (still refusing to recognize that these changes were being made for ethnic reasons) imposed its political will that the exiled population should return as a condition that there would be a UN presence installed there in due course. It was at best unrealistic and at worst pure hypocrisy to believe at that moment that there could be any such reflux of population so long as these regions remained totally insecure.

The ICRC opened an office in Sarajevo in January 1992. From the beginning of systematic bombardment, in April, humanitarian operations there were badly handicapped by the general lack of respect for hospital establishments and medical personnel. This, although medical evacuations were a matter of extreme urgency and ambulance drivers were daily risking their lives to reach the most dangerous areas of the capital and its outskirts, and take the wounded to hospital. An ambulance driver was killed on 24 April. He was the first of such victims, and his ambulance was fired on though clearly identified. There was an urgent need to decide how to escort the ambulances, whose number was dwindling under successive attacks. In less than a month the Emergency Medical Treatment Institute alone lost ten vehicles. The crews of the convoys were directly threatened, and had to suffer body searches at some roadblocks. If evacuations were nevertheless to continue general safety would have to be improved.

The belligerents had to be notified of the journeys the ambulances were to make. Dangerous areas had continually to be identified, and useful information on this point more efficiently circulated among the members of the health services. Above all, the combatants had to be made to understand that it was their duty to respect every aspect of the medical mission, and the ICRC set about doing this as soon as it received the first elements of information from delegates directly involved. As in the first conflict, the diplomatic approach adopted was that of asking the belligerents to appoint plenipotentiary representatives who could undertake to respect the rules applicable to the conduct of war and to grant humanitarian missions all the necessary mobility. In Bosnia-Herzegovina priority was given to access to victims and safe passage for extremely urgent aid.

The question of escorts for vehicles transporting the wounded remained open. The ICRC would have preferred a neutral accompaniment, by its own delegates, after due notification of the intended journey. The European Community and the United Nations (whose forces arrived in mid-April) recommended armed escorts. In a different context, in Lebanon, the ICRC tried out various ways of improving the safety and mobility of relief workers which, however, were only partly suited to Bosnian conditions. Even in Lebanon, they did not suffice to prevent all accidents, but their virtue was that they relied on an extremely dense network of contacts covering everyone involved in the conflict – militiamen, soldiers, the civil police and the occupying forces. These contacts were the fruit of several years of ICRC work in Lebanon and the close co-operation with the Lebanese Red Cross and its volunteers which grew closer as time passed; the delegates also had excellent logistic facilities. In Bosnia-Herzegovina and its capital, conditions were quite different. ICRC delegates had been permanently stationed there

for only a short time (but they were among the first representatives
of international organizations to arrive, and in some places, such
as Banja Luka, the only ones). A few months' work had not been
enough to weave a faultless web of official connections. Their
material resources were limited. In every approach the delegates
made, they had to work hard to win the other party's confidence
and get tangible results. They had to cross what may fairly be
called a humanitarian desert, realizing every time they made a new
contact what a long way there was to go before they could make
the rudiments of the laws of war known and accepted. They gauged
the vast distance that lay between official assurances on respect for
international humanitarian law and conditions in the field. And they
feared that on such barren soil there would be accidents and
blunders in plenty and that nobody would know how to stop them.

In spite of the meagre guarantees of safety obtainable, the
delegates had to find a way of stepping up programmes in aid of
the population, which was already living on its reserves and whose
most vulnerable groups needed greater help. They accordingly
organized a convoy of medical relief supplies, accompanied by a
team of ICRC delegates sent to reinforce those in Sarajevo. The
convoy left Belgrade on 17 May 1992. On the 18th, on leaving Pale,
it was attacked at the entrance to the old town. One delegate died
as a result the following day and two others were wounded.

One serious incident followed another, the deployment of ICRC
delegates within Bosnia-Herzegovina as a whole was severely
restricted, and the efficiency of humanitarian activity appeared to
be losing rather than gaining strength. After in-depth analysis of
the situation, the ICRC's top-level management decided[11] that all
its offices within the republic should be temporarily closed. The
EC's observers and those of the United Nations had already left.
With the departure of the ICRC, the last door closed on neutral
independent witnesses of the Bosnian scene. It was then that the
persecution of minorities was unleashed in all its violence.

The principle that worst is best

When the plenipotentiaries of the parties to the conflict in Bosnia-
Herzegovina met for the first time on 22 May 1992 at ICRC
headquarters in Geneva, it was originally to define the scope of the
law applicable and undertake to ensure its respect. But everyone
present had in mind the attack at Sarajevo four days previously,
especially as the ICRC's Bosnian guests attended the funeral
ceremony held on 23 May in Geneva Cathedral (which was crowded
to the doors) in memory of the delegate Frédéric Maurice.

Besides the purely legal aspects of the conflict, the protagonists had urgently to consider the question of safety guarantees without which humanitarian activities could not continue. At that time, the ICRC had not yet decided on its temporary withdrawal, whose duration would depend on the willingness and the time taken by the belligerents to satisfy its demands for an explanation of the attack, and on what had been done to prevent any recurrence of such serious incidents. Only ten days later, when the withdrawal was announced, was an *ad hoc* meeting held with the plenipotentiaries to fix the conditions on which the ICRC would resume its activities in the field.[12]

Meanwhile, the agreement of 22 May was put on the stocks in much the same way as the agreement concluded in the Croat–Yugoslav conflict. There, too, the aim was to circumvent the obstacle of formal designation of the conflict (which was open to various interpretations) and to agree on the substance of the rules applicable. There was no denying that armed hostilities were taking place. But were they part of an internal conflict? If so, there were different bodies in a republic newly recognized by the international community.[13] Or was this an international armed conflict, since the Yugoslav federal army, now a foreign army, was fighting on the side of the Bosnian Serbs? Three months later, without beating about the bush, the United Nations based the Security Council's resolutions on breaches of international humanitarian law firmly on the Geneva Conventions, treaties which apply specifically to wars between states. By so doing, they affirmed that the armed clashes taking place were international.

The ICRC, concentrating on essentials, took care not to set off a legal debate with the plenipotentiaries, but urged them to consider a draft on matters of concern to them as well as to the ICRC's wish to get on with its work. This Agreement of 22 May 1992 (see Appendix, Document VI) was based on existing law. It encouraged the parties to the conflict to go beyond the texts and offer the various categories of victims a degree of protection approaching that required in the international treaties. But there was one important omission: at the last moment, the parties refused to include in the agreement any admission that they were also responsible for the behaviour of the 'uncontrolled elements' fighting on their side. This is regrettable, remembering the atrocities later committed by some militias with full impunity. Another omission from the agreement was any provision for opening 'humanitarian corridors' through which to evacuate minority populations. The plenipotentiaries seemed ready to agree to this, but the ICRC did little to encourage them, fearing that it would facilitate the practice of separating communities. The agreement does not provide, as was the case for the first conflict, that working groups should be formed to consider

specific problems, such as prisoners and tracing missing persons.
The lack of any machinery for implementing the rules agreed on
was probably one of the reasons why international humanitarian
law was so frequently ignored in this conflict.

When they signed this text, the protagonists were aware that in
many provinces of Bosnia-Herzegovina, all the ingredients of
'ethnic cleansing' were present. They certainly knew this better than
the ICRC delegates who, when they temporarily left their bases all
over the republic, realized from the despairing looks cast at them
that the local inhabitants felt that they were being left to their fate.
'The people of Mostar wanted us to stay on, for we were the last
and they had no wish to be left alone to die', said François Bellon,
who had felt the tension rise in the region; his movements had already
been restricted by more than usually trigger-happy combatants. 'On
14 May, the United Nations received orders from its command to
withdraw. These they obeyed much against their will, lowering their
blue flag and hauling up ours in its place, between a couple of bursts
of sniper fire. The ICRC was left alone.' This went on until 28 May,
when it became possible to leave through the Croat rear lines, after
difficult negotiations for guarantees of safety that were meagre in
the extreme.

The worst atrocities against the civilian population – the only target
of martial frenzy – were around Banja Luka. The discovery of
detention camps, the tip of the iceberg of 'ethnic cleansing', hit
individual consciences like a thunderclap. 'We had a feeling that
something serious was happening but we would never have been
able to imagine anything on this scale,' said the delegates at their
posts when activities were resumed in July 1992. Their amazement
steadily grew as they visited the field and heard the flood of eye-
witness accounts of the most appalling outrages perpetrated on
civilians. And the world awoke.

What lay behind the mask of Manjaca

No sooner had they returned to the field in Bosnia than the
delegates were faced with a flood of reports on acts of violence against
the population, and of round-ups carried out in their absence.
According to rumour, there were 10–12,000 detainees in Manjaca
and Trnopolje, near Banja Luka. In the words of Patrick Gasser,
a delegate based in Zagreb since October 1991, who was to lead
the first team of delegates visiting Manjaca camp:

> We knew Manjaca as a big military farm on the heights, where
> we had already visited several hundred Croat prisoners in the
> first conflict, when we came from Belgrade.

The visit took place on 14 July. Eye-witness accounts told us to give priority to visiting Manjaca – we knew that we should be able to act quickly there. During the visit we learned more about Trnopolje and Omarska from our conversations with the detainees, and we decided to combine our visit to Manjaca with a visit to these two other camps.

During the three days of the first complete visit, the delegates managed to register the names of all the detainees (who in mid-July numbered over 2,300) in the six stables at Manjaca. This, they believed, was a first step to giving them protection:

> Every man there was living with a nightmare he could not erase from his mind. The general state of nutrition was lamentable; the detainees had lost a lot of weight in six weeks and were sliding down an extremely dangerous slope. But the worst thing was the scale of the horror that lay behind what you could see. We imagined the raids on villages, husbands and wives and children being separated and losing everything they had grown up with.

Beat Schweizer, the delegate in charge of the ICRC office in Banja Luka from July 1992 to February 1993, and his team were the only international humanitarian aid workers who were uninterruptedly in that region at this time. In the following passage, he tries to reconstruct what happened:

> At the beginning of May, the atmosphere was overheated by propaganda and pretty hysterical. There had been the vote on the independence of Bosnia-Herzegovina and recognition by the international community. Nationalist fever was rising everywhere. Here as in the UNPAs [United Nations Protected Areas], which the Serbs called Krajina, people felt more threatened than ever before. Then everything exploded without warning. That was why so many people died. Nobody was ready for anything like it. It all lasted three or four days. The aim was certainly to clean up the region, for the raids were not only on the men, but also on the women and children who were separated from the men and sent mainly to Trnopolje before being expelled to Croatia or central Bosnia via Travnik. At the same time, the villages were destroyed. The very memory of these villages was wiped out. All the men were arrested. Practically nobody escaped. They arrested everyone they hadn't killed. There are a lot of things we shall never know, for these villages were isolated. There was the notorious example of Kozarac, a town near Prijedor,[14] 95 per cent of whose 15,000 inhabitants were Muslim; hundreds of men were probably killed there. To some extent it symbolizes what happened. Going through the town, you won't see a single house standing. The only building more or less intact is the

Orthodox church. The town was attacked and bombarded, and then they went from house to house. In fact the detainees in all the prison camps were from two or three municipalities, Prijedor and Sanski Most, and to a lesser extent Kluj. This is where 'ethnic cleansing' struck early on; it was fairly regional and dominated by a handful of people. One of the factors was that in these municipalities a slight majority of the population was Muslim. The Serbian authorities felt threatened. Another factor was a memory of the past; from 1939 to 1945, the whole region of Banja Luka (and of Livno) was controlled by the Ustachis [the name given to Croat nationalist combatants in the Second World War], and terrible massacres of Serbs are said to have taken place at that time, with the bodies of murdered babies exposed in public places.

After the first series of visits to Manjaca, Patrick Gasser reported what he had seen to his head of delegation in Zagreb, who sent him off to Geneva by the first plane available to report his experiences by word of mouth and find reinforcements for the next round of visits. His close colleagues at ICRC headquarters were at once convinced of the gravity of the situation and the urgent necessity of doing everything possible to protect prisoners. The experts were brought in and so were the most important officials of the ICRC. But to Gasser, things were still not moving fast enough. He had seen events at first hand. He says:

I had never experienced anything like it. I did all I could to explain, but I could not get people to understand what lay behind the pictures. This was what mattered most to me and I felt that at this more subjective level my credibility, without being questioned, was being put to the test.

So far, no newspaper article and no television picture had made any impression on public opinion. Nevertheless there were journalists in Manjaca when the ICRC delegates made their first visit there, for the delegates asked the journalists not to follow them about at their work. Among the journalists was Roy Gutman of the New York newspaper *Newsday*, who took several days to write his article (the first to be published on Manjaca) and Ed Vuillamy of the *Guardian*; he too took time to think things over and postponed the publication of his article. Was this because of total surprise, or refusal to recognize the facts? Many prominent and war-toughened reporters did not fully realize what was going on in the camps before they saw the ITN documentary; nor did the public.

On the eve of the international meeting called by the UNHCR for 29 July 1992 to discuss the humanitarian consequences of the conflict in former Yugoslavia, the ICRC was putting the final touches to the speech its President was to make. It decided to denounce publicly the serious attacks on human dignity, the contempt shown for the elementary rules of behaviour in battle, and above all the ill-treatment of civilians, who were the first and almost the only victims – as well as the pawns and the target – of this war (see Chapter 3, p. 47).

From August onwards, report followed report on abuses of human rights, unfolding the sordid catalogue of the belligerents' inhumane methods. The table of contents of the *Livre Noir de l'ex-Yougoslavie* (*Black Book on former Yugoslavia*)[15] gives a short and non-exhaustive account of the scale of the tragedy suffered by the civilian population. As Tadeusz Mazowiecki says in the concluding remarks of his first end-of-mission report, 'All the parties to the conflict are violating human rights. There are victims on all sides, but the fate of the Muslim population is especially tragic, for it is threatened with extermination.'[16]

Amnesty International has published a very detailed account, covering the period April–August 1992, of flagrant ill-treatment and systematic taking of hostages, the immense majority of captured persons being civilians of no danger to 'state' security, who were detained solely as bartering counters.[17] It also mentions accusations of rape that were still insufficiently supported. Some newspapers (the *Guardian* and *Newsday*) reported these without arousing much interest in public opinion, which reacted only much later when the German media got hold of the subject.

In the field, reinforced teams of delegates were plotting a map of detention centres in the course of their visits. (See Appendix, Document VII.) This is not complete, and never will be. The entire eastern region – approximately 20 per cent of the territory of Bosnia-Herzegovina and places of detention, such as Brcko, famed for their harshness – remained closed to the delegates in spite of mounting pressure from the international community in August. The US State Department took charge of the matter, and its acting secretary appealed to the Commission on Human Rights to hold a special session to discuss the breaches of law committed in the detention camps.[18]

Access to the camps and the frequency of visits to them were matters much discussed in international circles, which were often ill informed of conditions in the field. These questions even became critical after some blitz visits such as the three-day mission by Paddy Ashdown, a British Member of Parliament. In a letter to Cornelio Sommaruga dated 12 August 1992, he expressed astonishment that the ICRC should have such limited means to deal with such a huge problem. To this the ICRC replied that delays and inadequacies in the frequency and extent of the visits were not due to material omissions but to the system of decision in the zones visited. Sometimes it was the military authorities who dealt with such matters, sometimes the regional civilian authorities, and sometimes the militias. As a result, there were unending fruitless attempts to get exact information on the prison scene and an agreement on a real programme of visits based on formal advance notifications, rather than having to make do with isolated unconnected visits. And there was of course the eternal question of the safety of the humanitarian mission.

One especially edifying example is that of Omarska camp, which the delegates were able to visit only on 12 and 13 August, that is, more than a month after the resumption of prison visits. There were then only 173 left of the thousands of detainees supposed to be in the camp. Several hundred of them had been transferred in appalling conditions to Manjaca and Trnopolje. There was no news of hundreds, perhaps thousands, of prisoners who had disappeared. 'We lost a lot of time negotiating our access to Omarska,' Beat Schweizer admits,

> for this regional camp was controlled by the commune of Prijedor, whereas Manjaca was controlled by military authorities with whom we were in touch and who very quickly gave us the green light. I never managed to get hold of the right person for Omarska, access to Prijedor having been closed to us in July. The military and the Banja Luka authorities all said they could not help us out of this deadlock.

The route was not opened until it was too late. Another camp the ICRC delegates could not visit was that at Keraterm, also emptied of its survivors before the Serbian authorities agreed to consider allowing the ICRC to visit it. A terrible question is still unanswered: how many detainees died when they were arrested, or from ill-treatment or lack of care, or especially in transfer to other places of detention? 'Manjaca prison consisted of six stables. The two occupied by the people from Omarska were not a pleasant sight,' said the ICRC nutritionist when she first visited the prison on 16 August. What shook Ariane Curdy in her consultations with these detainees was not only their general state of health but the look on their faces. It showed what they had just gone through, that they were haunted day and night by memories too dreadful for them to bear:

> The men detained at Omarska were young men regarded as fit for military service. The others, picked up here and there in the countryside, were more usually 'old grandads', originally stocky and well covered thanks to good food and slivovic, who held out much better than the young ones by drawing on their reserves of fatty tissue. But there were cases of vitamin deficiency,

even among the fat people, for vitamin B1 tends to disappear within two weeks, exposing the patient to beriberi and scurvy.

Before the ICRC arrived, the detainees had been surviving, most of them for the previous three months, on a diet of 500 to 600 calories a day, in the form of bread and a kind of soup. This represents one quarter of the normal nutritional requirements for a male population of an average height of 180 cm. Dietary deficiencies as considerable as these over a fairly long period cause impressive weight losses and greatly lower general resistance to cold and illness. There was an urgent need to increase the food ration and improve sanitary conditions in the camp. These are responsibilities of the detaining authorities, but the delegates soon realized that the ICRC would have to do something to make up for their lack of willingness to discharge them by drawing on its own resources to avoid the worst, especially as winter was approaching. Manjaca was by far the largest camp visited in terms of numbers of captives. The ICRC's assistance programme in this camp raised the energy value of the prisoners' diet from 600 to 2,200 calories daily. The target figure, 2,500 calories, could not be reached because the kitchens were not adequately equipped. Since there was an interval of some 15 hours between the main meal of the day and breakfast, this diet was supplemented by bread and biscuits for night-times, which had become cold. This assistance continued without a break until the prisoners were released, and enabled the ICRC to maintain a daily presence in the camp which gave extra protection. At the same time, Ariane Curdy was running a nutritional programme for the cases of malnutrition noted at her first consultations, which showed that about 15 per cent of the detainees were suffering from serious, 28 per cent from moderate, and 28 per cent from slight malnutrition. This operation ceased on 11 October because there were no patients – all of them were cured.

Conditional release

In August 1992, detainees, politicians, UN officials, humanitarian aid workers, journalists and belligerents unanimously agreed that the prisoners should be released and, their consciences being stirred, rushed to put forward widely differing proposals as to how and when this should take place.

The immense majority of the detainees were civilians whose only wish was to leave the camp and rejoin their families. They secretly hoped to recover their land one day, but they knew that they had no say in the matter. They knew, too, that they were lucky in comparison with prisoners who had not been fortunate enough to be registered by an independent organization. The belligerents, especially the Bosnian Serbs, wanted to rid themselves as soon as they could of a burden that every day was bringing down international censure on them and was a potential drain on their resources. The politicians in general wanted to show that they were capable of decisive action in a sphere where they had hitherto enjoyed little success. And the humanitarian workers, relying on their experience and understanding of the situation, maintained that the only proper thing to do was to close down the camps because they contained people who had no business to be there, being neither combatants nor seekers after power of any kind.

The London Agreements[19] confirmed that the international community unanimously wished to settle the question of the camps by unilateral unconditional releases. In the lobbies of the conference, Radovan Karadzic, the leader of the Bosnian Serbs, having exhausted all his arguments, was reduced to saying that all right, the ICRC was welcome to run the camps until they closed down. Meanwhile, preparations for the first evacuation of wounded and sick were going ahead nicely. Ever since their visits began, the doctors and nurses had taken note of the detainees whose state of health needed immediate hospital care. Their first concern was to see whether the local hospitals were equipped to look after seriously sick and wounded persons. On a purely professional level, a transfer of this kind was perfectly possible; but safety was quite another matter. At Banja Luka and other towns in Bosnia-Herzegovina, the delegates found that admittance to hospital was subject to ethnic discrimination, and that even if patients from a minority or 'enemy' community were accepted, their safety whilst they were in hospital was uncertain to say the least. Armed men intruded into hospitals on countless occasions and there were innumerable cases of brutality, some of them against patients. It soon became obvious that it was out of the question to expose people on whom frightful violence had already been inflicted in prison to the risk of reprisals.

While the framework agreement for the release of all prisoners was being prepared with the plenipotentiaries, negotiations for the emergency evacuation of wounded and sick were drawing to a close. The operation was postponed several times because of the difficulty of finding an airline willing to land at Banja Luka airport, but finally 68 sick and wounded from Manjaca camp took off for the United Kingdom on a Russian Tupolev aircraft on 15 September 1992. The operation went off smoothly. The delegates regarded this as a good omen for the success of the rest of the release programme, which was to absorb the energies of all concerned until December, for complete evacuation raised many problems, moral and logistic.

For example, were convoys to be under the armed protection of UNPROFOR troops? How was their safety to be ensured between the time they left prison and their arrival at Karlovac transit centre in Croatia, which had been chosen as a reception centre for those set free? Had host countries given sufficient guarantees that they would accept the persons set free? Rather than leave anything to chance, the ICRC tried to reach a detailed agreement with the parties to the conflict on the programme to be followed by the release operations. That agreement was concluded on 1 October 1992 in Geneva. It provided that the whole process would be finished on 31 October. A list of the camps covered by the evacuation plan was made out and approved by the signatories of the three Bosnian communities. It concerned eleven camps and nearly 7,000 people.

Between its first press release on the freeing of the prisoners, dated 15 September when the sick and wounded were flown to the United Kingdom, and that of 23 December 1992, temporarily suspending the application of the agreement of 1 October, the various stages of the plan suffered hiccups and delays which had disastrous consequences for the detainees. There were two main reasons for this chaos. The first was the host countries' vacillation in confirming and carrying out their promise of temporary asylum to the released prisoners and their families. The second was that the Bosnian Serb authorities disputed the figures of Serbian detainees submitted by the Muslim and Croat parties, arguing that persons confined in blockaded towns or regions should also be regarded as prisoners and benefit from the unilateral unconditional release agreement demanded by the London Conference. Immediately after the first releases at Trnopolje (on 1 October) and Manjaca (where evacuation began on 14 November) a third problem arose. This too was raised by the Bosnian Serbs, who pointed out that it was they who had released nearly all the persons set free, and called upon the Muslim and Croat parties to throw open their prison doors.

Sadako Ogata and Cornelio Sommaruga made a frontal attack on the first obstacle: the fact that the transit camp opened by the Republic of Croatia in Karlovac was crammed full after the first convoy of 1,560 civilians from Trnopolje and virtually remained so showed that the host countries were incapable of opening their frontiers more generously. Access to Karlovac was consequently forbidden to the thousands of other prisoners ready to be taken in charge by the ICRC and handed over to the UNHCR which, together with the International Federation of Red Cross and Red Crescent Societies, was responsible for running the transit camp. Both these high officials pressed the international community to overcome the obstruction so that the flow of releases could continue. They also took advantage of their joint press conference on 3 October to denounce the ravages of 'ethnic cleansing' and demand the cessation of grave breaches of international humanitarian law.[20]

Bickering over figures, together with the slowness of the Western countries, dashed the delegates' hopes of having all prisoners released before the worst of the cold weather. As for the deadline of 31 October, agreed upon for completing the release operation, this could naturally not be met. That became certain after the failure of the comprehensive campaign prepared for 26 October, when about 5,000 people detained in ten camps were to have been evacuated. Constant presidential pressure by the ICRC did little to get things moving, and meanwhile civilians in regions exposed to 'ethnic cleansing' were being treated worse than before.

It was only after President Sommaruga had talks with the leaders of the three Bosnian parties, each one separately, on 9 December 1992 at ICRC headquarters,[21] that the last stages of the evacuation were programmed, and carried out after a fashion, not always in ideal conditions of security. Beat Schweizer commented 'We could no longer pick and choose, it was already December and we had to get them out. The buses were fired on but we were lucky. One of the released prisoners was hit by a stone.' Pierrette Chenevard, an ICRC nurse with the Manjaca convoys, remembers the threats, shots, orders and counter-orders of the waiting period. She said:

> The soldiers were just playing with us, and the civilian population on the way was very aggressive. Panes of glass in the buses were broken. This was a terrible experience for the former detainees and a very anxious time for the delegates, who had to concentrate hard, take quick decisions and keep a grip on their nerves. I kept saying to myself: 'You mustn't crack up'.

After three months of effort the problem of the prisoners was far from being settled. True, the worst had been avoided for the people detained in the least liveable of the camps such as Trnopolje and Manjaca, but basically the same problems were still there. That is, the ICRC was still not being allowed access to all the places of detention, it was not notified of arrests, it could not supervise some of the release operations because they were being carried out without any of its delegates being present, it lacked reliable information on civilians kept in forced residence in their villages, and there was still an immense question mark over the fate of soldiers believed to have been taken prisoner. For the vast majority of persons visited were civilians, and it was still unknown whether combatants taken whilst bearing arms were being kept beyond the reach of humanitarian organizations, or whether the belligerents had liquidated them. The ICRC's reports submitted in April 1993 to the Republic of Bosnia-Herzegovina and the Croat and Serbian communities contain a detailed and severe commentary on every aspect of visits to detainees. These are confidential documents of about 20 pages, intended only for the detaining authorities. In language that leaves no room for doubt, they enumerate the principal infringements of international humanitarian law (that very law which the parties had repeatedly undertaken to respect), those of the delegates' recommendations that had some effect, and those that were ignored. They are intended not merely to catalogue over a given period – in this case from July 1992 to January 1993 – the uncertainty involved in protecting prisoners, but above all to improve their living conditions. Unfortunately, the delegates did not find that the competent authorities improved their treatment of prisoners to any great extent in the months following the submission of the reports.

In January 1993, although the ICRC had always publicly expressed its regret that it did not have access to all places of detention, it was faced with a new press campaign that obliged it to clarify its role. According to a sensational statement by the American secret service, at first published in the *New York Times* and later in the *International Herald Tribune*,[22] it was thought that 70,000 people were still being detained by the belligerents in Bosnia-Herzegovina, most of them by the Serbs, including some detained in Serbia itself, according to the American sources quoted. This exceeded by far all the estimates made by the humanitarian organizations present in the region. The ICRC was bombarded from all sides with demands that it should confirm or deny these statements, but it did no more than make clear what it was itself doing and repeat that the figures in its possession had been verified[23] but were incomplete. It refused to amplify this statement or to enter into controversy.

Lives in ruins

Rape is a war crime. To insist on quoting statistics as a means of emphasizing its enormity is to insult every woman and girl who has suffered the ultimate outrage upon her dignity in towns and villages isolated by war.

'It was already in the air in September 1992, but didn't make a stir', said Jane Howard of the BBC with regret. 'No follow-up, no pick-up. The story came back only in January 1993 and then hit the headlines. Why? Yes, it happened. The numbers are unbelievable … Nobody has a right to give numbers.' On Sunday 23 August, three weeks after his discovery of the 'camps of death',[24] Roy Gutman mentions eye-witness accounts of the rape of 40 Muslim women by soldiers acting under orders. Throughout the statements summarized by this American magazine relating to acts committed mainly in May and June, the words 'shame', 'anger' and 'moral injury' occur repeatedly. Then there was silence, or almost, until a number of women evacuated to Karlovac began to talk.

One of the first European newspapers to return to the subject was Munich's *Abendzeitung* on 4 November. It was followed on 13 November by the *Volkskrant*, a Netherlands newspaper, and then by the *Mona Lisa* television programme on the German channel ZDF on 15 November. Four days later, an action committee of members of the German parliament and German private associations[25] sent an open letter to Chancellor Helmut Kohl and to persons and organizations concerned by the conflict,[26] asking them to act without delay to prevent further rapes. According to this committee, there had been 'at least fifty thousand women and girl victims', and it expressed astonishment that the UNHCR and the International Red Cross should know nothing of them and do nothing to combat this outrage.

The ICRC delegation in Zagreb was frequently approached by journalists looking for confirmation or for independent statements. Disappointed in their quest, they often interpreted the lack of evidence as indifference by organizations supposedly fully aware of all the acts of violence committed throughout Bosnia-Herzegovina. To this the ICRC replied that it had been the first to denounce the crimes committed by the protagonists in this war to the international community, and to lament its own inability to restrain, if not stop, violations of the law. On 29 July in Geneva, it had addressed government representatives and the international press to this effect, speaking loud and clear but to deaf ears. It returned to the charge in London at the end of August, where all the responsible authorities in the world that were involved in the conflict had gathered for the Conference on former Yugoslavia, and again on 3 October in its appeal for 'Saving lives in Bosnia-Herzegovina'. And in dozens of statements and press releases and hundreds of interviews in Geneva and in the field, all of them for the same essential purpose of stopping violations of the law, doing away with hatred and putting in its place a humanitarian message of tolerance – with the help of the states signatory to the Geneva Conventions.

As the press campaign got under way, fed both from trustworthy sources and by propaganda, it became increasingly difficult for humanitarian witnesses on the spot to gain acceptance of the general argument on breaches of international humanitarian law, which although ranking rape as a war crime regards it as 'only' one aspect of 'ethnic cleansing'. It is true that by the end of 1992, delegates from the ICRC and other bodies had seen so many horrors that they did not feel able or entitled to indulge in statistical allegations. They knew that rape had been committed but respected the reticence of the victims. They had testimonies, few of them first-hand, but did not unilaterally attempt to confirm their truth. When, in a private interview, a detainee told an ICRC delegate that she had been raped, he had the decency to listen to her rather than think of guiding the interview along specific lines. Confronted with the distress of women forced to leave their homes, he well understood that, whatever they had gone through, what they wanted most of all was to rejoin their husbands and sons and everyone cruelly separated from them by the war. And as these interviews usually took place in Bosnia-Herzegovina, the delegates were particularly careful not to endanger people who would risk the worst by stating too precisely what outrages had been inflicted on them.

There was now a wide gulf between the experiences of humanitarian aid workers and journalists' expectations, and governmental and other groups or lobbies. This gulf existed less in terms of the facts than in their interpretation. One woman delegate said

> Villages, motels and houses were temporarily converted into field brothels; that is quite probable, but very difficult to verify. When we tried to get any information, we were told that the places concerned were private property, or were no longer used for that purpose.

Relatively few allegations and still fewer direct eye-witness accounts reached the ears of delegates, and the most serious incidents went back to a time when there were no international observers in Bosnia-Herzegovina. To this the ICRC President added, in February 1993:

> I do not know how many women suffered this tragedy, but the thing to do is to find out who is responsible and above all to take action to prevent any more atrocities of this kind. For this, many more international observers able to travel anywhere in the country would have been needed. The protected areas we proposed in August 1992, and on many later occasions, would have prevented horrible things like this from happening. We now have to make a major effort of rehabilitation, very tactfully and respecting the cultural environment. I much regret the way this matter has been turned into a political one, often by women. This has made the whole dreadful business much less credible and has sewn doubt in people's minds.

The Civil Affairs Bureau of UNPROFOR, the Commission on Human Rights, the European observers, the UNHCR, UNICEF, Amnesty International, MSF and the International Red Cross have all had to face the same difficulty, that of ascertaining the extent and character of that serious offence, the rape of persons who have fallen into enemy hands. That is also what the European Community Monitor Mission found when it came into contact with the main organizations from 18–24 December 1992 in Zagreb. Its preliminary report notes the great contrast between the scale of press coverage and the lack of documentary evidence held by those best placed to possess it. It was nevertheless the EC mission that produced the figure of 20,000 victims. Public opinion for a long time regarded this as almost official, whereas even Amnesty International, which produced a detailed report on the subject,[27] would express no opinion. In particular, it refused to confirm the figure put forward by the European mission of enquiry, and declared on 21 January to the *France Presse* news agency: 'All estimates concerning the number of women victims of rape and sexual abuse must be treated with caution.' This mission was led by Dame Ann Warburton of the United Kingdom; it aroused public controversy between its first and second missions (from 22–26 January 1993, in Bosnia-Herzegovina) when Simone Veil, the former President of the European Parliament, who took part in the first mission and being disappointed at the way the expedition was shaping, announced that she was withdrawing from the delegation on the grounds that 'she was a politician not a voyeur'.[28] The report made following the second mission confirmed the estimate of 20,000 victims and established that rape was deliberately used for strategic purposes. It also agreed that many eye-witness accounts stated that not only Muslim but also Serb and Croat women and children, as well as men in detention camps, had been raped. Amnesty International corroborated this last fact in its report and the ICRC delegates had always declared this to be the case.

Thierry Germond, the ICRC's Delegate General for Europe, was invited to take part in a hearing of the European Parliament's Commission on Women's Rights in Brussels on 18 February 1993. In the midst of a welter of passionate commentary flooding radio and television programmes of the previous few weeks, he attempted to bring a more humanitarian view to bear on a problem painful enough without being artificially inflated. 'Let us remember,' he said,

> that apart from the current inquiries on prisoners and rape, the essential point is that the whole of the civilian population of Bosnia-Herzegovina is the victim of acts of violence of every kind – summary execution, torture, rape, arbitrary internment, forced transfer, harassment of minority groups, hostage-taking, expropriation, threats and intimidation. All these evil practices are equally to be condemned and are absolutely unacceptable ... Nevertheless the ICRC is of the opinion that caution should still be used in denouncing them and that any action should be based on facts or eye-witness accounts objectively assembled in all regions affected by the conflict. For, as this war shows, every figure quoted as representing the number of victims of atrocities will inevitably be used to justify future acts of revenge ... The ICRC has exact information on the number of prisoners

it has visited. We know that several hundred prisoners have been hidden from us, but as regards the rapes, we have not enough information to confirm the allegation that these are systematically used for more extensive purposes ... The ICRC has condemned the practice of rape by all parties to the conflict, just as it has condemned the other acts of violence committed against civilians. Rape is regarded as a war crime and it is high time to find ways and means of stopping these unacceptable practices.

Once the sound and fury had died down, there was no more talk of these unfortunate women, who could in a more tranquil environment be given the care and attention needed to rebuild their shattered lives. Either taken in charge by local associations or supported by international aid, they were henceforth given post-trauma attention suitable to the maltreatment inflicted on them. For example, in April 1993 the International Federation of Red Cross and Red Crescent Societies opened its first centres providing care by specialist doctors and health visitors locally recruited in Croatia, Serbia, Slovenia, Montenegro and Macedonia, where there were tens of thousands of displaced persons. Other governmental organizations and NGOs were to follow.

Objective: civilians

One of the most painful features of the war is certainly the fate of civilians and non-combatants who fall into enemy hands. Measures that at first seemed necessary for state security and therefore justified, providing they were only temporary, soon became a means of reprisals and retaliation that turned the captured civilian into a mere pawn in the hands of his captor.

On re-reading a report submitted by the ICRC in 1921 to the tenth International Conference of the Red Cross,[29] when the community of states was preaching universal peace, it is clear that the Bosnia conflict did not invent systematic repression of the civilian population, although the tormentor's methods have become so efficient over time that they overwhelm humanitarian aid workers.

To propose rules for the protection of civilians immediately after the First World War might seem outrageous to people who believed that this was the 'war to end all wars', but not to others, more realistic, who knew that the civilian population was at risk from the fighting and that it was time to give it greater protection. Nevertheless, the idea ran into opposition from some of the victorious nations, especially France, the power that occupied Germany until the Treaty of Versailles came into force, and again when it occupied the Ruhr from 1923 to 1925. France long opposed any draft convention for the protection of the civilian population, including the ICRC's Tokyo draft of 1934, one year after the emergence of Nazi Germany and its first excesses. The diplomatic conference that was to have examined its text was scheduled to take place early in 1940. Four days after the outbreak of war, the ICRC proposed to the belligerents that the 'Tokyo draft' should be applied in advance and for the duration of the conflict only. However,

> Geneva received only one reply, from the German government, which stated that it was willing to discuss the conclusion of a convention for the protection of civilians based on the 'Tokyo project'. On so little a show of interest for the possible fate of civilians, the ICRC could not go ahead with its proposal. Only much later was this solitary reply revealed as the crowning point of Nazi hypocrisy and of indifference by the Western democracies.[30]

Nothing like this happened in the wars of former Yugoslavia. All the belligerents unanimously agreed, without restriction and with an open-minded attitude to negotiation such as is rarely encountered, to accept all the existing rules offering protection to the civilian population. Agreements were signed and undertakings publicly renewed. That was what the belligerents said. What they did is another matter.

As Marco Sassoli points out in an internal memorandum of 23 November 1992, more especially in relation to the agreements concluded on Bosnia-Herzegovina, 'Not only were all their provisions violated, but also even the most elementary rules of that minimum that should be respected in all circumstances', namely Article 3 (common to all four Geneva Conventions). He adds that, contrary to what one might expect,

> There is really nothing new about most of the problems facing international humanitarian law (IHL) and the ICRC in the conflicts in former Yugoslavia. Failure to respect IHL, lack of means to apply it, the international community's lukewarm commitment to enforcing it and the ICRC's safety problems, together with the subtle interplay of uncontrolled but controlled elements and the dilemmas facing the ICRC, which has to help provide a touch of humanity in profoundly inhumane circumstances, all this is as old as war, IHL and the ICRC themselves ... What is really unique is the gap between words and deeds ... You would think the war was on another planet, not only because of the gap between good intentions and conditions on the ground (which happens in all conflicts), but in nothing less than the virtual separation of these two spheres, and therefore

the existence of an enormous gulf that the ICRC alone cannot bridge.

Marco Sassoli points out another peculiarity of this conflict, which is that the parties unhesitatingly give the media full access, even when they commit the most outrageous abuses. Beat Schweizer confirms this, and saw it at Banja Luka. He says:

People are very clever. I've always been astonished to see that the military brought the press along to film atrocities. Why? Because what the soldiers wanted was to make everybody go away, but since all the surrounding frontiers were closed, other countries had to be persuaded to take the people the Bosnian authorities wanted to get rid of. The outside world had to be persuaded to save them, and this, in the end, is what we did. 'They' are very good at playing with the international media. They also showed it during the international negotiations on the Vance–Owen plan. They used CNN and prime time and got away with it for months on end. Even better than the Khmer Rouge.

There was no international presence in Cambodia for four years. The tragedy was played out behind closed doors. That is not so with Bosnia-Herzegovina, where humanitarian organizations, the United Nations and the NGOs are in despair after so many frustrations and, with the photojournalists busy, try to plug the breaks in the dyke to protect people and save them if possible. The terms of reference of these organizations sometimes overlap, but the words used are not necessarily interpreted in the same way, and the interpretation conditions the way operations are carried out on the ground. For example, at the height of 'ethnic cleansing' the UNHCR executive François Fouinat[31] said:

We have still not decided where we stand in relation to population displacement. Thousands of family reunions are being held up. To talk about people being free to move in such context is a delusion. And 'saving lives' does not mean the same to everyone.

Sadako Ogata is even more outspoken when she says that 'if you take these people you are an accomplice to ethnic cleansing. If you don't, you are an accomplice to murder'.[32]

The ICRC too has had to face this dilemma, but with its long experience soon resolved it; for ever since the Battle of Solferino in 1859, the Red Cross has had no doubt that the proper answer is to save lives – and if possible condemn the evil. By September, the delegates had decided which way their conscience pointed. They were convinced that even if they did nothing, 'ethnic cleansing' would go ahead. The only difference would be that there would probably be more victims. They had only to shoulder the blame for – or worse, stand accused of – lending a hand to a criminal practice contrary to the elementary laws of war, and aiding and abetting it. This was hotly debated at the ICRC, particularly within the Executive Board. The delegates' submissions were backed up unequivocally by the ICRC decision[33] that

> protecting thousands of civilians in Bosnia-Herzegovina from the effects of fighting before winter sets in is a matter of the utmost urgency. Added to the suffering caused by the war, the bitter cold will only worsen their tragic plight ... The ICRC has a moral duty to do all in its power to save thousands of civilians, even if that implies temporarily moving vulnerable groups out of their regions of origin.

At first everybody agreed that the civilian population should stay where it was, even if it were in a minority there, but as the months went by the more the face of war changed, with serious consequences for civilians. One need only quote the subtitles in a report on a mission in the Banja Luka region to show how completely the daily life of civilians in enemy hands was devastated: 'murders of civilians; beatings-up, armed robbery, rape, attacks, threats; destruction of homes; dismissals and expulsions from houses; reprisals following an ICRC visit,' etc.

In a note from Zagreb dated 31 May 1993, Urs Boegli, the ICRC official responsible for co-ordinating operations in Bosnia-Herzegovina, examines the slide towards the inexorable. To save their skin, 'people had no choice but to pay a baksheesh and abandon all they possessed to war profiteers. Only those rich enough managed to get abroad.' For others, the tragedy went on even when they were out of the danger zone. When they crossed the lines, families that had until then managed to stay together were dispersed. The men were recruited for the front and the women, children and elderly were sent to unsafe lodging, often in the middle of combat areas. This is what happened to people who left Banja Luka or its environs for central Bosnia, a region until then fairly quiet, when hostilities flared up there between the Croats and Muslims who were allies only hours before.

Months earlier, on 26 August 1992, the ICRC had proposed at the London Conference to set up protected areas much larger than the hospital and safety zones opened in the first conflict at Dubrovnik and Osijek. This was a broader concept of places able to shelter a population on whom 'ethnic cleansing' had been practised. It was therefore vital for the international community – either the United Nations, or other states – to make itself respon-sible for setting up and protecting these areas. It was also necessary to obtain the belligerents' agreement, implying their willingness and intention to respect those zones. The ICRC regarded an arrangement of this kind as urgent, and in October (nothing having been done at diplomatic level) it declared that zones of tranquillity were vitally necessary.[34] The Security Council did not specifically refer to this problem until 16 November, when it 'invited the Secretary-General to study the possibility and the requirements for promoting safe areas for humanitarian purposes'.[35] The capture of the town of Jajce on 30 October had previously caused an exodus of 50,000 people to the region of Zenica in central Bosnia, and convoys for the evacuation of bombarded civilians were being organized in Sarajevo. Nearly 5,000 people left the capital on 14 and 15 November under UNPROFOR protection.

On 16 December 1992 in Geneva, the ICRC returned to the charge, and its President addressed the Follow-Up Committee of the Conference on former Yugoslavia, repeating that new ways would have to be found to safeguard the civilian population, such as protected areas. He said:

> I still think that effective and efficient ways of protection should be introduced urgently within Bosnia-Herzegovina, without favouring population transfers but with a greater presence from outside, in spite of the attendant difficulties and risks. These measures should help to stop the abominable practice of 'ethnic cleansing'. And we must go on saving human life within the Republic of Bosnia-Herzegovina. I am speaking to you also on behalf of the 150 ICRC delegates in the region, who can see for themselves what is going on there.

The international community raised countless objections to this project. Some states feared that it would lead to the creation of an area such as that in northern Iraq, others were anxious to avoid the formation of 'Bantustans', and still others had plans to intervene that would be thwarted if the project came into being. But above all, the international community was not ready to make the necessary effort of providing large military forces to protect the minorities regrouped in this way, and was afraid of being drawn into operations that might involve the use of force. The ICRC and UNHCR specialists therefore sought a new approach (see Appendix, Document VIIIa). The UNHCR reasoned that it was better to make people safer where they were than to transfer them elsewhere, and it also wanted to back any plan that would end hostilities. It therefore recommended that the UN presence should be reinforced wherever the minorities were most exposed. To sum up, the UNHCR leaders regarded the setting up of protected areas as nothing more than a 'last resort', an opinion shared by many states.

The ICRC's conclusions, though based on the same premises, were distinctly different. The ICRC distinguished between besieged populations, for whom it agreed that more radical solutions (such as the cessation of hostilities) should be put forward, and civilian populations potentially in danger because they were in a minority in the towns and villages where they lived. A third category of persons comprised those who, as victims of 'cleansing', had already had to leave their homes and could find no real refuge elsewhere. The ICRC recommended that towns with minority populations should be designated as protected areas and have sufficient international protection to ensure their safety; people in this third category could then find temporary shelter there.

The Muslim pockets in territory conquered by the Bosnian Serbs, and towns like Mostar and Zenica, were to be granted protected-area status either too late or never. The Security Council voted Resolution 824 on 7 May 1993. It states what places are to be protected – Sarajevo and the five Muslim enclaves: Srebrenica, Zepa, Gorazde, Bihac and Tuzla – and is the result of amalgamating three kinds of parallel negotiations: political, with the plan for the carve-up of Bosnia-Herzegovina, military, which aimed at demilitarizing Sarajevo, and humanitarian. It covered only towns attacked by the Bosnian Serbs, forgetting towns like Mostar, and forgetting central Bosnia, where Croats and Muslims were at each other's throats.

Protection? What protection?

André Collomb took up his post as Deputy Delegate General for Europe in July 1992. As Thierry Germond's right-hand man, one of his most important functions was to liaise with the ICRC's heads of delegations covering Bosnia-Herzegovina as soon as the ICRC resumed its operations after the six-week suspension caused by the serious security incidents of May 1992. Reviewing the events of a year of war, he says:

> There are three phases in this war that are immutably linked: active war, harassment, and destruction, in that order. The latter two and all the kinds of behaviour they imply are completely contrary to the Fourth Geneva Convention on the protection of civilian persons. They are its almost exact opposite. You might even say that the Fourth Convention has been turned inside out, like a glove.

As proof, he says, one only has to consider the right of access, the right to assistance and, finally, the right to intervene which, as practised in Bosnia-Herzegovina, is tantamount to bargaining. He also recognizes that the ICRC has only an extremely limited experience of central and eastern Europe. Between the end of the Second World War and the fall of the Berlin Wall, the only armed clashes on European soil were in Hungary (1956) and Cyprus (1974). The presence of ICRC delegates was also required by the events in Poland (1981–82) and Romania (1989). The rulers of the then socialist states in the other troubled regions of that part of the world deliberately prevented the ICRC from stepping in, because they violently rejected any mediation, even for humanitarian purposes, by what they called western capitalist organizations. Generally speaking, European humanitarian aid workers therefore had no opportunity of transposing the experience they had acquired in Third World wars into the field in their own continent. They sadly lacked reference material.

Although the conflicts in former Yugoslavia are not necessarily a blueprint for future wars, as far as the civilian population is concerned, some patterns do repeat themselves and become more pronounced. Forcible transfer and regrouping of members of the same ethnic group have already been tried out on a large scale, as in South Africa. In Bosnia-Herzegovina, they have been still more radical, and the only break in them has been a 'minimal humanitarian service' good for no more than 'feeding the local mafias and maintaining the predatory economy that enables the war to continue'.[36] André Collomb tones this down by saying that

> our problem is not so much concerned with our competence as with the inexorability of the war machine and the incapacity of the international community to do more than deal with the humanitarian consequences of a conflict that only political and economic measures can stop.

What makes matters worse is that the sanctions imposed by the international community, however justified they may be on political and strategic grounds, bear hard upon the day-to-day existence of the civilian population, for whom the international community can find little pity. Indeed, it is suspicious of any aid for the Serbs. Whilst carrying out a parliamentary enquiry for the Council of Europe, the Swiss politician Michel Fluckiger was fiercely criticized by the Swiss media for his comments on the unenviable plight of the civilian population of the 'new Yugoslavia' after a year's embargo. Admittedly, almost the only course of action left to the international community (apart from military intervention, which the great majority opposed) was economic pressure, which primarily affects the most vulnerable strata of the population. The health service was badly hit. The ICRC physicians had no doubt that aggravating conditions already existed in former Yugoslavia, such as the disastrous state of its economy, the structure of its national services and the resulting political implications. But as far back as October

1992, they found that there was a lack of imported basic equipment in radiology and paediatrics, and for laboratories and chronic diseases. Psychiatric institutions had been neglected. Arrangements had to be made to rehabilitate amputees, and war surgery had to be improved.

The long, complicated procedures involved in the imposition of sanctions bore heavily on the health service, which at the same time was progressively weakened by the lack of state subsidies, rising unemployment and a greatly reduced yield from income tax. Blunders by international civil servants in interpreting the application of sanctions led to Belgrade Military Hospital being put on the blacklist, although the Geneva Conventions entitled that hospital to be treated in the same way as civilian hospitals. In November 1992, it had only three weeks' reserve stocks of blood-testing material and this shortage increased the risk of propagating diseases such as hepatitis B and AIDS. And whilst strategic materials easily evaded the embargo, the shortage of vitally needed products got worse and worse.

A special problem was that of Balkan nephropathy, a disease peculiar to the region, which causes an abnormally high incidence of renal insufficiency. The number of patients under dialysis was estimated at 5,000 for the whole of former Yugoslavia. A costly programme had to be followed to keep them alive.

The ICRC was aware that it risked burning its fingers, and it looked round for partners so as not to bear alone the weight of assistance programmes beyond its strength. It also knew that it would soon make itself unpopular by appearing to be critical of sanctions, although these are not supposed to affect humanitarian aid. As the only large-scale humanitarian organization, apart from the International Federation of Red Cross and Red Crescent Societies and the UNHCR, to be involved in helping the Serbian population to bear the suffering inflicted on it by the war, it supported the programmes introduced by the Red Cross of Yugoslavia and the Serbian Red Cross. At the same time it endeavoured to persuade international bodies such as the World Health Organization to take on greater commitments in the region.

The international community was more concerned with the medical and nutritional situation in Bosnia-Herzegovina, and this of course made it easier to finance assistance programmes there. But as regards medical aid, in the words of Dr Barthold Bierens de Haan,[37] 'in Bosnia-Herzegovina, lives do not come to an end in hospitals under the eyes of physicians, or in ruined buildings by fire and sword, but in secret hidden places where massacres, torture and rape eliminate thousands of people physically and psychically'. He adds that it is an insult to the vast numbers of highly competent medical practitioners of former Yugoslavia to flood their hospitals with unwanted equipment. But what is a matter of urgency is to think about setting up a service for psychological assistance to victims of war, ill-treatment and rape. This is being done by MSF which, ever since the first released prisoners arrived in France in 1992, has run a psychological aid programme whose first results have been the subject of extremely detailed reports.[38]

Protection of the civilian population resident in the UNPAs has its ups and downs because the field is complex and the UNPROFOR forces and UN Civil Affairs officials have difficulty in deploying there. There is no exact information on what has happened to dispersed families. There are still doubts as to the possibility of evacuating endangered minorities to Croatia or the interior of Bosnia-Herzegovina. Neither has there been any greater success in putting into effect the initial desire to create conditions for the return of the civilian population residing there before the fighting, because of a general lack of guarantees for their safety. The political status of the UNPAs and the unilateral proclamation of the Serb Autonomous Region did nothing to simplify matters. In short, it seemed to all the parties in those regions that they had got little out of the new arrangements and all they could do was to share their frustration. The Serb militias continued to operate illegally. The tension between Serbs and Croats was still high, causing all sorts of harassment and squabbles. The UN and ICRC observers could only look on, unable to stop the pursuit of political and military objectives in which the civilian population was at stake.

One positive note in this inventory of impotence to stop the worst from happening: the civilian population of Bosnia-Herzegovina received emergency material aid on a remarkable scale that enabled it to bear the rigours of winter, through the joint efforts of the UNHCR, the NGOs and the Red Cross (see Appendix, Document IX p. 216), and was also able to correspond regularly with family members who were either detained in camps or had gone abroad or had fled to other regions of former Yugoslavia. Their correspondence used the channel of the ICRC's Central Tracing Agency, which exchanged the record number of 50,000 family messages every week. During the year 1993, more than two million messages were sent or received by families separated by the conflict. This gave them an irreplaceable emotional link until they could be reunited – and for many of them this was unlikely ever to happen.

Law and morality

It is still too early to assess how far humanitarian law was respected and how far it was violated, and particularly to accuse those institutions that have assumed the thankless task of taking the place of defaulting political powers.

How is it still possible to believe Tahar Ben Jelloun when he writes:

> Perhaps we have kept only one of our illusions, a rare and essential one that admits of neither concession nor compromise. That is humanitarian law, an elementary law not always respected, but – let us face it – as this century nears its end, we have little to show that will save us a blush. This is a non-negotiable security that is still proof against personal selfishness, national indifference and political cynicism. It is our last card.

Later on, he asks, 'Where is the law today, and how are we to make humanitarian activities meaningful?'[39] The former UN High Commissioner for Refugees, Jean-Pierre Hocké, answers: 'Where international star performers have grabbed humanitarian activities and UNPROFOR to hide their lack of will and political unity', where 'the United Nations, now acting as maids of all work, are at a loss to know how they should start tackling the problems',[40] we must recover our freedom of action and stop playing 'video games' on relief convoys (will they or won't they get through?) which are games of chance and no longer even rank as 'charity business'. There are observers who, like Bernard Kouchner, think that the recent developments in Security Council resolutions show that humanitarian activities in their modern sense are a catalyst, and that the only way to save 'men and women survivors in Bosnia is to associate humanitarian activities more closely still with politics and diplomacy'.[41] Hocké favours a different concept, that of a genuine humanitarian partnership in which impartial non-political organizations would draw closer to one another and together form a force to be reckoned with.

The question is therefore not one of a war between ancient and modern but one of ethics. For the ICRC too, this mix of ideas opens a Pandora's box in which all excesses and all inaction are equally contained. The ICRC prefers to support initiatives that are fundamentally important, such as the creation of an international war crimes tribunal (Security Council Resolution 808 of 22 February 1993), provided that the tribunal now instituted on the occasion of the conflict in former Yugoslavia is not limited only to that theatre of war but becomes a permanent universal organ strengthening opposition to breaches of international humanitarian law wherever committed, and provided it does not reflect only the justice of the victors.

The jurist Mireille Demas-Marty says: 'Without the shock of the Second World War, human rights would probably not have taken the place they occupy today.' And she reminds us also that all rights are not protected to the same extent. Only some of them have an absolute value from which no exception, restriction or derogation is possible even in case of war. This is the case, not of the right to life, but of the prohibition of torture and inhuman and degrading treatment, and therefore the right to respect of human dignity.[42]

Suppose that the suffering and barbarism of the conflict in former Yugoslavia were to bring lost values back to life or invent new values, by giving humanitarian organizations an opportunity to recompose the present? As Jacques Freymond wrote after the humanitarian setback in Vietnam: 'The members of the ICRC consider that any criticism endangers the neutrality, impartiality and independence of the International Committee'.[43] Today the ICRC has changed. It knows that it is fallible and that it bears a heavy co-responsibility for the way in which humanitarian action will be rethought and remodelled to meet the priorities of the last years of the twentieth century.

CHAPTER 6

On the Proper Use of Propaganda

The information theory born during the Second World War has since made great strides forward. In form and spirit alike it has been so successful as to inspire those of former Yugoslavia's officials who have had the strategic mission of stamping reflexes of hate and revenge upon the human mind. They have fed primitive patriotic behaviour and blind faith in those – that is, the state – on whom material survival depends with a constant stream of ingeniously combined and grossly over-simplified pictures, slogans and catchwords.

Tadeusz Mazowiecki, as special rapporteur of the Commission on Human Rights, notes the pernicious role of the media in former Yugoslavia. He says that a great part of the population has been indoctrinated. Among the urgent measures he recommends is 'the establishment of an agency independent of the local authorities [which] might help to counteract the dissemination of hatred among the population'.[1]

Like others of his explicit injunctions, that seeking to control the propagandists' criminal ardour was not listened to, or was deliberately ignored and filed away among the curiosities put out by the international community. Later reports do not mention any willingness or intention to modify the standards of conduct in force.

This is all the more regrettable because the evil bites deep. The International Committee of the Red Cross (ICRC) delegates witnessed the vicious practices of the media over a long period, and saw this cancer of the mind develop even before the first shots were fired in 1991. Psychological manipulation and high tech gave the radio listener or television viewer little chance of escaping from the wave of warped information that grew more powerful every month. The isolated efforts of a handful of independent local journalists of course made no difference, any more than did those of people propagating humanitarian ideals that could not compete with the most graphic and ghastly pictures in modern history.

Communities were separated from one another by a furrow of hatred driven methodically between them. It blotted out individual memories and put new collective reflexes in their place that were primitive and passionate. Attempts to preserve information worthy of the name were grafted onto the stocks that this all-engulfing tide of forgetfulness had spared, but with scant success.

There were two things that institutions like the ICRC had to do. One was to make clear by word and deed what it was doing. The other was to give all combatants and persons responsible in any way whatsoever for enemies who had fallen into their hands some rudimentary knowledge of how they should behave towards them and of the elementary rules they should respect. This meant that a counter-propaganda machine had to be assembled.

Stage one: informing and educating

The violent demonstrations of March 1991 in Belgrade, followed by the first deaths in Krajina, set the pace. The war of the media had anyway already begun and its leading lights were indulging in extremely vigorous repartee.

On 10 May, the President of the ICRC sent a message to the Red Cross of Yugoslavia, referring to the Society's extremely active role in seeking peace since as far back as 1975, when it hosted the First World Red Cross Conference on Peace in Belgrade. He urged that Society to make even greater efforts to appease tension now that new dangers were threatening Yugoslavia.

The ICRC followed this up by holding two seminars on awareness of the situation for executives and leaders of the Red Cross of Yugoslavia. These took place in mid-June 1991, a few days after the conflict broke out in Slovenia. The tense atmosphere certainly encouraged awareness of what was coming, but it also made things very difficult for the ICRC officials running the seminars, who had to persuade the leaders of the Society to distance themselves from the political stance of the authorities and to make every effort to regain the trust of public opinion. They were in fact being asked to make a U-turn. This was not far from a revolution in the working habits inherited from the previous regime.

A few days later, 22 Red Cross executives from the six Yugoslav republics and the two autonomous provinces tackled (for the first time at this operational level and on such a scale) the formidable problem of overcoming ethnic barriers and working for victims from any and every camp. The persons seated around the table did not yet know that they were anticipating a working method that would be put to the test a few hours later. Everybody agreed to rank respect for humanitarian principles as more important than belonging to an ethnic group. This was a demonstration of impartiality, one of the seven Fundamental Principles of the International Red Cross and Red Crescent Movement. The plan was to put that principle into practice in joint operational teams.

The seminars achieved their aim of making those present aware of the problem. So much so that when a film on the Lebanese conflict of the 1980s was shown during the seminar, the participants said that this gave a foretaste of the intercommunal problems they would have to overcome if the situation got worse; they would have to cope with civilians expelled from all sides, thrown onto the roads, empty-handed and scared to death.

With the outbreak of the conflict in Slovenia and then in Croatia, it became clear that the usual methods of propagating humanitarian ideals and principles were inappropriate. The assurances given at the highest level of military hierarchies that the officers and rank and file of their forces were well aware of the laws of war were not borne out by their conduct on the ground. It was urgently necessary to find new ways of avoiding the worst. The ICRC's appeals for respect for international humanitarian law – three in less than a fortnight between 2 and 17 July 1991 – showed to what extent the laws of war were already being neglected. Reports were coming in of the first serious abuses of the Red Cross emblem.

The specialists in dissemination (the teaching of humanitarian principles and international humanitarian law) countered this speedy deterioration by launching an information campaign in the republics to drive home the elementary message, 'Don't fire on the Red Cross!' This injunction was accompanied by short descriptions of the work of ICRC delegates and members of the republican Red Cross Societies, translated into the appropriate languages and scripts and published by all the local media, with what success it is difficult to say. Optimists will note that the relief teams were harassed only a few times and were not pushed about too much. Pessimists will point to the serious security incident of 27 September 1991, on the road to Lipik in Croatia, where a properly marked convoy of which the authorities had been given advance notice was attacked by heavy weapons when preparing to evacuate patients from the psychiatric institute in Pakrac. Humanitarian activities were also subjected to countless hindrances, especially as regards access to towns under military blockade. And even worse incidents were yet to come in Bosnia-Herzegovina.

Running such a campaign solely to protect its humanitarian mission and the people carrying it out is not the normal practice of the ICRC which usually tries to make humanitarian principles widely known to all sections of the public. On the ground in Yugoslavia, this target quickly became out of range. The emergency was such that, to be able to act at all, it had to confine itself to going straight to the point.

Where are the journalists?

In the first few months of the war between Croatia and the Federal Republic of Yugoslavia, the wave of international journalists was not to be seen. It appeared only progressively. Even Vukovar, which had been shelled since 25 August, raised little interest, except for the anti-tank mine placed under the wheels of the *Médecins sans Frontières* (MSF) convoy of 18 October, and the capture of the town. On the other hand, the fate of Dubrovnik and the international heritage of its artistic treasures aroused more interest because the town was known and more people visited it. But none of the great international media except the BBC, *Le Monde*, the *Guardian* and a few others worried for long about the terrible events then happening in Slavonia. At the end of September 1991, Osijek too came under bombardment. A journalist from the local press centre almost resignedly described the media coverage as follows: 'A single shell on Zagreb makes the headlines; one hundred shells on Osijek rate a few lines on an inside page; but of one thousand shells on Vukovar there is nothing, no mention, no story.' The media really awakened only when the first pictures of the detention camps in Bosnia-Herzegovina were published. That was in August 1992. The war in former Yugoslavia had been going on for more than a year.

The silence of the international press, which with a few exceptions reported on the war only now and then, is not in itself blameworthy. It merely reflects the general anaesthesia of the western world at that time, and its refusal to revive the atrocious memories of past years in Europe. There was of course diplomatic activity, and European observers were on the spot, but not, as yet, any sufficient awakening of conscience in the circles most concerned. Against such a background, what could the public be expected to think?

This situation left the road wide open to the belligerents' official propaganda, which gathered pace and spread, giving some idea of the exponential disproportion that was later on to characterize the affairs of Bosnia-Herzegovina. It was ham-fisted, elementary in the extreme and effective. In some people it kept alive the feeling that they had been unjustly treated. It gave others a modest sense of triumph, or stifled their cries of protest. The only option open to intelligent people was not to watch television. A delegate advised them to avoid the endless procession of morbid pictures. 'This war,' he said, 'feeds on the media, and the media feed on this war.'

The local Red Cross Societies, still shy of putting out information to counteract state propaganda, even only partially, were ineffective. So was the ICRC, for it had only one Belgrade-based dissemination specialist helped by two locally recruited employees, and he was beginning to realize that the means at his disposal were tiny and his task tremendous.

Propaganda: its victors and its victims

At the end of 1992, Ivan Colovic read a report[2] at San Remo in which he took the works of official propaganda to pieces and pointed out how alike were the formulas used both by Croatia and Serbia in talking to a public that, although separated by war, shares the same historic and cultural heritage. It can even happen, he says, that the text of the messages used is identical.

Colovic takes as an example propagandist speeches supported by patriotic songs that are produced in two parallel versions. The words are the same, apart from place names in which the 'ladies of Belgrade' are replaced by the 'Zagreb girls', and except for references to nationalist subjects, when the Serbian flag is replaced by that of the Croat fatherland. That is what happened to a popular song much esteemed throughout former Yugoslavia. Its Serbian version bears the title of 'The March of King Peter's Guard'. The Croat version is 'Step by Step'.

Popular imagery is similarly disguised, apparently innocently, but it also takes more aggressive forms. For example, other popular songs, either previously existing or put together lock, stock and barrel in the style of traditional music, extol military virtues and instil hatred. Colovic adds that politicians, clerics and others use the same stratagem; they stuff their public speeches with popular sayings and quotations from epic poems, so as to strengthen the feeling that they belong to the nation and give the impression that it is the voice of the people that utters these propagandist verses. In this way the illusion is created – and perfectly synchronized – that the warmongers' interests are the interests of the nation. Take equal parts of charm, force and persuasion, flavour with a dash of familiar mythology, shake well and you have the perfect cocktail. It's a killer! The art of war can proudly take its place among the universal values.

Says an ICRC doctor, disgustedly:

> At the beginning, in 1991, from Zagreb to Belgrade within a few days of each other, you could see on the national television channels of the two republics the same pictures, the same village, the same burnt-out houses, the same gloating close-ups of the same disembowelled corpses. There was an absolutely incredible delight in being morbid. The only thing that was different was the commentary. I have never seen propaganda as crudely deployed and hammered home, full of references to the past and using library pictures. You suddenly realize that there are forces manipulating and inflaming public opinion so as to get people to fight without thinking.

Colovic believes that an even more perverse development of turning war into something ordinary and everyday lies in getting people to believe that massacres and outrages are normal. He calls this 'war propaganda by euphemism', of which there are three varieties: war as a means of meeting other people, enjoying oneself, making new friends and keeping fit; war as a chance of demonstrating your triumphant virility and leaving your mark and your smell on battle-fields; and lastly, war as an operation that glorifies the professional soldier as a rational, well-equipped being endowed with an unshake-able faith in the justice of his mission, for whom the ideal is a war without victims.

All this towering propaganda collapses the day an individual steeped in such nonsense finds himself facing real war on the ground, its stink, its pointless destruction and its madness. But then, as Colovic points out, it is too late.

The Yugoslav federal army is a particularly propitious terrain for implanting propaganda hitherto directed solely at the 'external enemy'. The rank and file, victim of the long communist interlude during which the teaching of humanitarian law must have been per-functory in the extreme, or indeed simply forbidden, does not know the elementary rules of behaviour in battle. Also, the decen-tralization introduced by Tito turned every commanding officer into an all-powerful chief, for good and above all for evil.

When Vukovar was captured, Judy Dempsey wrote in the *Financial Times* that the extraordinary hardships suffered by its inhab-itants would not end the hatred there. On the contrary, there would be more and more clashes because the Croats would want to avenge Vukovar: 'The war has entered a new phase. It is unstop-pable.' And she adds that, against this background of propaganda and death, the reasons for this war become confused and distorted.[3]

The spiral of revenge that sprang into life after the fall of Vukovar did not spare the ICRC. Croat public opinion was so deeply shocked by the fall of the city that a humanitarian institution became an ideal culprit for the local media, one that could be accused of all evils because it had not been able to prevent the worst from happening. This reprobation even became lasting resentment against the ICRC delegates who were regarded as incapable of tracing missing persons or gaining access to the secret detention camps where they were doubtless languishing.

Official pronouncements

Between 2 July 1991, during the Slovene war, and 13 August 1992, when it condemned conditions in detention camps in Bosnia-Herzegovina, the ICRC issued 34 press releases to the international community and the public. This represents 40 per cent of all the ICRC's statements published during that period. This percentage is unprecedented, considering the major crises in which the ICRC was simultaneously engaged (in Liberia, Sudan, Somalia, Afghanistan and the aftermath of the Gulf War, etc.). During the same period, it made numerous approaches to official circles such as the governmental representatives accredited to the office of the United Nations in Geneva, and sent many letters to the leaders of the parties concerned, reminding them of their obligations.

There is no escaping the fact that the ICRC's explicit and repeated appeals, as it daily witnessed serious acts of violence, were not listened to, or if they were, that they were deliberately ignored to a great extent. This new propensity to expose itself publicly during the first year of war, shown by an institution better known for its caution and indeed its restraint, is remarkable, but it was hardly noticed. Governments showed scant inclination to take action and were not constrained to do so by the pressure of their public opinion, which was virtually non-existent; but week after week the ICRC took major initiatives in language that left no room for doubt.

The ICRC's determined attempt to provoke discussion culminated in a speech by its President, Cornelio Sommaruga, on 29 July 1992 at the International Conference on Aid to the Victims of the Conflict in Former Yugoslavia, convened by the UNHCR in Geneva. The event was an exemplary one. The text of the speech was weighty and well documented from observations by ICRC delegates, it was delivered at a suitable place and time and to a suitable public, and it was simultaneously circulated to the international media. And it went completely unnoticed. Or almost. Not until 2 August, when the first trenchant article on the detention camps appeared, followed by the ITN television programme, was the torpor shaken and what was until then only 'the Yugoslav file' came to life.

Stage two: dissemination

'The civilians don't like us!' – many delegates on either side of the front lines made this heartfelt remark. It sums up the particularly delicate situation prevailing since the outbreak of the conflict in Bosnia-Herzegovina and which stems partly from the Marxist-Leninist education hammered into its victims for dozens of years, leaving indelible traces. Everything bearing a western hallmark – including an organization with headquarters in Geneva, neutral and independent though it might be – was therefore by definition suspect, even dangerous.

ICRC delegates are not famous for their unbridled emotions, but they were deeply distressed by the hostility of the public towards the ICRC, its emblem, and the men and women serving it. They were all the more shocked by this because the humanitarian work that they had been trying to do for long months, first from Belgrade and Zagreb and then in Bosnia-Herzegovina, was particularly frustrating. Ambushes, traps and direct attacks made their mission hazardous and considerably lessened their efficiency. This diagnosis of unpopularity was one of the four observations made by the dissemination specialist Daniel Masse, when he took on responsibility for dissemination in the Belgrade delegation in May 1992. He tackled this together with the other three problems, the first of these being that breaches of international humanitarian law were widespread and committed both by the regular forces and bands of irregulars, also known as 'weekend combatants', because they were partly composed of individuals who came to fire a few shots and sniff the gunpowder at the front line during their weekend leave. The second problem was that, shown on a scale of nought to ten, respect for the Red Cross emblem was at best three or four, in all regions where flagrant abuses had been recorded; and, lastly, that local Red Cross sections, being wholly dependent on the public authorities in regions where there was fighting, had fallen into the trap of partiality and were choosing victims worthy of receiving aid.

The Sarajevo ambush made delegates' safety a matter of the utmost urgency, for assistance programmes cannot be carried out unless the mission is safe, and on such assistance programmes depends any improvement in the living conditions of the people the ICRC is trying to protect – civilians in enemy hands, prisoners, wounded and sick.

Daniel Masse says that the attack on the ICRC convoy at Sarajevo on 18 May 1992 was

> the flash of light that showed things as they were. We began to be more and more safety conscious – there were still a whole lot of attacks. We were shot at several times. Some of our employees felt that they would not come out alive. Sarajevo cast a psychosis over convoys. Nevertheless the insecurity had become an everyday fact for delegates.

The same kind of uncomfortable awakening had led to the first mass-information campaigns on the ICRC *in situ* when three ICRC delegates were machine-gunned in Rhodesia/Zimbabwe in 1978, when carrying out their mission. Perhaps they were not deliberately attacked for what they represented, but only out of ignorance. All the same, something had to be done.

How were combatants in Bosnia-Herzegovina to be persuaded not to attack the Red Cross? The delegates thought a television spot would be a good idea, but now they had to think again. People who were told 'Don't fire on the Red Cross!' used to answer that they would never dare to do such a thing, and that this exhortation must have been intended for the adverse party, which had no respect for anything. They did not feel concerned.

Lectures to the troops on the laws of war, a well-tried method in many other conflicts, had only very limited impact. They managed to raise polite interest only on the part of a few officers whose duty it was to go through the motions. This did not mean that they had been persuaded to apply the rudimentary rules of humanity in battle, or that they would order their subordinates to do so, or that they would repress breaches of those rules. And indeed, what officer would of his own accord agree to take disciplinary action against his men when this might endanger their fighting spirit as a unit? Some army corps even went as far as to decline the offer of lectures because they believed that the information given some years previously by the Red Cross of Yugoslavia was amply sufficient. Besides, the soldiers fighting in Bosnia-Herzegovina are not necessarily professionals. They are more likely to be men recruited from day to day, aged 40 and over, whose very acute instinct is to stay alive. They know what fear is. They know that death exists and is not merely an abstract idea. Nearly all of them have had friends or relatives who have been liquidated by the enemy. The result is that, in this life-and-death struggle, the rules of international humanitarian law, which require respect for other human beings, are thrown completely out of joint.

Other arguments, more down to earth or more moralistic, had therefore to be thought up to get through to brains busy with other thoughts and heavily conditioned by propaganda. One delegate of a realistic turn of mind recounts that

> I was in a garrison to 'put over' my talk about disseminating law, when I saw some buses arrive and unload men in civilian clothes – men aged from 18 to 60. A couple of hours later they came along wearing half a uniform and carrying a rucksack and a rifle, and boarded the same buses. Fifty minutes later they were at the front, for the front was only ten kilometres away. The whole business lasted between two and three hours. They haven't the least idea what war is. The only thing they have remembered about international law is 'sauve qui peut.' And so they drink hard, to be less scared. Some of the officers told me they would never have had any military success at all if they had not let their men drink. And so there are limits to the extent to which humanitarian law principles are digested.

Another delegate heartily shared this opinion, and launched into a colourful description of the ordinary militiaman, euphemistically known as a 'reservist', a man who usually swaggers about with a complete arsenal round his waist and breath smelling strongly of drink. He is usually the chap who does the fighting. The younger ones have got more sense (they work, or go abroad, or are at university) and it is he who makes this war a particularly disgusting one, for there are just two things that keep him going: he hates the other chap and he boozes slivovic.

In this context, we still have to find a moral justification, a sense of values that resists wartime excesses. Daniel Masse says: 'The only sense of values I have been able to identify so far is that of violence, of survival at any price, or in other words destroying the other chap so as to survive, and ensuring national survival by eliminating or expelling all the others.' This testimony seems to indicate that the ICRC's last resort is to speak out more vigorously, to adopt a still firmer attitude, and to make the troops face up to their responsibilities by telling them that they are personally responsible for all war crimes.

One of the ICRC's major handicaps in its approach to the kinds of behaviour it has encountered in central and eastern Europe is that people no longer put any trust in institutions because previous regimes have systematically resorted to lies. International credibility does not count for much, but when any individual attached to that institution puts a foot wrong the unpopularity he provokes falls on the institution as a whole, which therefore loses on both counts.

Another conceptual weakness is that the ICRC did not begin working in central Europe until 1991, having previously been denied access to it because of the opposition of the ruling regimes, in which the Red Cross was reserved for the governing classes and international humanitarian law was to be seen more in a showcase than on the battlefield. As one delegate said, 'This is Potemkin-style humanitarian law.' In many countries in that part of the world, before the Cold War ended, the officers usually regarded humanitarian law as a western tool for weakening the Warsaw Pact's military forces. It became strategic *a contrario*. Governments called it 'an emanation of bourgeois culture' and labelled the ICRC an 'agent of western imperialism'. The Red Cross utopia, although built on a doctrinal plan resembling the political systems then in use, was, they found, alarming. Better not say too much about it. Since 1989 those ideological arguments have gone out of fashion and the time has come to be more enterprising.

From groping in the dark to stepping on the gas

War broke out between Yugoslavia and Croatia and then in Bosnia-Herzegovina 'in a mixture of high technology and the irrational', to quote a delegate, who said:

The way this war is being fought is utterly insane. Humanitarian law is seized on as a pretext for haggling of the most sordid kind: 'I'll give you a lorry-load of petrol for an old folks' home.' It's just cruel bargaining. You see people behaving in a medieval way, but without the knightly code of honour, and you can do nothing about it. People don't realize how effective propaganda is when it observes no limits and does not have to worry about anything that would restore the balance, such as 'tolerance' or 'respect for human rights'. People don't give each other any way of fighting propaganda. All sides plead enemy behaviour to justify their own excesses.

One delegate said: 'Why are we not being shot at so much for two or three months? Perhaps because it gets dark earlier.' This may seem rather a comic way of looking at things, but there is a touch of realism about it, and it raises a lot of questions and doubts as to what should be done in this conflict, and perhaps in future conflicts too, to disseminate principles and law.

Delegates say that in the light of the Yugoslav experience, methods need to be reconsidered and the new realities of the situation taken into account. One thing is obvious, namely that the deserving efforts of a delegate isolated in a world ruled by anarchy are utterly wasted. Something else has to be found.

To talk about 'differentiated target publics', the jargon hitherto used in the ICRC to mean the armed forces, medical circles, youth and Red Cross volunteers, is to show one is lamentably out of touch with what is happening on the ground. This is especially true of the characteristics of combatants, above mentioned, and the break-up of the chain of command caused by the emergence, according to one delegate,

> of discretionary life-and-death powers in the hands of any and every little district warden and night watchman. You can never get hold of the armed forces; they are nowhere to be found ... Nowadays the risks we run are due primarily to anarchy, everybody carrying a gun, universal drunkenness and the unlimited powers allowed anyone from the rank of corporal upwards.

There still remain the duly established central powers, whether or not the international community recognizes them. What help can be expected from them in disseminating humanitarian ideals? At the very least they should grant access to the media, which are mainly under their control. These of course are largely rotten to the core because of the all-pervading presence of heinous propaganda that, as a matter of principle and efficiency, denies that there is any such thing as a victim. To inspire hatred is to deny that there is any reason for the existence of international humanitarian law, whose essential purpose is to protect enemies that have become war victims. Nevertheless, the local media are still the most direct means of reaching the population, and they have to be used for that reason.

Before tackling the local media, the experts on dissemination in Bosnia-Herzegovina wondered whether they would not get better results by having their own broadcasting station that could cover the regions at war. Advocates of an independent station point out that a 'humanitarian radio' would for example make it possible to monitor programmes and the area in which they were broadcast and so protect them from propaganda. A neutral broadcasting station of this kind could also be used to pass on family news, a system much used by the ICRC, with some success, at the end of the Second World War in renewing contact between hundreds of thousands of dispersed families. Others have retorted that the experiment was bound to fail because of the topography of the regions it aimed to reach. Moreover, they thought it preferable to select different transmitters and programmes to suit the various audiences they were intended for. Incidentally, *'Droit de Parole'* (*The Right to Speak*), the floating radio station belonging to *Reporters sans Frontières*, which cruised off the Dalmatian coast, had its ups and downs. When it was started, the European Community gave it considerable financial backing, and it did its best to keep going by appealing to its generous donors so that it could carry on. But it ran into official opposition from the International Tele-communications Union (ITU), which went so far as to prohibit it from broadcasting.

The use of the local media does not confer immunity from accidents either, as UNPROFOR found to its cost. In the words of John Mills:[4]

> We found that some of our programmes broadcast in the Croat language had been edited in such a way as to change their meaning ... In the past, complete programmes were prohibited from being broadcast over the Croat radio, without the competent authorities giving any reason for their decision.

The danger of official intervention and even manipulation exists, but it has not prevented the ICRC from working out a plan of action whereby its humanitarian message would be inserted in the local media.

A pilot experiment was tried out in the region of Banja Luka in the self-proclaimed 'Serbian Republic of Bosnia', where the ICRC has had a well-established delegation since July 1992. Its delegates were in great demand throughout the period of the discovery of the detention camps in the region, the subsequent visits to them and the ultimate release of their prisoners. This high degree of operational visibility was at the root of the approaches made by Beat Schweizer, the head of the delegation, to the local media. It was first of all necessary to improve the public image of the ICRC and explain what it was there for, remembering that, for the man in the street, the enemy in descending order of importance was as follows: the Bosnian Muslims, the Croats and then the 'international community', represented by the United Nations who were regarded as responsible for the anti-Serbian resolutions adopted in New York. The ICRC had to defend its neutrality and impartiality. This was the job of an underground mineworker who has to hack his way through useless seams of propaganda, win a hearing from his audience, gain their interest and convince them. But above all, he has to gain access to broadcasting programmes and to the local newspaper, without his humanitarian message being distorted. This was a daily problem for the delegate, who had to use charm and exert pressure, and buy advertising space when necessary. Week after week, he built up relations with people who were not in the habit of compromising. Although it is not possible to prove it beyond doubt, publications and broadcasts did help to improve the general atmosphere. Delegates were less often insulted in the street, vehicles marked with the Red Cross were not spat on as much as before, and people were much less hostile. Of course this was not a perfect idyll, there were relapses into hostility, but it is an example of what can be done. It laid the foundations of the future dissemination plan by radio, television and the press throughout Bosnia-Herzegovina. The main emphasis was on local broadcasting stations, of which there are more than 50 in the republic, for television reception varied a great deal and newspapers were too expensive for many a tight family budget.

The information transmitted to the public remained straightforward and easy to understand although it became more elaborate than the first publicity 'spot'. Its purpose was to make people understand that the ICRC was in the region for the good of the local population, which had, incidentally, already derived great benefit from its material and medical assistance programmes. For the 1992–93 winter months alone, aid to the 27 municipalities in the Banja Luka region amounted to DM 5 million. People easily understood what DM 5 million meant at a time when the average monthly wage was about DM 20. The press campaign also appealed to the dignity of the fighting man and tried to make him understand that when he attacked civilians he was not a hero but a coward.

In broadcasting programmes, pre-recorded features were supplemented by local documentaries and interviews with delegates. These help to bring the subject nearer home and satisfy parish-pump preoccupations. On the other hand, the ICRC soon realized that the short filmed passages it produced rarely found their way on to television screens because they were so low-key. 'They're too tame,' said local journalists, who were used to productions that were much less sedate. In that respect it's an uneven match. To talk of respect for humanitarian law and try to show what it means makes little impression on television audiences, now thoroughly used to pictures that shock them into attention, but are only distorted reflections of a world in whose tragedy they are inexorably involved. The humanitarians seem to have lost their battle before it began.

In quest of that rare commodity, truth

Repeat a lie a hundred times and it becomes a truth. In times of war, facts that are not misrepresented are few and far between. Former Yugoslavia is in the lead, but not alone, in doctoring the truth.

The Bosnian camps, the number of prisoners, the cases of rape, everything serves as a pretext for distortion, either by the perpetrators themselves or by some other nation wanting to throw a sop to its public's opinion. And then there is the brutish leapfrogging that inflates statistical data, or its contrary, the sudden withdrawal of interest when a given situation no longer attracts media attention. The parties to the conflict have made full use of this leapfrogging to reach their objectives by fostering a climate of terror in minority populations.

Add to this the recent traumas of the international press, which burned its fingers in the Timisoara affair in Romania, which was shoved about by the news cameras in the Gulf War, and embarrassed by the tele-landing in Mogadishu.

What then can be said of the prospects of those primarily concerned, the journalists of former Yugoslavia who, as the last survivors of the shipwreck of the media, strive to uphold a demand for quality? They asked themselves all these questions, and other more important ones besides, at a meeting held by the International Federation of Journalists and the International Federation of Newspaper Publishers early in 1993 at Ljubljana.[5]

Being aware that they were isolated and therefore that their responsibilities were all the greater, the independent journalists coming from all the former Yugoslav republics and autonomous provinces, speaking together for the first time since the conflict began in 1991, described the struggle in which they were engaged every day. A journalist working for the Serbian newspaper *Borba* said that the threshold of honesty must never be overstepped, and that if you are a correspondent at Sarajevo, the first thing to do is to stay alive. You have to use your reason and intelligence to find strength to resist what is going on around you, and to absorb emotion without lapsing into indifference. A Slovene woman journalist said how hard it was, when war broke out in one's ōwn country, not to slant language. The representatives of isolated independent media in Croatia, Kosovo, Montenegro and Serbia spoke of purges and privations. Much was said too of the heroic struggle of *Oslobodenje*, the Sarajevo daily newspaper that had not ceased publication for a single day although a hail of fire was falling on the city. On the initiative of *Reporters sans Frontières* and the 'World Media Network', and with the help of UNESCO, dozens of newspapers from London to Tokyo had united to give it moral and material support. Its editor, Zlatko Dizdarevic, had travelled all over the world to bear witness to the horror of the siege of the Bosnian capital with his *Journal de guerre* (*War Diary*).[6] Other media in Sarajevo and elsewhere are still publishing honest information at their risk and peril.

Foreign correspondents run risks of a different kind. If they publicly express doubt that certain atrocities were committed, or give the impression that they are clearing the aggressor of blame because it has just been discovered that the party suffering aggression has committed atrocities, then they are guilty of revisionism. In the same way as prior to 1989 it was possible to conceive of a just war, the champions of propaganda in the 1990s designate good victims and bad victims. If ever a correspondent takes it upon himself to swim against the tide, all too often 'marketing gets the better of editorial vision,' say Jacques Lesourne and Bruno Frappat, and

> that being so, working as a journalist inevitably varies enormously from one editorial chair to another. It could even be asked whether wage-earners who have to write publicity articles, go-getter journalists with showbiz travel programmes, specialized copywriters on the look-out for news, special correspondents who risk their lives in hot spots, and star-turn news producers with their eyes glued to audience ratings can still legitimately be regarded as belonging to a homogeneous corporation. Can the same ethical principles apply to them all?'[7]

The first drift away from unanimity is a cleavage desired by some and refused by others. Says Alain Woodrow:

> There are not on the one hand responsibly-minded media that habitually investigate, analyse and comment – the sole preserve of the printed press – and on the other the frivolous media given over to stage and screen, entertainment and hit-or-miss statements – the audiovisual landscape.[8]

However, Woodrow goes on to say 'Whilst speed is the essence of news, its enemy is untimely urgency. We must cry halt to the tyranny of technology to re-establish an interval between the journalist and the current event he is reporting.'

Resisting this elimination of time, allowing for a period of reaction and learning to separate the wheat from the chaff are vitally necessary to journalists unwilling to be manipulated. Yet 'Manipulation is an exercise practised by the most honourable institutions' because 'no institution is indifferent to its image, nor can it afford to neglect its interests by failing to make known how its activities are faring, what results it is getting and how its plans are developing'.[9]

Does talking about oneself, in the good sense of the term, inevitably involve bending the truth, arranging it to suit one's own convenience, or concealing it? In any case, it must captivate. Paul Virilio says of the most famous charmer of them all: 'You can't understand Kouchner without the camera. Kouchner is a victim of the camera just as the camera is the victim of Kouchner. They are predestined to go together.'[10] Claude Torracinta says ironically: 'Whatever has become of Bernard Kouchner? This globe-trotter in the interests of humanitarian aid, this visiting fireman in the tragedies that are tearing our world to bits has disappeared from the television screens. I haven't seen him for a whole week.'[11] This cathodic revolution has put humanitarian aid right in the middle of the news. It made General Philippe Morillon such a public idol that his superior officers hauled him over the coals because they were jealous of his being so outrageously famous that it seemed he would go down in history as the Hero of Srebrenica. It influences and even determines political decisions of the greatest importance.

In the United States, it is becoming difficult to imagine any time in which television did not occupy a predominant place in foreign policy decision-making. According to Michael R. Beschloss, had the Cuban crisis taken place in the 1990s, John Kennedy would not have been able to hold the American and world public at arm's length for six whole days, and then choose exactly when and how to reveal how tremendous the crisis was. CNN television would be on the spot and might even have discovered the missile launchers before the CIA. Nowadays, for better or for worse, television can bring decisive pressure to bear on the American leaders.[12]

In Bosnia, whether there is or is not media coverage makes all the difference in the world. In his fifth, May 1993, report on human rights in former Yugoslavia, Tadeusz Mazowiecki states his regret that violations of humanitarian law are neither filmed any more nor publicly condemned. This is for lack of journalists. As *Libération* points out, 'Where there are no United Nations troops, there are no pictures. And when there are no pictures, little by little, war loses its reality.'[13]

Thierry Germond says that in comparison with other hot spots in the world 'There has been a misinterpretation because everything has happened in the full view of everybody.' The influence on international negotiations of this total and well-nigh permanent exhibition of what is happening on the ground, as digested and passed on by the media, has been strong enough to influence the content of policy speeches. Thus, at the London Conference (26–28 August 1992), although all the protagonists were present, the real humanitarian issues were only touched upon and generally evaded. The speeches made were for the news cameras. The indirect pressure exercised by the hundreds of accredited journalists was considerable, although they were physically parked well away from the holy of holies. Countless press conferences and interviews emptied the hall of the principal speakers, who were irresistibly attracted by the honeyed bait of media coverage. Everyone – aggressors and aggressed, and intermediaries whether neutral or otherwise – took part in this endless ballet.

In the midst of this media-induced cacophony, the ICRC continued to stiffen its attitude. It issued repeated warnings, reminding the states signatory to the Geneva Conventions of their responsibilities, taking the risk of tiring or irritating them. But what was happening in former Yugoslavia required the ICRC to at least change its language and be more incisive and precise in its public statements. This it did from Geneva by taking the initiative in diplomatic negotiations and approaches to the public.

On the spot, things looked rather different. At the beginning, in the first conflict, the ICRC's part in the war was to react to what happened; it gave information on incidents involving security, provided background material and helped visiting journalists. Then came the camps and the ITN television pictures, and all the floodlights focused on humanitarian assistance. The ICRC looked over its shoulder, remembered certain painful episodes in the past[14] and decided to attack. Its delegates were instructed to go public, as several had already done without waiting for the order. This was the age of media inflation. Régis Debray has called humanitarian assistance a better source of pictures than ecology, 'direct stuff', a subject instantly understood without any need for explanations of the why and wherefore. However, images of the suffering people and humanitarian assistance become so profligate that those who actually *are* suffering are obliterated by a tide of media hype.[15]

Then the ICRC ran out of steam and lost the initiative. It was overtaken by the UNHCR, which was more aggressive in its relations with the media and took advantage of the airlift to Sarajevo. It invited journalists to accompany its convoys which, by travelling under military escort, often gained speedier access to reportedly dangerous regions. These were great advantages of which the UNHCR never hesitated to make use. The Geneva-based co-ordinator of UNHCR operations is convinced that this high profile which it won for itself in the field has done much to lend the UNHCR greater weight in negotiations.

For the delegates, the most perverse result of this abundance of media material on the market was that the world was led to believe that humanitarian aid workers were there and active, whereas all too often their presence was an alibi, something only second-best. They were hostages of a situation that was far beyond their powers to control. They were tolerated in some places and refused entry to those where the worst abuses had taken place. Meanwhile, public opinion, as if anaesthetized, forgot that diverting attention to humanitarian aid enabled states to conceal political issues. By the grace of the media, humanitarian aid, which used to be exclusively a matter of 'action', has become a 'phenomenon' – one that henceforth occupies the entire screen.

CHAPTER 7

1993 – Brief Chronicles

On 20 January 1993, after the Croats and the Muslims, the Bosnian Serb Parliament declared that it accepted in principle the peace plan drawn up in Geneva by the two co-presidents of the International Conference on Former Yugoslavia. This plan proposed to divide Bosnia-Herzegovina into ten provinces. It was the end result of a diplomatic process that began in London in August 1992, but no sooner was it signed than it aroused a medley of passions in its advocates and detractors. Controversialists, leader-writers and politicians whether active or retired examined its advantages and disadvantages in the minutest detail, but it was never unanimously accepted and its signatories had already plotted its demise.

The Vance–Owen peace plan was entering upon its death-throes. In the meantime, acts of violence, far from abating, continued their headlong course around the Muslim pockets of eastern Bosnia blockaded by the Bosnian Serb forces, and then in central Bosnia, where Croats and Muslims were locked in furious hand-to-hand fighting to capture or recapture scraps of territory before the final carve-up.

When, on 30 July 1993, the Geneva negotiations produced a fresh agreement for a new state to be known as the 'Union of the Republics of Bosnia-Herzegovina', the scenario was just the same – fighting was going on practically everywhere. There was extreme tension in the UNPAs, Mostar had been cut off from the outside world since the end of June, and Sarajevo, where more than 3,000 shells had fallen in a single day only a week before, was licking its wounds, but they never had time to heal.

The generals and negotiators came and went, their regular arrivals and departures resembling a game of ping-pong between blindfold players. And so, between the making and breaking of promises interrupted by hard fighting all over the region, Bosnia-Herzegovina no longer hit the headlines. It was not even a matter of compassion fatigue, well known to humanitarian aid workers seeking support, but simply that the accumulation of lies and repeated setbacks had made the public sick and tired of the subject. The only palpable fact for people harassed by 18 months of war was that they were starting their second winter or, worse still, the third for those unlucky enough to have moved from one conflict to another since Yugoslavia began its descent into hell.

A quick review of the eleven months following the agreement on the first peace plan yields only a caricature, in which humanitarian endeavours are enmeshed in the tangled skein of political intrigue.

An assault course for the 'Warrior Without Weapons'[1]

30 January 1993. The International Conference on Former Yugoslavia was suspended. Only the Bosnian Croats accepted the peace plan in its entirety, including the map of the carve-up into ten provinces. The Bosnian Serbs and Muslims refused to accept parts of the plan.

10 February. The International Committee of the Red Cross (ICRC) delegates made their first visit to the detainees in Sarajevo since the start of the conflict in Bosnia-Herzegovina. They registered the names of 48 persons but were not allowed access to six of them, who were in hospital.

The meeting of the plenipotentiary representatives of Bosnia-Herzegovina, which was to have taken place in Geneva on **11 February** at the invitation of the ICRC, was cancelled. The tension in UN circles in Sarajevo since the assassination on 8 January of Vice-Prime Minister Turajlic, of Bosnia-Herzegovina, who was under UNPROFOR protection, prevented the Bosnian representatives from using UN flights to Geneva. On the other hand, the plenipotentiaries of the first conflict between Croatia and federal Yugoslavia, who were also invited, discussed how best to wind up the file on the remaining prisoners still detained in spite of the Budapest agreement of August 1992.

17 February. In retaliation for the prohibition of access to the Muslim pockets in eastern Bosnia, Sadako Ogata suspended all UNHCR humanitarian operations. These resumed a few days later on the injunction of the UN Secretary-General. Also on 17 February, UNPROFOR evacuated 380 Croat civilians from the UNPA-South zone, where the Croat military forces were about to intensify their operations.

On **18 February**, the ICRC Delegate General for Europe testified on the question of rapes to the European Parliament's Commission on Women's Rights in Strasbourg, at a public hearing.

On **19 February**, the Security Council extended the mandate of UNPROFOR until 31 March (Resolution 807). This was a provisional measure so that the UN could reconsider the way in which it should in future intervene on the ground, where there was hardly any peace left to maintain.

On **22 February**, the Security Council decided on the principle of setting up an international tribunal to try persons who had committed grave breaches of humanitarian law (Resolution 808).

On **23 February**, the Commission on Human Rights held its 49th session, at which it adopted a resolution condemning the practice of rape and mandated its special rapporteur to continue his enquiry and report on 30 June.

In the Banja Luka region and in eastern Bosnia, especially at Cerska, Gorazde, Srebrenica and Zepa, 'ethnic cleansing' was in full swing. On **25 February** the ICRC made representations to Radovan Karadzic in an attempt to improve protection for the civilian population.

On **28 February**, for the first time, American military aircraft dropped relief supplies by parachute at Cerska and other eastern Bosnian towns. On **2 March**, the Bosnian Serb forces took control of Cerska.

On **5 March**, General Philippe Morillon went to Srebrenica on a rescue mission. Concurrently, Dr Simon Mardel, a WHO physician, heard alarming information on the fate of 70,000 persons given shelter in that town, whose pre-war population was only 6,000.

On **5 and 6 March** in Geneva, the plenipotentiary representatives of Bosnia-Herzegovina gave their verbal agreement to the release of all the prisoners visited by the ICRC, which asked for access to all the regions of the republic including eastern Bosnia. The ICRC drew up a plan of action for the release of the prisoners and sent it to all three parties, who were expected to reply on **15 March**. On that date only the Bosnian Croats confirmed that they were willing to put the plan into effect, and its execution was accordingly postponed until further notice.

On **25 March** in New York, where the Conference on Peace in Former Yugoslavia had temporarily been transferred, the Bosnian Croat Mate Boban and President Alija Izetbegovic signed the peace plan. The Bosnian Serbs did not sign the plan.

On **31 March**, when visiting the camp at Batkovic, which was in Bosnian Serb hands, the ICRC delegates discovered that 17 prisoners who had been sent to dig trenches at the front had died on 26 March. The ICRC publicly denounced this grave breach of the Geneva Conventions.[2]

On **31 March**, the Security Council authorized the use of force to close Bosnian air space.

On **2 April**, at the request of the Security Council, the former Norwegian Minister of Foreign Affairs, Thorvald Stoltenberg, who was also briefly United Nations High Commissioner for Refugees after the resignation of Jean-Pierre Hocké and before the appointment of Sadako Ogata, agreed to replace the negotiator Cyrus

Vance who had resigned his post of co-president of the peace conference. On 3 April, the Bosnian Serbs rejected the peace plan.

On 13 April, at Bjeljina, at the first meeting of the ICRC with the head of the Bosnian Serb armed forces, General Ratko Mladic, supported by 14 members of his General Staff, and Thierry Germond, the ICRC Delegate General for Europe, discussed for eight hours the whole range of humanitarian questions concerning prisoners, besieged towns, neutralized zones, humanitarian corridors and suchlike.

On 16 April, the Bosnian Serbs intensified the siege of Srebrenica, and in Sarajevo Thierry Germond held talks with General Halilovic, officer commanding the Bosnian forces. Meanwhile the ICRC delegates based in Jablanica in central Bosnia had to leave the town, which was under bombardment.

In the night of 16 April, the United Nations proclaimed Srebrenica a safety zone and medical evacuations were organized. The town was having immense difficulty in obtaining supplies of food and medicaments, a difficulty alleviated to some extent by dropping them by parachute. On the same day at Vitez, UNPROFOR presided over the signature of a cease-fire in central Bosnia between the Croat and Muslim forces.

On 17 and 18 April, General Wahlgren, the officer commanding UNPROFOR, successfully arranged a meeting at Sarajevo airport between Generals Halilovic and Mladic, who concluded an agreement concerned mainly with medical evacuations and releases of prisoners, and the parts to be taken in these by the armed forces, UNPROFOR and the humanitarian institutions.

On 18 April, the UN forces entered Srebrenica and the Muslim combatants laid down their arms.

On 20 April, the ICRC appealed for international humanitarian law to be respected in central Bosnia, where bitter fighting was taking place.

On 22 April, ICRC delegates began to visit a total of about a thousand prisoners in Muslim hands at Zenica and in Croat hands at Vitez.

From 22–27 April, representatives of states' members of the Security Council carried out an exploratory mission on the ground, especially at Srebrenica. Meanwhile, on 25 April, Radovan Karadzic again rejected the peace plan.

On 30 April, General Mladic and Thierry Germond of the ICRC again met to discuss the hazardous conditions prevailing in the Banja Luka region that were making the conduct of humanitarian operations difficult, and the impossibility of access to Srebrenica by relief convoys.

On 1 and 2 May, the meeting said to offer the 'last chance' of saving the peace plan drawn up by the co-presidents of the

International Conference on Former Yugoslavia was held in Athens, in the presence of the parties to the conflict, the United Nations and the European Community. The Bosnian Serbs, who were the last party that had not yet accepted the plan, undertook to do so subject to the agreement of their parliament, which was to give its decision in the next few days.

On **6 May**, the Bosnian Serb Parliament declared that it was not competent to take a decision and demanded that a referendum should be held.

Also on **6 May**, after Srebrenica, the Security Council declared Sarajevo, Zepa, Gorazde, Bihac and Tuzla safe areas.

On **11, 12 and 13 May**, the ICRC Delegate General for Europe met, one after the other, Mate Boban, Alija Izetbegovic and Radovan Karadzic, to all of whom he handed the reports on the respect or non-respect by each party of the humanitarian rules laid down for the protection of prisoners and the civilian population. These confidential reports were based on observations made in the field by ICRC delegates and covered the period from April 1992 to January 1993 as regards the treatment of civilians, and July to December 1992 as regards visits to detainees.

On **11 May**, at the entrance to Mostar, a Spanish member of the UN contingent was wounded while escorting a relief convoy. He died in Madrid four days later.

'Ethnic cleansing' continued in Mostar, where humanitarian action was still difficult. On **13 May**, ICRC delegates were allowed access for the first time to Rodoc, where Croat forces were holding nearly 2,000 Muslim civilians.

On **16 May**, the Bosnian Serbs rejected the peace plan by referendum. Also on **16 May**, the Bosnian Serbs and Croats concluded an agreement on the cessation of hostilities and the exchange of all prisoners (before 1 June) and mortal remains (before 1 July). They also gave every guarantee for the free passage of individuals and convoys in the areas under their control.

On **18 May** at Medjugorje, in the presence of President Tudjman and the two co-Presidents of the International Conference, David Owen and Thorvald Stoltenberg, the Croats and Muslims confirmed that they would respect a cease-fire in the Mostar region. On the same day, the Croats and Serbs concluded a cease-fire agreement covering southern Krajina.

On **20 May**, Rodoc camp was emptied. Women and children were released and large numbers of men were transferred to other places of detention.

On **22 May** Spain, France, Russia, the United Kingdom and the United States adopted a 'Joint Programme of Action' in which they renounced any resort to military operations. The plan provided for

American support for the protection of the safe areas proclaimed by the United Nations.

On **25 May**, for the first time since the forces of the Republic of Croatia intervened on 22 January 1993, the Serbs in Krajina and the Croats made a first exchange of prisoners at Otocac in the UNPA zone. On the same day, the Security Council decided to establish an international tribunal to try persons believed to be 'responsible for serious violations of international humanitarian law committed in the territory of the former Yugoslavia between 1 January 1991 and a date to be determined' (Resolution 827).

On **28 May**, the situation in Gorazde deteriorated. Although this town was one of the six safe areas designated by the Security Council, it had no effective protection from UNPROFOR. Fierce fighting took place in the town of Travnik in central Bosnia.

On **29 May**, an Italian humanitarian convoy was attacked at Gornji Vakuf in central Bosnia. Three volunteers were killed.

On **1 June**, a European Community and UNHCR convoy was bombarded between Zenica and Maglaj. Two Danish drivers and an interpreter died.

From **4–6 June**, ICRC delegates who went to Zepa in eastern Bosnia found that UN air drops had made the situation there less disastrous than at Srebrenica, where shortage of water was so serious that only three to five litres of water per person were available instead of the twenty litres necessary by WHO standards. Sarajevo and Gorazde were still under strong pressure. Also, a convoy escorted by the United Nations travelling to Tuzla was attacked by the Croat forces. UNPROFOR returned the fire, and two Croat soldiers were killed.

The Muslim assault on the town of Travnik led to considerable population movements. Between **9 and 11 June**, the ICRC evacuated more than 3,000 civilians to Croatia and requested the authorities of the Republic of Croatia to give up their plan of re-installing some of the evacuees in Mostar, where there was fighting every day. Men of military age who had left Travnik as refugees were taken prisoner by the Serbs and regrouped at Manjaca.

On **12 June**, the specialists of the ICRC Central Tracing Agency announced that they had forwarded more than a million Red Cross messages in less than six months. Members of families dispersed by the conflict were able to get in touch with each other again, or to keep in touch, by means of this humanitarian postal service.

On **14 June**, UNHCR and ICRC representatives personally witnessed an 'ethnic cleansing' operation that had just taken place on the road to Kiseljak, where a village was burnt to the ground in the full view of its inhabitants, who were assembled outside by the Croat forces before being transferred.

On the same day, the Bosnian Croats and Serbs concluded a cease-fire agreement at Celebici.

On **15 June**, the military commanders of all three sides signed a cease-fire agreement which was to enter into force on 18 June.

On **16 June** in Geneva, the three parties to the conflict attended a summit meeting to approve the division of Bosnia-Herzegovina into three confederate states. President Izetbegovic walked out of the summit meeting, declaring that his government would not take part in the next meeting, scheduled for 23 June.

Also on **16 June**, the ICRC made a public appeal for an end to the destructive chaos in Bosnia-Herzegovina, with particular reference to the situation in central Bosnia.

On **18 June**, when the UNPROFOR contingent numbered 9,400 men, the Security Council approved the despatch of an extra 7,600 UN troops to improve the protection of the safe areas.

On **20 June**, ICRC delegates succeeded in entering Gorazde with medical supplies. On **23 June**, the delegates were granted access to Foca, where they had not been able to go for the past year, and visited 73 persons who were detained by the Bosnian Serbs.

On **24 June**, the Bosnian Serbs and Croats announced in Geneva their agreement to the partition of Bosnia-Herzegovina into three regions forming a confederation, under the aegis of the co-Presidents of the International Conference.

At the **beginning of July**, the town of Maglaj was held in a stranglehold by the Croat and Serb forces and was still out of the reach of humanitarian organizations.

On **3 and 4 July**, the ICRC was informed that the Bosnian Croats had arrested 7,000 people aged between 16 and 60.

On **8 July**, the World Health Organization made an appeal concerning the deplorable health situation in Sarajevo.

On **8, 9 and 10 July**, ICRC delegates made three attempts to gain access to the prison camp at Rodoc, near Mostar, in which most of the persons arrested at the beginning of the month had been regrouped.

On **9 and 10 July**, at Makarska, south of Split, on the initiative of Vice-Prime Minister Mate Granic of the Republic of Croatia, an agreement for the free passage of humanitarian convoys in the areas controlled by the Croats in central Bosnia was first negotiated and then concluded in the presence of UNPROFOR, HCR and ICRC representatives.

On **12 July**, the Bosnian Croat forces halted an ICRC convoy between Split and Zenica and refused to allow it to proceed.

On **13 July**, the Organization of the Islamic Conference decided to send 18,000 soldiers to protect the safe areas.

On **14 July**, the ICRC succeeded in opening an office in Gorazde after many previous attempts had failed.

A tense situation prevailed in Krajina. On **15 July**, the Croat forces announced that the airport at Zadar, and the bridge at Maslenica would shortly be reopened. However, on the same day, ICRC delegates were still denied access to the 7,000 Muslims arrested at Mostar. According to one report, more than 400 Croats whom the delegates had visited at Manjaca in June had been exchanged for diesel fuel.

On **15 July**, the Belgian Minister of Foreign Affairs, who had been sent to Belgrade as the envoy of the European Community, left that city, having been shown the door by Slobodan Milosevic.

Between **15 and 23 July**, a series of operations for the release of prisoners took place, with or without the presence of ICRC delegates. In the largest, held on **21 July** under ICRC auspices, 433 detainees were released by the Serbian forces at Batkovic at the same time as 245 Serbs held by the Muslims at Tuzla.

On **16 July**, the UNHCR convened a special session in Geneva of the working group on humanitarian questions, because of financial difficulties. The calibre of the governmental representatives attending, and the content of the discussions, presaged disappointing results.

On **17 July**, in Geneva, Presidents Tudjman and Milosevic came to an agreement on the withdrawal of Croat forces from Maslenica by 31 July. Maslenica is situated in a UNPA.

On **22 July**, the worst day since the siege began in April 1992, more than 3,000 Serbian shells fell on Sarajevo. Fighting became fiercer in all regions except the UNPAs, where for the moment greater calm prevailed. New fronts were opened, especially in the north-east on the border with the Republic of Croatia, between Bosanski Brod and Brcko. The Croatian authorities appealed publicly to the Croatian forces in Bosnia to respect the laws of war and facilitate the work of the humanitarian organizations.

On **25 July**, the three parties to the conflict signed a cease-fire agreement so that the negotiations in Geneva could be resumed as intended on 27 July. On that day, the negotiations were resumed in Geneva.

On **29 and 30 July**, the co-Presidents of the Geneva Conference proposed that a 'Union of the United Republics of Bosnia-Herzegovina' should be established. On the ground, fighting went on. The Security Council and NATO stated that they were considering carrying out air strikes. The Croat forces were not ready to respect the deadline of 31 July for their withdrawal from Krajina.

On **30 July**, the belligerents concluded a constitutional agreement in Geneva for the establishment of the 'Union of the Republics of Bosnia-Herzegovina'. The ICRC Central Tracing Agency announced a new record, namely that 350,000 Red Cross messages were transmitted in a single month (July).

By **31 July,** ICRC delegates had still not been granted access to Mostar.

Early in August, the American Secretary of State announced that the United States were prepared to carry out air strikes on their own. In Geneva, the 'carve-up of Bosnia-Herzegovina'[3] continued. At the front, ICRC delegates observed that, contrary to humanitarian law, the belligerents were still sending civilian prisoners to dig trenches at the risk of their lives.

On **3 August,** the 16 member countries of NATO decided in principle to carry out air strikes 'subject to the agreement of the Secretary-General of the United Nations'.

On **5 August,** WHO made a new appeal concerning the health situation in Sarajevo, which had become extremely critical because of the shortage of energy supplies. One hospital burnt its records, the only immediately available combustible material, so that it could go on operating. In central Bosnia, at Mostar, Travnik and Kiseljak, fighting raged unabated. In Krajina the Croat forces declared that they would not leave unless the Serbian heavy weapons were handed over to the United Nations and that this was followed by a cease-fire.

The Bosnian Serb forces delayed their withdrawal from the Igman Mountains and Bjelasnica, and on **6 August** the Geneva negotiations came to a halt.

On **9 August,** NATO repeated that it was determined to intervene. World attention focused on Sarajevo.

On **10 August,** ICRC delegates were granted access to Mostar. They registered the names of 2,000 prisoners in Rodoc camp and received confirmation that 5,000 other persons had been transferred to other detention centres (at Ljubuski, Gabela, Dretelj), in addition to the 800 already transferred to the island of Obonjan and to Gacinci.

On **11 August,** the military section of the peace agreement was signed in Sarajevo by all three parties, under the aegis of UNPROFOR.

On **14 August,** a UNHCR driver was killed at Vitez, on the Prozor–Gornji Vakuf–Zenica route. The humanitarian organizations were still without access to the principal towns of central Bosnia. ICRC delegates had been unable to return to Jablanica since 28 June.

On **16 August,** in a BBC broadcast, the ICRC delegation in Zagreb condemned the repeated use of prisoners by all parties to carry out dangerous work at the front line.

On **16 August,** the Geneva negotiations were resumed. On **18 August,** they became bogged down. Their only result was an agreement on the future of Sarajevo, which provided that it should come under UN administration for up to two years.

On **18 August**, a public debate took place on the merits of the medical evacuations from Sarajevo, following 'Operation Irma', named after the little girl flown out of Sarajevo for treatment in Great Britain.

On **19 August**, the ICRC convened a meeting of the representatives of the permanent missions in Geneva to inform them of the serious shortages of water and energy in the hospitals of Sarajevo and central Bosnia. Supplies of gas and diesel oil were urgently needed to improve the functioning of the hospitals.

On **23 August**, the President of the ICRC had talks in Geneva with the minister of foreign affairs of the Yugoslav Federation concerning the prisoners of the first conflict with Croatia who had still not been set free, and on the effect of sanctions on the civilian population of Serbia and Montenegro.

On **24 August**, the Security Council unanimously confirmed the principle of sovereignty and independence of Bosnia-Herzegovina and condemned war crimes and violations of international humanitarian law (Resolution 859). Some of the ambassadors present departed from the usual sedate tone of the debates by embellishing their speeches with references to great men of the past such as Blaise Pascal, Shakespeare and Benjamin Franklin.

On **25 August**, the ICRC announced its recognition of the Red Cross Societies of Slovenia and Croatia and confirmed its recognition of the Red Cross of Yugoslavia, which was continuing the work of the Red Cross Societies of Serbia and Montenegro, and recommended that the position of the Kosovo Red Cross, which was responsible to Belgrade, be clarified by balancing the composition of its management so as to be representative of the population.

On **28 August**, at Vitez, armed Croats took three Muslim wounded from an ICRC ambulance and later included them in an exchange operation.

On **30 August**, the three parliaments of the parties to the conflict conditionally approved the draft map of the three entities proposed by the constitutional agreement. Sarajevo was again quiet for the time being, but it was Mostar, where relations between the Muslims and Croats were still tense, that engrossed public opinion. Visits to prisoners and access to towns and villages were increasingly subjected to the requirement of reciprocity. 'Ethnic cleansing' continued at Banja Luka. Confirmation was received of a barbarous assault on a grandmother aged 102, whose limbs were broken.

On **1 September**, the Geneva negotiations which had resumed on 30 August again came to a halt. The Muslims insisted on possessing the port of Neum and a corridor of access leading to it. In central Bosnia, numerous mopping-up operations, massacres and acts of violence of all kinds were committed by all parties.

On **30 and 31 August and 1 September**, ICRC delegates made their first visit to the camp at Gabela, where they interviewed 1,043 detainees.

On **1 September**, the ICRC office in Mostar was plundered by Croat women.

On **6 September**, ICRC delegates were given access to Dretelj camp, in which there were 1,230 detainees.

On **14 September**, it was alleged that 35 Croats, most of them elderly, had been massacred by Bosnian forces in the village of Briz, near Uzdol, in a sector controlled by the HVO (the Bosnian Croat armed forces). The Bosnian authorities in Sarajevo ordered the opening of an inquiry.

On **21 September**, Geneva Conference co-Presidents Owen and Stoltenberg were at Sarajevo airport to witness the signature of a peace agreement by the representatives of the three parties to the conflict. The Bosnian Republic was ready to sign on condition that it retained its international rights and its seat at the United Nations.

On **22 September**, ICRC delegates made their first entry into Zepce, in territory controlled by the Muslim forces.

On **23 September**, 516 prisoners were released from Dretelj and transferred to the island of Korcula. This was the largest release operation effected in a single day by the ICRC since that at Manjaca camp at the end of 1992.

On **27 September**, Fikret Abdic proclaimed the autonomy of the Bihac enclave. A wave of arrests followed.

Beginning on **1 October**, ICRC delegates visited the political detainees in Kosovo for the second time in that year.

On **4 October**, the Security Council extended the mandate of UNPROFOR for six months until the end of May 1994 (Resolution 871).

On **12 October**, a relief convoy of 14 lorries organized by the ICRC, which was on the way to Tesanj, had to turn back after its leading vehicle, which was armoured, was blown up by a mine. Nobody was wounded.

On **19 October**, the ICRC's many requests to free prisoners held by all three parties were partially successful, when releases began between the Muslims and Croats, who freed 1,080 persons. The process was interrupted by various incidents and the need to re-negotiate some provisions.

On **21 October**, Fikret Abdic, the head of the Bihac enclave whose autonomy he had proclaimed, signed a peace agreement at Zagreb with Mate Boban, in the presence of President Tudjman. On the same day, NATO repeated that it was ready to apply the 'concept of air strikes' if the United Nations gave it the green light.

On **22 October**, Fikret Abdic signed an agreement for lasting peace with Radovan Karadzic in Belgrade, in the presence of Slobodan Milosevic.

The United Nations reported that, on **28 October**, renewed tension between Muslims in the Bihac pocket led to the death of some 20 persons in that single day.

In Stupni Do, a Muslim village near Vares in central Bosnia, UNPROFOR found 25 people lying dead among the rubble. On **29 October**, about a hundred of the 250 inhabitants of that village were said to be listed as missing following this reprisal operation carried out by Bosnian Croat forces on **23 October**.

On **27 October**, the plane chartered by the ICRC made its first round-trip between Zagreb and Sarajevo in support of the relief programme organized for the second winter of the war in Bosnia-Herzegovina.

On **31 October**, the ICRC delegation in Zagreb issued a press release deploring the deterioration in the situation at Vares, a Croat town besieged by Muslim forces on the west and Serbian forces on the east, where its delegates had been informed of forced departures, ill-treatment and summary executions.

The negotiations begun at the end of September by the ICRC with the Bosnian Serbs and Muslims for the release of all prisoners continued. On **2 November**, another meeting took place between President Momcilo Krajisnik of the Bosnian Serb Parliament, and Siladjzic, the Bosnian prime minister. They announced that they agreed in principle that a release operation should take place in mid-November. But discussions between the Bosnian Croats and Muslims for the release of prisoners were still deadlocked.

On **4 November**, the Bosnian Muslim forces captured the town of Vares. The situation was chaotic. The inhabitants fled in their thousands to the neighbouring towns and forests. The ICRC sent emergency assistance to Sokolac, a Serbian-controlled town, where 5,000 Croats had taken refuge. Another team went to Kiseljak, a town in Croat hands in which several hundred displaced persons had taken refuge.

The same day, near Vares, the vehicle belonging to *Solidarité*, a French NGO, was blown up by a mine. One person was killed and another seriously wounded. The UNPROFOR vehicle that went out to rescue it was also damaged by a mine. Three men were wounded.

Fighting went on as fiercely as ever in central Bosnia, where the Croats captured the town of Bakovici on **13 November** and the town of Fojnica on **14 November**, whilst maintaining their pressure on Gornji Vakuf.

Sarajevo suffered its most lethal bombardments since July on **9 and 10 November**, which left a dozen dead and many wounded.

On **18 November** in Geneva, the UNHCR held a meeting attended by the political and military heads of the three parties to the conflict in Bosnia-Herzegovina, for the first time since negotiations were broken off in September. The meeting was one of the Working Group on Humanitarian Questions of the International Conference on Former Yugoslavia. The ICRC attended the meeting, and exhorted the responsible officials to give due attention to humanitarian matters. They undertook to do so, and signed a joint declaration guaranteeing that humanitarian organizations should have free access to victims of the conflict by the most direct routes, and confirmed that the belligerents intended to release all the civilians in their hands.

Between **19 and 28 November**, the President of the ICRC, Cornelio Sommaruga, visited Sarajevo, Pale and Grude (the headquarters of the three parties to the conflict), Skopje, Belgrade, Podgorica, Zagreb, Ljubljana and Banja Luka. He handed the belligerents a report based on observations made by ICRC delegates concerning the use of prisoners to do dangerous work at the front line, a practice prohibited by the Geneva Conventions. This was his first visit to the region since the breakup of Yugoslavia, and he put in a strong plea for the welfare of the civilian population and all persons who had fallen into enemy hands. He also met UN officials on the spot.

In spite of the promises made in Geneva on 18 November, the humanitarian organizations were still coming up against numerous obstacles to the dispatch of relief. UN convoys, suspended since 25 October, were officially resumed a month later on **25 November**, but met with great difficulties.

A food assistance programme for persons most in need of aid began in Sarajevo. It was to entail the opening of 14 soup kitchens run by the local Red Cross with ICRC backing. They were to serve hot meals as from **25 November** in the Muslim zone and **29 November** in the Serbian zone.

On **27 November**, Radovan Karadzic declared that the Bosnian Serbs would not make any territorial concession until the international community recognized their right to control two-thirds of Bosnia-Herzegovina.

On **29 November**, after an interval of more than two months, tripartite negotiations were resumed in Geneva under the aegis of the European Union and in the presence of David Owen and Thorvald Stoltenberg. Apart from yet another promise to allow relief convoys to pass through, no tangible result was achieved as regards the carve-up of Bosnia-Herzegovina. The Muslim delegation rejected the principle of partitioning Sarajevo, and the European Union proposed that sanctions against Serbia and Montenegro should be relaxed in exchange for territorial concessions to the

Muslims. On **3 December** the representatives of the three parties broke off their talks with an admission of failure.

On **30 November**, the Kosevo hospital in Sarajevo was hit by shells. Four persons were killed, including two nurses and a doctor.

On **6 December**, another meeting of Croats and Yugoslavs was held at ICRC headquarters in Geneva, to settle the question of the prisoners of the first conflict in 1991. The Croats said that they were ready to go ahead with this and the Yugoslavs undertook to accelerate their consideration of the matter.

On **7 December**, an ICRC convoy on the way to Mostar was fired on and had to turn back.

No progress having been made in the negotiations on the release of all prisoners, the Bosnian Croat leader Mate Boban announced that he intended to release the majority of his Muslim detainees in a unilateral operation to mark International Human Rights Day (**10 December**). ICRC delegates prepared for this but were refused access to one of the principal detention camps, Gabela, by the local commandant. The first releases were nevertheless made on **14 December** at Rodoc (where more than 2,000 persons were set free) and Gabela (more than 1,000).

Before dawn on **15 December**, the last remaining Muslim religious monuments in Banja Luka were blown up. Two days later, an Islamic cemetery was razed to the ground by a bulldozer. Both these acts are contrary to humanitarian law, which requires that the cultural and spiritual heritage of peoples shall be protected.

On **15 December**, an ICRC convoy conveying 441 detainees released from Rodoc on the left bank of Mostar came under fire. It nevertheless managed to reach its destination, but the incident obliged delegates to suspend the operation for 48 hours, until the Bosnian Croat forces had arrested the culprit.

On **16 December**, six European countries established diplomatic relations with the former Yugoslav republic of Macedonia.

On **19 December**, President Slobodan Milosevic's Socialist Party took the lead in the Serbian parliamentary elections.

On **23 December** in Brussels, the belligerents decreed a Christmas truce, in negotiations under the auspices of the European Union. The truce hung fire.

Conclusion

The more odious war is, the more difficult it is to claim to mitigate its effects. How can anything so unacceptable possibly find a place in humanitarian endeavours that draw their strength from laws and decent standards of behaviour? How can one stop the yawning chasm of human distress without asking oneself why and however such barbarism began? And how can one dare be content with a political and military status quo, sprinkled with procedures intended more for containment than for the resolution of conflicts?

After over three years of hostilities, all the belligerents, whether they are regular soldiers, unofficial militias or impromptu guerrillas, have fabricated so many reasons for paying off old scores that it is impossible to know when the spiral of reprisals is going to slow down, peace treaty or no peace treaty. The acts of violence and hatred that have accumulated over the months and years have left no family unharmed, drawing them all into the vicious circle of retaliation:

> Of course everyone has found that what is happening amply confirms what he sees as the truth. He saw himself attacked, the victim of atrocities, and he believes he is entitled to fight in any way he pleases against an enemy he rates as bloodthirsty. Interminable quibbles develop about each party's share of the blame. The argument becomes particularly distressing when it concerns the number of civilians deported, or girls and women raped – all this to show which of the parties is 'the most barbaric'.[1]

The conflicts in former Yugoslavia by no means hold the monopoly for brutality and behaviour contrary to the elementary rules that should be applied on the battlefield, but the Yugoslav context is such that it aggravates their consequences still more. There is the weight of history which, over the centuries, has drawn a shifting map of alliances and divisions in this country that is both of the East and of the West, in which orthodox tradition is at odds with Latin roots and Islamic influence and where religions and nationalities intermingle and confront each other. There is the weight of all past wars, and especially of that World War in which horror was piled on horror by both sides and whose memory Marshall Tito's regime was obstinately determined to keep alive individually and collectively in a population trapped by the language of propaganda.

The 1990s, rid of communist oppression, enabled all these tensions to find expression in the worst possible way, one that broke up this jigsaw puzzle of a nation that had been put together with so much difficulty. The conflict in former Yugoslavia is an unavowed civil war for the defenders of national unity and an international war for the partisans of independence. It is the arena in which profiteers carry on their pernicious exploitation, selling to the highest bidder thousands of people rounded up indiscriminately – preferably civilians, no matter whether they are men or women, old or young, or children, for they are easier to capture than combatants, and they are bought and sold in haggling of the most sordid kind between any pair of scoundrels toting Kalashnikovs who happen to come along.

In such circumstances, the battle waged by humanitarian workers has drawn its strength from the revealed truth of international humanitarian law and from the pragmatic truth that inspires action on the ground. Well aware of the difficulty of imposing the elementary rules of conduct in waging war, even one between two duly constituted states and their organized armed forces, and *a fortiori* in an environment as fragmented as that of former Yugoslavia, they have endeavoured to follow the straight and narrow path between the immediate interests of the belligerents and the demands of humanity. On the ruins of Vukovar, then, which was the grave of Yugoslav unity and the theatre in which western shame was silently enacted, a new form of diplomatic and humanitarian action was born.

The International Committee of the Red Cross (ICRC) has endeavoured, with varying degrees of success, and by working out non-legalistic approaches, to persuade the parties to the conflict that the laws of war are important. Far from denying humanitarian law, it has tried to restore its original meaning. A recognized law that combatants can apply unhesitatingly for the benefit of the wounded, civilian and military prisoners, besieged populations, displaced persons and dispersed families.

The humanitarian balance-sheet of the first war is tinted grey, but that of the war in Bosnia-Herzegovina is much nearer black, in spite of the tremendous joint efforts of charitable organizations, either responsible to the United Nations or non-governmental. The word most frequently heard in the ranks of humanitarian workers is frustration. Their leaders are powerless to settle by themselves the problems involved with security and they have worn themselves out negotiating and renegotiating with opposite numbers of the most unlikely kind agreements that lose all their meaning even before they are reached. This struggle to obtain the slightest respect for the engagements entered into by the belligerents continued throughout 1993. No one could say whether the screw would be loosened for any length of time after NATO's intervention in February 1994 and the Washington agreement of 1 March between the Bosnian Muslims and Croats. If the confrontations in Bosnia-Herzegovina were to come to an end, willy-nilly, the situation in the UNPAs (the zones now claimed both by the Republic of Croatia as part of its territory and by the Serbs) would again come to the fore. These frontiers are, indeed, the real barometer of conflicts in former Yugoslavia. It is there that the first shots were fired and the first dead of the 1990s are buried. The international community has preferred to forget them by handing them over to the United Nations and calling them 'protected areas'. Disturbances have never ceased there and secessionist tendencies have increased, provoking reaction from the Croat armed forces. Although it has a large contingent on the spot, the United Nations has difficulties every day in trying to pacify these territories, and has not yet managed to do so. The cauldron of the Krajina, like the Kosovo one, is therefore still as explosive as ever, while the situation in the former Yugoslav republic of Macedonia, which bears the seeds of foreign intervention, is temporarily contained by the presence of a UN contingent of a few hundred men.

Some observers have chosen to regard humanitarian action as perpetuating the war. This reproach has been heard in other theatres of intervention. It is undeserved and all the more unjustified as regards former Yugoslavia, because of all the organizations working there it is certainly the charitable agencies that can show a record of solid achievement, even if this has not matched the vital needs of civilian victims of war, and the efforts put into it. Figures speak eloquently of the material assistance given in food and staple commodities, and equally eloquently as regards the mail exchanged between members of dispersed families: millions of messages have been handled by volunteers from the Red Cross and Red Crescent Societies in the region and in host countries, which had not been the channel for any comparable flood of family news for more than 40 years.

On the other hand, as regards the protection of persons exposed to the worst atrocities, the scales tip sharply to the wrong side. The humanitarian agencies have been in contact with men, techniques and environments whose brutality has often appalled their most war-hardened representatives. One explanation for this is that, as Jean-Christophe Rufin writes, today more and more

> the centres of violence are moving towards the towns, either in conventional wars as in Yugoslavia or in guerrilla operations as in Peru. These new terrains have to be approached with extreme caution. The intimate connection between grinding poverty

and war, the enormous numbers of civilians affected, and the difficulties of access peculiar to town life baffle the NGOs. All the indications are that this new tendency of conflicts is bound to get worse and will soon give rise to very difficult problems.[2]

In former Yugoslavia, all these criteria are present: war on towns, to which access is cut off; voluntary or forced movements on a vast scale of populations seeking safety; the destitution of people who have had to leave behind them all they possessed, destitution made worse by the prolonged hostilities; and the extreme climatic conditions prevailing over several months of the year.

In 1992, when violence was erupting in the neighbourhood of Banja Luka, ICRC delegates had regretfully to leave the region for six weeks, from the end of May to early July. They long imagined that their mere presence would have had a chance of preventing the worst excesses, even if they were not allowed to come directly to the help of inhabitants of towns and villages who had been driven away from their homes, or arrested in round-ups or massacred. Then, once they were back, they found that not only did such acts of violence continue but seemed to follow a plan that nothing would stop. Neither the representatives of the humanitarian agencies, who were much thicker on the ground from the winter of 1992–93 onwards, nor international journalists, nor the experts in human rights were able to change the course of history, let alone the politicians who much too long ago had given up any attempt to do so. From February to April 1993, the Muslim pockets of eastern Bosnia were besieged one after another. Public opinion had hardly recovered from these successive shocks when serious disturbances broke out in central Bosnia. Croats and Muslims, in a reversal of alliances that transformed the pattern of the war, waged fierce battles, sowing terror in the villages and cutting the supply lines of the principal urban centres – before the eyes of the world.

The ICRC delegates were used to trying to improve the daily living conditions of prisoners in political and military gaols all over the world without interfering in the reasons for their internment; but here the reasons for which arrested persons, most of them civilian males, were detained were such that the delegates had to change their methods. The urgency of the situation required intervention of another kind, for which the ICRC had not prepared itself. Once the delegates had registered the detainees' names, they had to move heaven and earth to get them released without delay, if necessary by protesting that their imprisonment was illegal. Even before there was any international pressure caused by the discovery of the detention camps in Bosnia-Herzegovina, the delegates were sure that this was the only possible approach, for they realized that many people arrested in round-ups were going to be used as bartering counters and that their arrest more resembled the taking of hostages than an act permissible under the laws of war. Developments proved that they were right. Although their action led to the release of thousands of people, the reasons for which detainees were held were still not clear. The combatants, regular or irregular, had continued to detain for their own purposes large numbers of prisoners for use in more lucrative bargaining. Other detainees (it is not known how many) had been liquidated and had disappeared without trace. It was a long and difficult business to get to the bottom of this, as it was to find out about 'ethnic cleansing'. The name of this policy does not accurately describe what it entails. It served as an excuse for brutally uprooting tens of thousands of people and despoiling them of the land their ancestors had lived on for generations. Women were raped and human dignity set at nought. All this was done on such a scale and with such determined violence that nobody was able to intervene.

Since the war began in 1991, humanitarian workers have faced countless natural and artificial difficulties that became all the greater as conditions on the ground steadily deteriorated. Come hell or high water, in spite of the anarchy around them, they battled to keep their activities going in an orderly way. And in this they succeeded to a large extent, whilst feeling deep within themselves a sense of extreme bitterness for all the failures and slip-ups they experienced.

As for the UN forces, when their advance guard arrived in the region in April 1992, they had received no orders relating to Bosnia-Herzegovina, which was still considered as a rear base. Only as from July, when Sarajevo airport was reopened, were they given a mandate out of phase with the reality of the clashes occurring on the ground. Their small numbers and the lack of preparation of the contingent for situations of this kind greatly restricted their powers of intervention. The international community, although well aware of the inadequate numbers of the UN forces, of which successive commanding officers of UNPROFOR had complained, could not or would not correct this major handicap. As a result, UNPROFOR's role was confined to that of a pseudo-humanitarian convoy escort, and also of civil engineer, a particularly welcome activity that did much to clear away obstacles along the main roads used by UNHCR, ICRC and NGO relief convoys.

When a decision had to be taken for or against the establishment of protected areas, at the end of 1992, so as to protect the civilian population of Bosnia-Herzegovina from the fighting and give temporary shelter to people who had lost all their possessions, that same international community took refuge behind the excuse that it could not make sufficient forces available to ensure effective military control. Some quarters estimated that more than another 200,000 men, about 10,000 of them for Sarajevo, would be needed to protect the safe areas called for by the ICRC, at a time when large-scale preventive measures could have made all the difference between life and death for many inhabitants of Bosnia-Herzegovina. The few towns later placed under UN protection were only a weak and tardy palliative to the suffering endured by the Bosnian civilian population.

Nearly four years of war in former Yugoslavia have shown that it is fatal to confuse the duties of politicians, soldiers and humanitarian workers. Merely adding these components together does not lead direct to a new golden age of peacemaking, and to think that it does is to underestimate the differences in structure, function and behaviour of the forces involved. Where the humanitarian organizations were entitled to expect their political counterparts to show real determination in making the belligerents respect their international commitments, western leaders found it easier to wave the flag of humanitarian assistance. Where the situation demanded that a modicum of law and order should be restored, whether or not under the name of 'a new world order', guerrilla leaders distinguished only by their bloodthirsty feats continued to wage their kind of war and go completely unpunished, in contempt of the most elementary rules of humanitarian law, while negotiators outside contented themselves with merely symbolic measures, that made the horror experienced every day seem almost normal and banal.

It may seem faint-hearted to urge that the roles of political, military and humanitarian bodies should be redefined so as to prolong indefinitely so culpable a drift off course, unless one considers that true courage lies in affirming basic truths that have proved their worth, and in daring to give short shrift to concepts that at first sight appear generous but are far removed from crude realities. In modern war as in the struggles of the past, the only men and women who can lay claim to impartiality, neutrality and independence are those who are capable of making these their guiding principles and who serve only one master at a time: the victim.

Landmarks 1991

May

10   Message from the President of the ICRC to the presidency of the Red Cross of Yugoslavia.

15–18   Exploratory ICRC mission led by the Delegate General for Europe, in the region of Knin and in Slavonia.

21   Second series of visits to 'persons arrested in relation to the political situation and detained under the responsibility of the Secretariat of Justice in the Republics of Croatia, Bosnia-Herzegovina, Macedonia and Serbia'. In all, 307 detainees seen for the first time in 23 places; this was the second visit for 58 detainees already seen in 1990 (the visits ended on 18 July).

June

27   War in Slovenia (until 6 July).

July

2–11   Visits to members of the Yugoslav armed forces and other representatives of the federal administration detained by the Republic of Slovenia. Releases of rank and file as from 3 July. No exact statistics of persons arrested. The Slovene authorities notify about 3,000 detainees.

7   The Brioni Declaration, under the auspices of the European Troika.

8   The Brioni Agreement, mentioning the ICRC, on the release of prisoners (Article VI).

17–19   Mission to Belgrade of the ICRC Delegate General for Europe.

Visits to detainees in Croat hands, continuing until December. 1,491 persons, placed under the responsibility of the Ministries of Justice, the Interior and Defence, are visited.

12   Until 30 December, visits to persons detained by the Yugoslav People's Army, the territorial defence forces and the civilian authorities, in Bosnia-Herzegovina, Montenegro, Serbia, Baranja and Krajina.

August

Beginning of the releases/exchanges of persons whether visited or not by the ICRC, but without its participation.

25   Vukovar under continuous artillery bombardment.

30   Letter from the President of the ICRC to all the leaders involved (Stipe Mesic for the Federal Republic, Franjo Tudjman for the Republic of Croatia, Milan Kucan for the Republic of Slovenia and Slobodan Milosevic for the Republic of Serbia) reminding them of their obligations to respect international humanitarian law.

September

13   Continuous mortar bombardment of the Osijek, Valpovo and Vinkovci region.

25   Resolution 713, the first resolution by the United Nations Security Council on the Yugoslav conflict, supports European efforts to settle the conflict and orders an embargo on deliveries of weapons to the region.

27   Attack on the ICRC convoy near Lipik, in Croatia.

October

Disintegration of the federal government, which asks the ICRC to place a delegate in Sarajevo (10 October).

18   Vukovar: on 18 October, attack on an MSF convoy. ICRC plan for a convoy due to travel on 19 October postponed indefinitely.

22   First meeting of the Tripartite Commission on prisoners, attended by representatives of the Croat Defence Ministry, the Yugoslav Federal Army, the European Community and the ICRC.

24   Memorandum prepared by the ICRC proposing rules for the release of all prisoners.

24   The 'Crisis Committee' of the Republic of Bosnia-Herzegovina agrees to the opening of an ICRC office in Sarajevo.

27   Agreement of both parties to the conflict for an ICRC convoy to Vukovar.

28   Council of Europe resolution calling for the humanitarian activities of the ICRC, the UNHCR and other aid organizations to be facilitated.

November

1   First talk between the ICRC Delegate General for Europe and Lord Carrington, Chairman of the Conference on Yugoslavia.

2   Discussion with the Federal Army of a plan for an ICRC convoy to Vukovar.

3   First ICRC evaluation mission to Dubrovnik.

5   All the parties present at the Hague Conference sign a declaration on the respect of humanitarian principles. The declaration was inspired by the ICRC and published in its press release No. 1688 of 6 November.

6   Agreement on the release of prisoners, signed by members of the Tripartite Commission, on the principle 'all for all'.

8   Letter from the President of the ICRC to the leaders of the parties to the conflict repeating the demand that they should respect international humanitarian law and offering to appoint plenipotentiaries to deal with urgent humanitarian matters.

11   Hail of fire on Dubrovnik.

15   Meeting at ICRC headquarters in Geneva of the Red Cross of Yugoslavia and the Red Cross Societies of the republics.

16   As a follow-up to the joint UNICEF/UNHCR mission, the Secretary General of the United Nations gives these organizations a mandate to prepare an appeal.

16   Vukovar: two quadripartite meetings of the European Community, the ICRC, Croatia and the Federal Army on the plan for a humanitarian assistance convoy and medical evacuations.

17   Even fiercer fighting at Vukovar. Public appeal by the ICRC in Zagreb.

18/19   Fall of Vukovar.

21–23   Osijek heavily bombarded.

23   Geneva agreement on the 14th and last cease-fire and on the blockade of barracks, in the presence of the leaders of the parties to the conflict.

24   Notification to the parties to the conflict that the ICRC has taken up residence in Dubrovnik in the Franciscan monastery and the Medarevo hospital, and of the possible neutralization of these buildings.

26–27   First meeting of the plenipotentiary representatives of the Federal Republic, the Federal Army, Croatia and Serbia, under ICRC auspices in Geneva. Signature of a Memorandum of Understanding on humanitarian priorities.

28–30   Meeting of the Council of Delegates of the International Red Cross and Red Crescent Movement, in Budapest. It adopts a resolution on the Yugoslav conflict entitled 'Budapest Appeal: Peace in People's Hearts'.

29   Fourth extraordinary session of the Council of Europe on Yugoslavia, which adopted a resolution supporting United Nations action for the installation of a peace-keeping operation.

December

3   Joint appeal by the UNHCR, UNICEF and WHO for assistance to persons displaced by the conflict between Croatia and Yugoslavia.

6   The UNHCR, having been granted a mandate by the Secretary-General as the agency responsible for the entire

UN operation in Yugoslavia, appoints José-María Mendiluce as its special envoy.

6   Dubrovnik: the hospital and monastery declared protected zones. Attack causing major damage and loss of life. Intensive bombardment of the town and port.

7   Conclusion by the parties to the conflict of the 'Cavtat Agreements' for a cease-fire in the region of Dubrovnik. They are not respected.

8   Agreement for an exchange of prisoners, put into effect between 10 and 12 December. 1,075 Croat soldiers and 558 members of the Federal armed forces are released.

11   Javier Perez de Cuellar submits his report to the Security Council following the four missions by Cyrus Vance, his special envoy, (on 11–18 October, 3–9 November, 17–24 November and 1–9 December 1991). This report is the first step towards the acceptance of the 'Vance Plan' on stationing UN troops in the regions of Croatia in which the Serbs formed a majority or a significant minority (Krajina and Baranja), but not in Bosnia-Herzegovina for preventive reasons. The report also provides for the return of all refugees who so wish.

13   First meeting in Sarajevo of the head of the ICRC delegation based in Belgrade and Dr Miljenko Brkic, the president of the Red Cross of Yugoslavia and a member of the government of Bosnia-Herzegovina.

13   Meeting of the Tripartite Commission to examine the question of the remaining persons covered by the exchange of 10 December, the possibility of local exchanges (in Slavonia), the supremacy of local commanders and the persons missing from Vukovar.

15   Security Council Resolution 724, which gives its agreement to the Vance Plan on the peace-keeping operation but asks that prior to the deployment of UN troops, the cease-fire agreement of 23 November should be respected. Meanwhile it endorses the offer to send an exploratory mission to Yugoslavia. The resolution also calls for a report on the implementation of the embargo on deliveries of weapons and military equipment (see Resolution 713) and draws attention to the great need for humanitarian assistance, the number of displaced persons having reached half a million.

16   The Joint Commission on Missing Persons and Mortal
        Remains is formed at Pècs in Hungary, and holds its first
        meeting there, which is attended by representatives of the
        Republic, the Federal Army, Croatia and Serbia, and the
        ICRC.

18,19   Preliminary contacts made by the ICRC with the three
        political parties' members of the governmental coalition
        of Bosnia-Herzegovina, with a view to opening an office
        in Sarajevo.

23   Germany announces its recognition of Slovenia and
        Croatia, with effect from 15 January 1992.

27   The parties to the conflict sign an agreement in Pècs for
        the establishment of a protected zone at Osijek Hospital.

Landmarks 1992

January

3   The neutralization of Osijek Hospital becomes effective at midnight. It coincides with the worst day of bombardment.

4   Entry into force of the 15th[1] cease-fire between Croatia and Federal Yugoslavia, which is long-lasting.

8   Security Council Resolution 727 approves the dispatch to Bosnia-Herzegovina of 50 liaison officers. It deplores the death of five members of the European Community Monitoring Mission on 7 January and welcomes the cease-fire agreement, which is respected.

18   As at this date, Croatia and Slovenia recognized by 33 countries, not including either Russia or the United States.

24   Third meeting of the Joint Commission for Tracing Missing Persons and Mortal Remains.

31   Third meeting of the plenipotentiaries at ICRC headquarters in Geneva.

February

Agreement between the ICRC and the UNHCR whereby the UNHCR takes over the operation for assistance to persons displaced by the conflict between Croatia and Yugoslavia.

11   Tripartite Commission on the prisoners, at Sarajevo.

15   The first shell hits Osijek Hospital.

21   Resolution 743 on the establishment of a United Nations Protection Force (UNPROFOR) in Yugoslavia for a period of twelve months, renewable.

29   Referendum on the independence of Bosnia-Herzegovina.

March

Immediately after the referendum, the Bosnian Serbs erect the first barricades in Sarajevo.

5   The United Nations Secretary-General appoints Lieutenant General Satish Nambiar to command UNPROFOR, Major General Philippe Morillon as deputy commander, and Cedric Thornberry as UNPROFOR director of civilian affairs.

7   Some 20 shells fall in the perimeter of Osijek Hospital.

19–20   The Tripartite Commission meets in Pècs (Hungary). Agreement on the release of prisoners between the Federal Army and the Republic of Croatia.

26   Slovenia lodges its instrument of accession to the Geneva Conventions and their Additional Protocols.

27   Fourth meeting of plenipotentiaries in Geneva. The Republic of Serbia not represented.

April

5   Fighting flares up in Bosnia-Herzegovina.

7   Resolution 749 on the deployment of UNPROFOR.

10   ICRC appeal for the protection of the civilian population in Bosnia-Herzegovina.

10   José-María Mendiluce convenes a meeting of the diplomatic representatives in Zagreb to discuss UNHCR projects in Bosnia-Herzegovina.

11   Under UNHCR auspices, the directors of the three governmental parties sign the Sarajevo Declaration on humanitarian treatment of displaced persons in Bosnia-Herzegovina.

22–23   Meeting of the Tripartite Commission on Prisoners.

23   Conclusion of a cease-fire on Bosnia-Herzegovina negotiated by Lord Carrington. It is not respected.

23   Osijek Hospital hit by several shells.

24   First UNHCR meeting and first UNHCR report on Bosnia-Herzegovina.

27   The ICRC delegates based in Bosnia-Herzegovina and Belgrade arrive in Sarajevo for an operational meeting.

May

Between 1 and 11 May, shells continue to fall in the perimeter of the neutralized hospital at Osijek.

1–5   Operational meeting of ICRC leaders at Sarajevo, the scene of fierce fighting.

3–9   CSCE end-of-mission report on the situation in former Yugoslavia.

9   The Serbian militias requisition an ICRC four-wheel-drive vehicle and an ICRC lorry in the Sarajevo region.

11   Appeal by the twelve nations of the European Community on Bosnia-Herzegovina.

12   Joint appeal by Sadako Ogata of the UNHCR and Cornelio Sommaruga of the ICRC on respect for war victims.

15   Resolution 752 calling for the organizations responsible for forwarding humanitarian assistance to have access to the victims.

18   ICRC convoy attacked at Sarajevo. Three delegates wounded.

19   One of the wounded delegates, Frédéric Maurice, dies of injuries sustained in the attack.

21   International conference on the refugees from Bosnia-Herzegovina held in Vienna.

22–23   First meeting of plenipotentiaries on Bosnia-Herzegovina at ICRC headquarters in Geneva. Signature of a framework agreement, and request made to the ICRC to start an airlift to Sarajevo.

23   Fifth meeting of Croat and Yugoslav plenipotentiaries.

27   Decision of the ICRC Executive Board to withdraw temporarily from the territory of Bosnia-Herzegovina.

30   Resolution 757 deploring the attack of 18 May on the ICRC convoy, announcing the closure of Sarajevo airport, condemning the Federal Republic of Yugoslavia and the Yugoslav People's Army, and imposing a commercial blockade of, and forbidding flights over, Serbia and Montenegro.

June

2–4   Meeting of the Tripartite Commission on the prisoners taken in the conflict between Croatia and Yugoslavia.

4–6   Second meeting of the plenipotentiaries of Bosnia-Herzegovina, studying the procedures for the redeployment of the ICRC.

13–18   Operational meeting of the ICRC in Zagreb with a view to resuming activities in Bosnia-Herzegovina.

17–18   First extraordinary meeting of the Organization of the Islamic Conference on Bosnia-Herzegovina, held in Istanbul, which adopts a resolution referring to the Geneva Conventions and the obligation to respect international humanitarian law.

18   Resolution 760 of the Security Council, stating that the sanctions do not apply to the import of 'staple commodities and products for essential humanitarian needs'.

20   The government of the Republic of Bosnia-Herzegovina confirms that it accepts the agreements concluded with the ICRC in Geneva on 22 May and 6 June and awaits the resumption of humanitarian operations.

24   Beginning of the first phase of resumption of activities in Bosnia-Herzegovina.

29   Resolution 761, announcing the despatch of reinforcements to UNPROFOR and the reopening of the airport at an early date.

30   Osijek Hospital de-neutralized.

July

1–2   Operational meeting of the ICRC in Zagreb on Bosnia-Herzegovina.

6–9   Mission by Sadako Ogata to Ljubljana, Zagreb, Sarajevo and Belgrade.

6–10   The ICRC delegates resume their visits to prisoners.

7–10   Organization of relief convoys.

8–17   Mission of the ICRC Delegate General for Europe to Belgrade, Zagreb and Sarajevo.

13 and The Delegate General pays two visits to Sarajevo.
16

14   Yugoslav application to the Sanctions Committee to
            mitigate the effects of the blockade on the social insurance
            sector. The application is rejected.

14–16   First visit of ICRC delegates to Manjaca prison, during
            which they registers the names of 2,353 prisoners in
            Serbian hands.

28   Second visit to Manjaca.

28   Talks by the President of the ICRC with Yugoslav Prime
            Minister Panic and the Croatian Vice-Prime Minister
            Granic on the question of persons still detained in relation
            with the conflict between Croatia and Yugoslavia.

29   International meeting on humanitarian aid to the victims
            of the conflict in former Yugoslavia convened by the
            UNHCR in Geneva.

29   Under ICRC auspices, the agreement for the release of
            prisoners taken in the conflict between Croatia and
            Yugoslavia (at the close of hostilities under the terms of
            Article 118 of the Third Geneva Convention) is signed
            in accordance with the principle of 'all for all'.

August

2   Roy Gutman's article in *Newsday*, with the first testi-
            monies by prisoners of the Bosnian Serbs.

7   Budapest: in the presence of the president of the ICRC,
            the prime ministers of Yugoslavia and Croatia initial the
            agreement on the release of all prisoners taken in the
            conflict between Croatia and Yugoslavia.

10   The ICRC is refused access to Omarska detention camp.

10   The ICRC's Deputy Director of Operations gives the
            European Commission in Strasbourg an account of grave
            breaches of international humanitarian law.

13   Resolution 770 on the delivery of humanitarian assistance
            and Resolution 771 on respect for international humani-
            tarian law and the treatment of detainees.

13 and   Extraordinary session (at the request of the United States)
14   of the Commission on Human Rights on the situation in
            former Yugoslavia, following the revelations on the
            detention camps. Tadeusz Mazowiecki, former prime

minister of Poland, appointed special rapporteur of the commission.

13   Solemn appeal by the ICRC on the situation in Bosnia-Herzegovina, with particular reference to the treatment of prisoners.

14   Nemetin, near Osijek: simultaneous release of 1,131 Croat and Yugoslav prisoners.

16–18   Official visit by the President of the ICRC to Warsaw, where he also meets with Tadeusz Mazowiecki.

18–23   The ICRC Delegate General for Europe visits Zagreb, Sarajevo and Belgrade, where he has talks successively with Mate Boban, Alija Izetbegovic and Radovan Karadzic.

26–28   London Conference on former Yugoslavia.

27   Public statements by Mazowiecki on his return from his first mission, condemning all the parties to the conflict committing serious abuses and flouting human rights.

27   Closure of the ICRC delegation in Ljubljana.

29   CSCE visits to places of detention in Bosnia-Herzegovina (until 4 September).

September

4   Meeting of the Follow-Up Committee of the London Conference on former Yugoslavia in Geneva. The United Nations presents its plan of action and consolidated appeal.

13 and 14   Internal discussion by ICRC delegates on the problem of 'ethnic cleansing'.

14   Resolution 776 giving UNPROFOR the green light to escort convoys of released prisoners if the ICRC so requests.

15   Evacuation of 68 wounded and sick ex-prisoners to Great Britain in a Russian airplane chartered by the ICRC.

22   Resolution AG 47/1 of the General Assembly of the United Nations, excluding the Federal Republic of Yugoslavia from the 47th Session of that Assembly.

30 and 1 October   Third meeting of plenipotentiaries on Bosnia-Herzegovina and continued consideration of the humanitarian programme of the London Conference.

October

1   Agreement signed under ICRC auspices by the three
           parties to the conflict for release of all prisoners, in
           accordance with the 'all for all' principle.

1   Evacuation by the ICRC of 1,560 detainees from Trnopolje
           to the Karlovac transit camp in Croatia.

3   President Sommaruga of the ICRC convokes the
           diplomatic representatives accredited to Geneva to a
           meeting at ICRC headquarters. The appeal 'Saving Lives
           in Bosnia-Herzegovina' is launched and is followed by a
           press conference held jointly with United Nations High
           Commissioner for Refugees Sadako Ogata.

6   Resolution 780 on the constitution of a United Nations
           Enquiry Commission on War Crimes in former Yugoslavia.

7   Speech by the President of the ICRC to the Assembly of
           the Council of Europe in Strasbourg.

9   Resolution 781 on the ban on military flights in the
           airspace of Bosnia-Herzegovina.

18   Meeting in Geneva on the initiative of the ICRC of two
           ministerial delegations of the Yugoslav Federation and of
           the Republic of Croatia to settle the question of persons
           reported missing and residual cases of prisoners.

20   ICRC appeal to the diplomatic representatives, asking them
           to facilitate the reception in host countries of prisoners
           freed from camps in Bosnia-Herzegovina.

23   Security incident in Bileca: two delegates molested in
           public.

23   Beginning of an ICRC campaign to heighten public and
           official awareness of the need to expedite procedures for
           the reception of freed prisoners.

30   The ICRC convenes a further meeting of diplomatic rep-
           resentatives in Geneva to increase pressure for the reception
           of prisoners.

30   Fall of Jajce; 50,000 displaced persons make for Zenica.

November

11   The first mission of ICRC delegates to Pale, the seat of
           the Bosnian Serb authorities, since the attack of 18 May.

| 14 | 755 detainees released from Manjaca and evacuated by the ICRC to Karlovac. |

14 and 15   Civilians evacuated from Sarajevo: 400 by the Jewish community and 4,700 by the Bosnian Red Cross, under UNPROFOR protection.

16   Resolution 787, tightening the embargo, particularly by sea, and condemning breaches of international humanitarian law. It refers to the Commission of Experts established by Resolution 780, and 'invites the Secretary-General to study the possibilities and needs concerning the promotion of safe areas for humanitarian purposes'.

23   ICRC mission to Sarajevo and meeting with the generals of the three parties to the conflict under the aegis of General Philippe Morillon.

26 and 27   First visit of the ICRC delegates to Tarcin, where prisoners in Muslim hands are being detained in a silo designed for the storage of wheat.

30 and 1 December   Second extraordinary session of the Commission on Human Rights. Discussion of the three reports made by the special rapporteur Tadeusz Mazowiecki. Publication of a resolution condemning the Serbian party for 'ethnic cleansing'.

December

1–3   Second extraordinary session of the Organization of the Islamic Conference in Jedda and adoption of a resolution more severe than its predecessors.

4   Follow-up meeting to the London Conference, during which several delegations express doubts as to the validity of the project for safe areas.

7 and 8   Meeting in Budapest with their International Federation of the Red Cross Societies involved in assistance to refugees from the conflicts of former Yugoslavia, to take stock of their activities during the preceding six months.

9   The ICRC President receives the leaders of the three parties to the conflict in order to expedite the release of the prisoners detained in Bosnia-Herzegovina.

9   The ICRC Director of Operations meets the military commander of the Bosnian Serbs, General Mladic, at Banja Luka in order to obtain easier access to the victims.

14   1,008 detainees evacuated from Manjaca by the ICRC.

16   1,001 prisoners released from Manjaca.

18   The last 418 prisoners leave Manjaca with the ICRC delegates.

Appendix

List of documents

I   Brioni Declaration, 7 July 1991.

II   Letter from the President of the ICRC to the leaders of the Republic of Croatia, the Republic of Slovenia, the Republic of Serbia and the Federal Socialist Republic (FSR) of Yugoslavia, 30 August 1991.

III   Agreement between the Republic of Croatia and the Armed Forces of the FSR of Yugoslavia on the exchange of prisoners and persons deprived of liberty, 6 November 1991.

IV   Memorandum of Understanding on the procedures for the application of the applicable rules of international humanitarian law by the Republic of Croatia, the Republic of Serbia and the Armed Forces of the FSR of Yugoslavia, 27 November 1991.

V   Statement by the President of the ICRC at the opening of the International Meeting on Humanitarian Aid for Victims of the Conflict in the former Yugoslavia, held under the auspices of the United Nations High Commissioner for Refugees, 29 July 1992.

VI   Agreement on respect for the rules of international humanitarian law by the plenipotentiaries representing the parties to the conflict in Bosnia-Herzegovina, 22 May 1992.

VII   Map of the places and dates of the visits made by the ICRC delegates to persons detained in relation to the conflict in Bosnia-Herzegovina, as at 6 August 1992.

VIIIa Protecting vulnerable ethnic minorities in Bosnia-Herzegovina, a project drawn up by the ICRC, 14 December 1992;

VIIIb Safe areas for humanitarian assistance (SC res. 787), position of UNHCR, 14 December 1992.

IX   Statistical tables on protection and assistance activities.

Document I

FEDERAL EXECUTIVE COUNCIL

Brioni Declaration

Secretariat for Information
of the Federal Executive Council

Belgrade, July 1991

JOINT DECLARATION

At the invitation of the Yugoslav Government, the European Community Ministerial Troika met on July 7th 1991 at Brioni, with representatives of all parties directly concerned by the Yugoslav crisis.

The objective of the Troika mission was to create the appropriate conditions for a peaceful negotiation between all the parties. All the parties concerned took note of the European Community and its Member States' declaration of July 5th 1991 and reaffirmed their commitment to full implementation of the European Community's proposal of June 30th, 1991 in order to secure the cease-fire and enable negotiations on the future of Yugoslavia.

In regard of these proposals modalities were agreed in **Annex I**.

Parties agreed that in order to ensure a peaceful settlement, the following principles will have to be fully followed:

- it is upto and only to the peoples of Yugoslavia to decide upon their future,
- a new situation has arisen in Yugoslavia that requires close monitoring and negotiation between different parties,
- negotiations should begin urgently, no later than August 1st 1991, on all aspects of the future of Yugoslavia without preconditions and on the basis of the principles of the Helsinki Final Act and the Paris Charter for a new Europe (in particular respect for Human Rights, including the rights of peoples' self-determination in conformity with the Charter of the United Nations and with the relevant norms of International Law, including those relating to territorial integrity of States),
- the Collegiate Presidency must exercise its full capacity and play its political and constitutional role, namely with regard to the Federal Armed Forces,
- all parties concerned will refrain from any unilateral action, particularly, from all acts of violence.

The Community and Member States for their part will assist in reaching a peaceful and durable solution to the present crisis, provided and as long as the commitments undertaken above are fully abided by.

In this context, the European Community and its Member States accept the request by the other parties to assist and facilitate the negotiating process.

Their help could be extended to a monitoring of the progress of the negotiations, expertise for the working groups to be established by the parties concerned, inter alia legal, human rights, including the rights of minority populations, economic, commercial and security relations.

In the wake of the decision taken in Prague in the framework of the CSCE, they agreed that a monitoring mission should become operational as soon as possible in order to help stabilize the cease-fire and to monitor the implementation of the remaining elements of the agreement reached between Yugoslav parties with the contribution of the European Community. Guidelines for the preparatory mission are set out in **Annex II**.

They welcome the expected arrival on July 9th of this preparatory mission of High Officials.

All Yugoslav parties committed themselves to support the envisaged monitoring mission by, inter alia, providing full protection and guaranteed freedom of movement.

They all agreed that the protection of minority populations is critical to a successful outcome of the negotiations. They also reconfirmed that they will fully respect in this matter their commitments under International Law.

The European Troika is prepared to inform all the CSCE Participation States about developments in the negotiating process.

ANNEX I

FURTHER MODALITIES IN PREPARATION OF NEGOTIATIONS

I – Border regime
   Control of border crossings will be in the hands of Slovenian police. They will act in conformity with federal regulations.

II – Customs
   The agreement signed by the representatives of the federal government and the government of the Republic of Slovenia on June 20th 1991 is reconfirmed and shall be implemented. Custom duties shall remain a federal revenue and be collected by Slovenian

custom officials. They shall be paid into a joint account to be controlled by the federal and republican ministers of finance plus one or two external controllers.

III Air Traffic Control

There is a single air traffic control for the whole of Yugoslavia. All domestic and international air traffic over Yugoslavia is controlled and guaranteed by the competent federal authority.

IV Border security

The situation prevailing before June 25th 1991 shall be reestablished. Within the suspension period (of three months) negotiations shall be completed in order to ensure an orderly transfer of the competencies of the YNA in this field. A border regime based on European standards remains a firm objective.

V Further modalities for the implementation of the cease-fire

*   lifting of the blockade of YNA units and facilities
*   unconditional return of YNA units to their barracks
*   all roads to be cleared
*   return of all facilities and equipment to YNA
*   de-activation of territorial defence units and return to quarter.

All these measures shall be effective as soon as possible, but no later than July 8th at 24.00 hours.

VI Prisoners

All prisoners detained in connection with hostilities since June 25th 1991 shall be released at the earliest but no later than July 8th at 24.00 hours. The International Red Cross should be associated with the implementation of this decision.

ANNEX II

GUIDELINES FOR AN OBSERVER
MISSION TO YUGOSLAVIA

Introduction

The situation in Yugoslavia is of concern to all CSCE Participating States. The Committee of Senior Officials meeting in Prague discussed the dispatch of a multinational Observer Mission into Yugoslavia. Obviously, such an Observer Mission can only operate with full consent of all Parties concerned. To ensure that the Observer Mission can fulfil its tasks, it is necessary to define its mandate and to determine its rights and duties. The financing of the operation and a number of practical aspects have to be decided upon. For this purpose, the following elements are suggested:

MANDATE

An Observer Mission will be established with the objective to monitor the situation in Yugoslavia, in particular by monitoring activities in Slovenia – and possibly also Croatia. The aim of these activities is to monitor the implementation of the remaining elements of the agreement reached between Yugoslav parties with the contribution of the European Community.

DURATION OF THE MANDATE

The Observer Mission should be able to take up its activities as soon as possible. The Observer Mission could continue its operation as long as this is deemed necessary by all Parties concerned.

AREA OF DEPLOYMENT

Under the current circumstances, the Observer Mission would geographically limit its activities to Slovenia and possible Croatia. If need arises, the area of deployment could be reviewed in agreement with all Parties concerned.

COMPOSITION AND OPERATION

The Observer Mission would be of mixed composition, i.e. both military and civilian personnel.

The Mission could consist of 30 to 50 people. Since it is important to act as expeditiously as possible, selection of personnel should not be allowed to delay the beginning of the Observer Mission's activities. A practical solution could be to recruit observers from the civilian and military members of the Vienna CSBM delegations where expertise on the CSCE is available. They could be supplemented with other civilian and or military officials.

The Mission would establish a Coordination Centre within Yugoslavia. From this Centre smaller units – of e.g. two men – would be deployed in different sectors. One liaison-officer of each of the opposing parties would be assigned to escort such observer units at all times.

COMMAND STRUCTURE AND SUPERVISION

The observer units would work under the responsibility of the Head of the Observer Mission.

The Head of the Observer Mission would submit a daily report, through the Prague CSCE Secretariat, to the Committee of Senior Officials.

The Committee could be the appropriate venue to take stock of the activities of the Observer Mission and to decide on the prolongation of the mandate of the Mission, if this is necessary.

LEGAL ARRANGEMENTS

Legal arrangements would be necessary to ensure that the Observer Mission can carry out its tasks. These arrangements include provisions concerning diplomatic immunity as well as the freedom to travel and communicate freely within Yugoslavia, i.e. with the Coordination Centre and with embassies.

PRACTICAL ARRANGEMENTS

Amongst the many practical arrangements to be decided upon are questions regarding the means of transport and interpretation services that will have to be made available to the observer units and the way in which the observers will identify and distinguish themselves as members of the CSCE Observer Mission.

Since the Observer Mission is not a peace-keeping force, the observers would not carry arms.

Document II

Geneva, 30 August 1991

Mr President,

The International Committee of the Red Cross (ICRS) has been working in Yugoslavia since 21 May last. It has visited persons detained in the six Republics and two Autonomous Provinces and furnished material assistance to the victims of the current tragic events.

I should like to thank you for the support that your government has extended to my staff in the performance of their tasks.

As you know, the seriousness of the situation and its consequences in humanitarian terms prompted the ICRC to appeal on 2 July 1991 to all the parties to the conflict, urging them to respect international humanitarian law and to ensure that it is respected by all persons taking part in the hostilities.

In view of the escalation of the fighting, which is directly affecting the civilian population, and by virtue of its humanitarian duty and the mandate conferred on it by international humanitarian law, the ICRC calls on all parties to the conflict and the authorities concerned:

- to cease all attacks against civilians and civilian property;

- to spare the lives of those who surrender and to ensure that all captured enemy combatants are humanely treated;

- to respect and ensure respect for the Red Cross emblem so that those displaying it in the course of their humanitarian activities can work in safety;

- to ensure that all Red Cross personnel and medical staff called upon to assist the civilian population and persons *hors de combat* enjoy the necessary freedom of movement;

- to inform combatants of the basic humanitarian rules relating to the conduct of hostilities and to facilitate the work of the ICRC in this regard.

The current situation necessitates an extensive humanitarian operation on behalf of all the victims. Such an operation can be carried out by the Red Cross only with the resolute support of all political forces concerned.

Convinced of the urgent need to continue and expand the operation already under way, I am taking the liberty of approaching you personally. I have no doubt that you will grant Mr Jean de Courten, member of the ICRC Executive Board and Director of Operations, all the facilities needed for the Red Cross to pursue its activities for all the victims of the current conflict.

Please accept, Mr President, the assurance of my highest consideration.

Cornelio Sommaruga

Unofficial Translation

Document III

The Government of the Republic of Croatia, represented by Ivan Milas, Deputy Minister of Defence, and the armed forces of the FSR of Yugoslavia, represented by Major-General Andrija Rašeta, after harmonizing their positions have reached the following

AGREEMENT

on the exchange of prisoners, that is, persons deprived of their freedom during armed hostilities in the Republic of Croatia or in connection with those hostilities, as follows:

1. The two parties jointly declare that they will exchange all prisoners, that is, persons deprived of their freedom, in accordance with the 'all-for-all' principle.

2. The term prisoner comprises all persons deprived of their freedom who are currently in prison, in detention or in prison camps, regardless of whether criminal or other proceedings have been instituted against them, charges brought or an enforceable or unenforceable sentence pronounced, and regardless of the territory on which they are or of the places in which they were captured, arrested, restricted in their movements or held hostage.

3. Each side will hand over to the other a list of all prisoners, with precise indications as to the places where they are being held, and both sides will hand over copies of those lists also to the representative of the International Committee of the Red Cross (ICRC).

4. The signatories hereto agree to carry out the exchange of prisoners immediately after the ICRC has registered and visited the prisoners in accordance with the ICRC's specific criteria.

5. The signatories hereto will accept as authoritative the list of prisoners registered by the ICRC.

6. The signatories hereto agree that no prisoner may be returned against his will and that each prisoner will be allowed to state his wishes freely to the ICRC representative.

7. The signatories to the agreement undertake not to put pressure of any kind on the prisoners as regards persuading them to reject or accept their return.

8. The signatories to the agreement solemnly undertake not to take any reprisals against prisoners who refuse to return or against their families.

9. The signatories also agree to carry out the exchange of prisoners in the presence of EC observers.

10. The signatories to the agreement will start the exchange of the lists of prisoners immediately, and within two days of the signing of this agreement will appoint persons authorized to carry out the exchange.

11. The signatories undertake to place all prisoners immediately under the protection of the ICRC and, as regards the treatment and housing of prisoners, to defer in all respects to the requirements and standards of the International Red Cross.

12. The authorized persons mentioned in point 10 of this agreement will clarify any questions that might arise in the implementation of the agreement.

13. In the event of disputes concerning the interpretation and application of the present Agreement, the ICRC shall be competent.

Zagreb, 6 November 1991

DEPUTY DEFENCE MINISTER OF THE REPUBLIC OF CROATIA

Ivan Milas

PLENIPOTENTIARY REPRESENTATIVE OF THE ARMED FORCES OF THE SFRY

Major-General

Andrija Rašeta

AMBASSADOR

Dirk-Jan Van Houten

Document IV

MEMORANDUM OF UNDERSTANDING

We the undersigned,

H.E. Mr. Radisa Gacic, Federal Secretary for Labour, Health, Veteran Affairs and Social Policy
Lt. General Vladimir Vojvodic, Director General, Medical Service of the Yugoslav People's Army
Mr. Sergej Morsan, Assistant to the Minister of Foreign Affairs, Republic of Croatia
Prim. Dr. I. Prodan, Commander of Medical Headquarters of Ministry of Health, Republic of Croatia
Prof. Dr. Ivica Kostovic, Head of Division for information of Medical Headquarters, Ministry of Health, Republic of Croatia
Dr. N. Mitrovic, Minister of Health, Republic of Serbia

taking into consideration the Hague statement of 5 November 1991 undertaking to respect and ensure respect of international humanitarian law signed by the Presidents of the six Republics; having had discussions in Geneva under the auspices of the International Committee of the Red Cross (ICRC) on 26 and 27 November 1991 and with the participation of:

Mr. Claudio Caratsch, Vice-President of the ICRC
Mr. Jean de Courten, Director of Operations, Member of the Executive Board of the ICRC
Mr. Thierry Germond, Delegate General for Europe (Chairman of the above mentioned meeting)
Mr. Francis Amar, Deputy Delegate General for Europe
Mr. François Bugnion, Deputy Director of Principles, Law and Relations with the Movement
Mr. Thierry Meyrat, Head of Mission, ICRC Belgrade
Mr. Pierre-André Conod, Deputy Head of Mission, ICRC Zagreb
Mr. Jean-François Berger, Taskforce Yugoslavia
Mr. Vincent Lusser, Taskforce Yugoslavia
Mr. Marco Sassoli, Member of the Legal Division
Mrs. Cristina Piazza, Member of the Legal Division
Dr. Rémi Russbach, Head of the Medical Division
Dr. Jean-Claude Mulli, Deputy Head of the Medical Division
Mr. Jean-David Chappuis, Head of the Central Tracing Agency

have agreed to the following:

(1) *Wounded and sick*
     All wounded and sick on land shall be treated in accordance
     with the provisions of the First Geneva Convention of August
     12, 1949.
(2) *Wounded, sick and shipwrecked at sea*
     All wounded, sick and shipwrecked at sea shall be treated in
     accordance with the provisions of the Second Geneva
     Convention of August 12, 1949.
(3) *Captured combatants*
     Captured combatants shall enjoy the treatment provided for
     by the Third Geneva Convention of August 12, 1949.
(4) *Civilians in the power of the adverse party*
     Civilians who are in the power of the adverse party and who
     are deprived of their liberty for reasons related to the armed
     conflict shall benefit from the rules relating to the treatment
     of internees laid down in the Fourth Geneva Convention of
     August 12, 1949 (Articles 70 to 149).
     All civilians shall be treated in accordance with Articles 72 to
     79 of Additional Protocol I.
(5) *Protection of the civilian population against certain consequences
     of hostilities*
     The civilian population is protected by Articles 13 to 26 of
     the Fourth Geneva Convention of August 12, 1949.
(6) *Conduct of hostilities*
     Hostilities shall be conducted in accordance with Articles 35
     to 42 and Articles 48 to 58 of Additional Protocol I, and the
     Protocol on Prohibition or Restrictions on the Use of Mines,
     Booby Traps and Other Devices annexed to the 1980 Weapons
     Convention.
(7) *Establishment of protected zones*
     The parties agree that for the establishment of protected
     zones, the annexed standard draft agreement shall be used as
     a basis for negotiations.
(8) *Tracing of missing persons*
     The parties agree to set up a Joint Commission to trace
     missing persons; the Joint Commission will be made up of
     representatives of the parties concerned, all Red Cross
     organizations concerned and in particular the Yugoslav Red
     Cross, the Croatian Red Cross and the Serbian Red Cross
     with ICRC participation.
(9) *Assistance to the civilian population*
     The parties shall allow the free passage of all consignments
     of medicines and medical supplies, essential foodstuffs and
     clothing which are destined exclusively for the other party's
     civilian population, it being understood that both parties are

entitled to verify that the consignments are not diverted from their destination.

They shall consent to and cooperate with operations to provide the civilian population with exclusively humanitarian, impartial and non-discriminatory assistance. All facilities will be given in particular to the ICRC.

(10) *Red Cross emblem*

The parties undertake to comply with the rules relating to the use of the Red Cross emblem. In particular, they shall ensure that these rules are observed by all persons under their authority.

The parties shall repress any misuse of the emblem and any attack on persons or property under its protection.

(11) *Forwarding of allegations*

The parties may forward to the ICRC any allegations of violations of international humanitarian law, with sufficient details to enable the party reportedly responsible to open an enquiry.

The ICRC will not inform the other party of such allegations if they are expressed in abusive terms or if they are made public. Each party undertakes, when it is officially informed of such an allegation made or forwarded by the ICRC, to open an enquiry promptly and pursue it conscientiously, and to take the necessary steps to put an end to the alleged violations or prevent their recurrence and to punish those responsible in accordance with the law in force.

(12) *Requests for an enquiry*

Should the ICRC be asked to institute an enquiry, it may use its good offices to set up a commission of enquiry outside the institution and in accordance with its principles.

The ICRC will take part in the establishment of such a commission only by virtue of a general agreement or an ad hoc agreement with all the parties concerned.

(13) *Dissemination*

The parties undertake to spread knowledge of and promote respect for the principles and rules of international humanitarian law and the terms of the present agreement, especially among combatants. This shall be done in particular:

- by providing appropriate instruction on the rules of international humanitarian law to all units under their command, control or political influence, and to paramilitary or irregular units not formally under their command, control or political influence;
- by facilitating the dissemination of ICRC appeals urging respect for international humanitarian law;

 – via articles in the press, and radio and television programmes
    prepared also in cooperation with the ICRC and broadcast
    simultaneously;
 – by distributing ICRC publications.

(14) *General provisions*

The parties will respect the provisions of the Geneva
Conventions and will ensure that any paramilitary or irregular
units not formally under their command, control or political
influence respect the present agreement.

The application of the preceding provisions shall not affect the
legal status of the parties to the conflict.

(15) *Next meeting*

The next meeting will take place in Geneva on 19–20 December
1991.

Geneva, 27 November 1991

Document V

COMITÉ INTERNATIONAL DE LA CROIX-ROUGE

Statement by Mr. Cornelio Sommaruga
President of the International Committee of the Red Cross
at the opening of the International Meeting on
Humanitarian Aid for Victims of the Conflict in the
former Yugoslavia, held under the auspices of
the United Nations High Commissioner for Refugees

Geneva, 29 July 1992

The magnitude of the Yugoslav tragedy hardly bears contempla-tion. After more than a year of increasingly violent fighting, the consequences are horrendous and already bear the mark of the greatest human disaster in Europe since the Second World War. And who knows when and where it will all end?

Today's meeting gives us the sadly necessary opportunity to reassess the humanitarian activities carried out for the victims of the conflict in the former Yugoslavia. Here I should like to con-gratulate the United Nations High Commissioner for Refugees on her timely initiative to being together all those most closely involved in such work, and to stress the excellent cooperation, based on regular and constructive consultation, that has prevailed between our two institutions since the beginning of the Yugoslav conflict.

Allow me first of all to make two observations. The *first*, which is far from exhaustive, relates to the situation in humanitarian terms as it unfolds almost before our eyes. I am talking about the more than two million victims who have fled violence and perse-cution in appalling conditions, all the dead, the wounded, the sick, the prisoners – in a word, all those who bear the brunt of hatred and intolerance; the ordinary women and children whose lives have been ruined along with their homes, their social relationships and, in many cases, their very roots. But this is not the worst of it.

Behind this nightmare situation, nourished by revenge and hate, there is a deliberate plan based on the exclusion of other groups. For a man of the Red Cross like myself, this is quite abhorrent. Indeed, we are only too well aware of the practical consequences of such an idea, especially when it is being trumpeted by the media and put into effect by the many local demagogues who have emerged from the chaos. I am referring, of course, to the terrible ravages of "ethnic cleansing", in whose name whole populations are being terrorized, minorities intimidated and harassed, civilians interned on a massive scale, hostages taken, and torture, deporta-tion and summary executions are rife. Such methods, which we thought had been consigned to museums showing the horrors of the Second World War, have become almost common practice in the war-torn territory of what was Yugoslavia. They are used by all the parties involved, to an extent determined by the means at their disposal, in flagrant violation of the most basic rights which the victims, as protected persons, are entitled to enjoy under the Geneva Conventions and their Additional Protocols.

This state of affairs is all the more revolting in that the vast majority of the victims are civilians who take no part in the hostilities and are thus especially vulnerable. The large number of elderly people who have been arrested or displaced is a particularly disgraceful aspect of the tragedy. Some of them survived the First World War as children and the Second World War as adults, only to be treated like cattle in their old age. Their grandchildren, when they have been able to stay by their side, are going through the same experiences, which may even contain the seeds of strife for further generations. Once again, the prospect is staggering.

My *second* observation relates to the role of the International Committee of the Red Cross in this conflict.

Since June 1991 the ICRC has, in accordance with its mandate, been running large-scale and diverse programmes for the victims. Its activities focus on providing protection for prisoners and for civilians affected by the fighting, tracing missing persons and arranging for the exchange of news between the members of separated families, distributing food and other aid to displaced people and vulnerable groups, providing medical and surgical assistance for the war-wounded; and of course spreading knowledge of international humanitarian law, especially among the armed forces of all parties to the conflict.

In addition to its daily work, the ICRC acted as a neutral intermediary in the midst of the conflict. On no fewer than six occasions it brought together in Geneva, around the same table, plenipotentiary representatives of the parties involved in the conflict in Croatia, and more recently in the conflict in Bosnia-Herzegovina, to work out practical solutions to questions of humanitarian concern. These meetings, and the work of *ad hoc* commissions set up to deal with the tracing of missing persons and the release of prisoners, led to tangible results in favour of the victims.

With the outbreak of hostilities in Bosnia-Herzegovina nearly four months ago, the Yugoslav conflict reached a new level of violence. Substantial additional means have been mobilized in an attempt to bring aid to the new victims, who are scattered around the republic, ravaged by ethnic divisions.

And then suddenly, at the height of its humanitarian involvement, the ICRC suffered a terrible blow: on 18 May, at the eastern gate of Sarajevo, an ICRC relief convoy came under deliberate attack. Three of our staff were wounded, among them Frédéric Maurice, who died of his injuries during the night. His death is not only a tragic loss for his family and friends, it represents an outrage against the very symbol of the Red Cross, the symbol which embodies humanitarian endeavour at its most noble, *inter arma caritas*. A few days later, on account of the growing insecurity which paralysed nearly all our activities, the ICRC withdrew from Bosnia-Herzegovina. It stayed away for a month, until the parties to the conflict adopted a plan of action laying down strict security conditions indispensable to the resumption of our operations. Five weeks ago our delegates went back to carrying out their many protection and assistance tasks in the regions of Bihać, Banja Luka, Trebinje, Mostar and Zenica.

I must stress that all those endeavours and the results achieved fall far short of the exponential magnitude of needs, especially in Bosnia-Herzegovina. We may ask ourselves what is the point of an operation that cannot assist all the victims of the conflict, for some areas, notably those in eastern Bosnia-Herzegovina, still cannot be reached by the ICRC since they do not offer minimum security guarantees for our staff.

More generally, over this last year of conflict the ICRC has been forced to recognize that breaches of international humanitarian law and of human rights have become almost commonplace, especially as regards the civilian population, despite numerous public appeals and confidential approaches at all levels and to all the parties. There is no doubt that the vicious circle of hatred and reprisals erodes basic humanitarian values more and more each day, although these values are universally recognized. The humanitarian message must be heard and understood in its entirety, it must ring out loud and clear to reach all those concerned and suppress rumour, propaganda and disinformation. As we all know, it is first and foremost up to the States and their governments to respect and ensure respect for the basic rules of humanitarian law.

It is at this point that humanitarian action reaches its limits. Despite the immense efforts made by UNHCR, the ICRC and other humanitarian agencies, and despite the dedicated work of local Red Cross organizations, it has become increasingly clear that humanitarian activities, which have gained sudden prominence in the past year, will not be able to resolve the problems generated by a crisis that continues to spread and gather momentum.

Prompted by awareness of our limitations, which are largely dictated by our mandate, we must express our deep concern about the prospect of remaining powerless to deal with suffering on such an immense scale. It is on behalf of the victims that we are voicing this preoccupation. Today more than ever, priority must be given to tackling the causes of the crisis, not only its effects. As President of the ICRC, I would like to take this opportunity to appeal to the

States, especially those which are the most directly concerned, to use every means at their disposal to seek a peaceful settlement to the conflict. Much has already been done, but it is not enough! There will be no hope for an end to this senseless violence until States make firm commitments and fully assume their political responsibilities. Otherwise, humanitarian efforts may gradually be reduced to nothing but ineffective stop-gap measures.

Until a political solution to this tragic conflict is found, all efforts to alleviate the unbearable suffering of the victims must continue and be stepped up. It is imperative that the aims of this meeting receive wide support and be followed up by more effective long-term programmes to help displaced people and refugees. We must not lose sight of the fact that humanitarian activities undertaken on the spot – including the protection and assistance work carried out by ICRC delegates – help to attack the causes of emigration and thereby slow the exodus.

The ICRC is determined to pursue its emergency operations and to continue seeking ways of reaching all the victims and potential victims of the conflict. It will spare no effort in making representations at the highest level to promote dialogue on humanitarian issues among the parties concerned.

If the endeavour to alleviate the untold distress of the victims of the Yugoslav conflict is to receive a new impetus, UNHCR and the ICRC – which will continue to work together, each respecting the other's independence – must be able to count on the active solidarity and support of the entire international community. On behalf of all the victims of this conflict, I thank you in advance.

Document VI

AGREEMENT

At the invitation of the International Committee of the Red Cross,

Mr. K. Trnka,	Representative of Mr. Alija Izetbegovic President of the Republic of Bosnia-Herzegovina
Mr. D. Kalinic,	Representative of Mr. Radovan Karadzic President of the Serbian Democratic Party
Mr. J. Djogo,	Representative of Mr. Radovan Karadzic President of the Serbian Democratic Party
Mr. A. Kurjak,	Representative of Mr. Alija Izetbegovic President of the Party of Democratic Action
Mr. S. Sito Coric,	Representative of Mr. Miljenko Brkic President of the Croatian Democratic Community

met in Geneva on the 22 May 1992 to discuss different aspects of the application and of the implementation of international humanitarian law within the context of the conflict in Bosnia-Herzegovina, and to find solutions to the resulting humanitarian problems. Therefore

- conscious of the humanitarian consequences of the hostilities in the region;
- taking into consideration the Hague Statement of 5 November 1991;
- reiterating their commitment to respect and ensure respect for the rules of international humanitarian law;

the Parties agree that, without any prejudice to the legal status of the parties to the conflict or to the international law of armed conflict in force, they will apply the following rules:

1. *General principles*
The parties commit themselves to respect and to ensure respect for Article 3 of the four Geneva Conventions of 12 August 1949, which states, in particular:

1) Persons taking no active part in the hostilities, including members of armed groups who have laid down their arms and those placed *hors de combat* by sickness, wounds, detention, or any other cause, shall in all circumstances be treated humanely, without any adverse distinction founded on race, colour, religion or faith, sex, birth or wealth, or any other similar criteria.

To this end, the following acts shall remain prohibited at any time and in any place whatsoever with respect to the above mentioned persons:

a) violence to life and person, in particular murder of all kinds, mutilation, cruel treatment and torture;
b) taking of hostages;
c) outrages upon personal dignity, in particular, humiliating and degrading treatment;
d) the passing of sentences and the carrying out of executions without previous judgment pronounced by a regularly constituted court, affording all the judicial guarantees which are recognized as indispensable by civilized peoples.

2) The wounded and sick shall be collected and cared for.
   An impartial body, such as the International Committee of the Red Cross, may offer its services to the Parties to the conflict.
   The Parties to the conflict should further endeavour to bring into force, by means of special agreements, all or part of the other provisions of the present Convention.
   The application of the preceding provisions shall not affect the legal status of the Parties to the conflict.

2. Special agreement

In accordance with Article 3 of the four Geneva Conventions of 12 August 1949, the Parties agree to bring into force the following provisions:

2.1 Wounded, sick and shipwrecked

The treatment provided to the wounded, sick and shipwrecked shall be in accordance with the provisions of the First and Second Geneva Conventions of 12 August 1949, in particular:

– All the wounded, sick and shipwrecked, whether or not they have taken part in the armed conflict, shall be respected and protected.
– In all circumstances, they shall be treated humanely and shall receive, to the fullest extent practicable and with the least possible delay, the medical care and attention required by their condition. There shall be no distinction among them founded on any grounds other than medical ones.

2.2 Protection of hospitals and other medical units

Hospitals and other medical units, including medical transportation may in no circumstances be attacked; they shall at all times be respected and protected. They may not be used to shield combatants, military objectives or operations from attacks.

The protection shall not cease unless they are used to commit military acts. However, the protection may only cease after due warning and a reasonable time limit to cease military activities.

2.3 Civilian population

The civilians and the civilian population are protected by Articles 13 to 34 of the Fourth Geneva Convention of 12 August 1949. The civilian population and individual civilians shall enjoy general protection against the dangers arising from military operations. They shall not be the object of attack. Acts or threats of violence the primary purpose of which is to spread terror among the civilian population are prohibited.

All civilians shall be treated in accordance with Articles 72 to 79 of Additional Protocol I. Civilians who are in the power of an adverse party and who are deprived of their liberty for reasons related to the armed conflict shall benefit from the rules relating to the treatment of internees laid down in the Fourth Geneva Convention of 12 August 1949.

In the treatment of the civilian population there shall be no adverse distinction founded on race, religion or faith, or any other similar criteria.

The displacement of the civilian population shall not be ordered unless the security of the civilians involved or imperative military reasons so demand. Should such displacements have to be carried out, all possible measures shall be taken in order that the civilian population may be received under satisfactory conditions of shelter, hygiene, health, safety and nutrition.

The International Committee of the Red Cross (ICRC) shall have free access to civilians in all places, particularly in places of internment or detention, in order to fulfil its humanitarian mandate according to the Fourth Geneva Convention of 12 August 1949.

2.4 Captured combatants

Captured combatants shall enjoy the treatment provided for by the Third Geneva Convention.

The ICRC shall have free access to all captured combatants in order to fulfil its humanitarian mandate according to the Third Geneva Convention of 12 August 1949.

2.5 Conduct of hostilities

Hostilities shall be conducted in the respect of the laws of armed conflict, particularly in accordance with Articles 35 to 42 and Articles 48 to 58 of Additional Protocol I, and the Protocol on the prohibitions or Restrictions on the Use of Mines, Booby Traps and

Other Devices annexed to the 1980 Weapons Convention. In order to promote the protection of the civilian population, combatants are obliged to distinguish themselves from the civilian population.

2.6 *Assistance to the civilian population*

The Parties shall allow the free passage of all consignments of medicines and medical supplies, essential foodstuffs and clothing which are destined exclusively to the civilian population.

They shall consent to and cooperate with operations to provide the civilian population with exclusively humanitarian, impartial and non-discriminatory assistance. All facilities will be given in particular to the ICRC.

3. *Red Cross Emblem*

The Red Cross emblem shall be respected. The Parties undertake to use the emblem only to identify medical units and personnel and to comply with the other rules of international humanitarian law relating to the use of the Red Cross emblem and shall repress any misuse of the emblem or attacks on persons or property under its protection.

4. *Dissemination*

The Parties undertake to spread knowledge of and promote respect for the principles and rules of international humanitarian law and the terms of the present agreement, especially among combatants. This shall be done in particular:

- by providing appropriate instruction on the rules of international humanitarian law to all units under their command, control or political influence;
- by facilitating the dissemination of ICRC appeals urging respect for international humanitarian law;
- by distributing ICRC publications.

5. *Implementation*

Each party undertakes to designate liaison officers to the ICRC who will be permanently present in meeting places determined by the ICRC to assist the ICRC in its operations with all the necessary means of communication to enter in contact with all the armed groups they represent. Those liaison officers shall have the capacity to engage those groups and to provide guarantees to the ICRC on the safety of its operations. Each party will allow the free passage of those liaison officers to the meeting places designated by the ICRC.

Each party undertakes, when it is informed, in particular by the ICRC, of any allegation of violations of international humanitar-

ian law, to open an enquiry promptly and pursue it conscientiously, and to take the necessary steps to put an end to the alleged
violations or prevent their recurrence and to punish those responsible in accordance with the law in force.

6. *General provisions*
The parties undertake to respect and to ensure respect for the present
agreement in all circumstances.

The present agreement will enter in force on 26 May at 24h00
if all parties have transmitted to the ICRC their formal acceptance
of the agreement by 26 May 1992 at 18h00.

Geneva, 22 May 1992

Mr. K. Trnka   Mr. D. Kalinic

Mr. J. Djogo   Mr. A. Kurjak   Mr. S. Sito Coric

Document VII

VISITS
since activities resumed, 7 July 1992

[See map on p. 214]

C = in Croatian hands: 921
M = in Muslim hands: 289
S = in Serbian hands: 2,822

situation at 6 August 1992

1. Bosanski Brod prison
   139 prisoners, visited
   9 July 1992; 15/16 July 1992 (C)

2. Mostar prison
   192 prisoners, visited
   9/10 July 1992 (C)

3. Bileca detention camp
   456 prisoners, visited
   9/10 July 1992 (S)

4. Manjaca camp
   2,366 prisoners, visited
   14/16 July 1992; 28 July 1992 (S)

5. Ljubuski prison
   92 prisoners, visited
   23 July 1992 (C)

6. Zenica prison
   289 prisoners, visited
   18/20 July 1992 (M)

7. Bosanski Brod Krindija
   362 prisoners, visited
   20 July 1992; 24 July 1992 (C)

8. Capljina
   80 prisoners, visited
   31 July 1992 (C)

9. Livno
   56 prisoners, visited
   29/30 July 1992 (C)

Total: 4,032 prisoners visited in nine places of detention

Document VIIIa

14 December 1992

PROTECTING VULNERABLE ETHNIC MINORITIES IN BOSNIA-HERZEGOVINA

The International Committee of the Red Cross (ICRC) is deeply disturbed by the fact that, despite sustained efforts by the international community and humanitarian organizations, the situation in Bosnia-Herzegovina continues to deteriorate. The hostilities during the past few months and countless breaches of international humanitarian law have forced hundreds of thousands of people to leave their homes and seek refuge elsewhere in Bosnia-Herzegovina or abroad. As winter sets in, many of these people are without any shelter at all.

Above and beyond any legal considerations, the ICRC feels that the current situation of the civilian population, and that of the displaced people in particular, is unacceptable, just like the policy of 'ethnic cleansing' which is largely to blame for the scale of the problem.

It is the responsibility of the international community to do all in its power to remedy this situation. The immediate priority is to save lives before it is too late.

Various proposals have been put forward to bring help to the civilian victims of the conflict in Bosnia-Herzegovina, and to displaced people in particular.

On 30 October 1992 the ICRC proposed that protected zones be set up for the civilian population at risk, away from combat areas. They would not be intended for the inhabitants of besieged towns, for whose protection other solutions should be found, such as a cessation of hostilities.

In the ICRC's view, the following practical measures could be envisaged:

1. In order to protect the most vulnerable groups, United Nations forces or other forces not involved in the conflict could be deployed in certain towns, away from the fighting, and humanitarian organizations should be allowed to provide assistance for

the inhabitants on the spot. The ICRC believes that such forces should be deployed in all the towns in Bosnia-Herzegovina where minority groups – whether Moslem, Croat or Serb – are at risk.

2. In addition, where large numbers of people have left their homes because of hostilities or persecution and are unable to find refuge in neighbouring countries, they too should be offered temporary shelter in these zones, according to the ICRC's proposal of 30 October 1992.

The zones should be relatively small and placed under the protection of United Nations forces, or other forces not party to the conflict.

In either case, any decision on the setting up of protected zones should be reached with the agreement of the parties to the conflict. In the ICRC's view, the above measures could in no way be regarded as contributing to the policy of 'ethnic cleansing' since they would involve, in the first case, protection of minority groups in their places of residence and, in the second, aid to people who are already displaced.

Moreover, the measures would be of a temporary nature, intended to deal with an emergency situation. They would have no effect on the legal status of either the areas in question or the people within them.

The ICRC cannot assume responsibility for such protected zones, but would be ready to play a role in carrying out tracing activities and participating in the relief effort.

The ICRC is not competent to assess the strength of the armed forces which would have to be deployed to ensure the security of such protected zones, but it is aware of the difficulties involved.

The institution is nonetheless convinced that even greater difficulties are bound to arise if vulnerable groups are not given protection in their home areas and if shelters offering sufficient security are not provided for displaced people.

In any event, the ICRC intends to pursue its protection and assistance activities in Bosnia-Herzegovina and its efforts to ensure greater compliance with international humanitarian law.

Document VIIIb

14.12.92

'SAFE AREAS FOR HUMANITARIAN ASSISTANCE'
(SC resolution 787)
POSITION OF UNHCR

1. In UNHCR's opinion the overriding principle in Bosnia and Herzegovina should be to bring safety to the people, rather than to bring people to safety. The first priority should remain to improve the level of safety and to provide assistance *in situ*.

2. To the extent human suffering and displacement are caused primarily by armed conflict, notably in areas and cities under siege or threat, this means that a genuine and durable cessation of hostilities is imperative. UNHCR sees no viable alternative. The establishment of safe areas risks to distract from the necessity to bring all fighting to a halt.

3. In areas where displacement is caused by ethnic persecution, measures should be taken to improve the safety and material conditions of the remaining minority groups. Both assistance and protection mechanisms should be enhanced through a strategy of three complementary elements: deployment of peace-keeping forces, human rights monitoring and humanitarian assistance. Such measures should include military protection, and would involve a highly visible and mobile international presence. This approach should be followed without discrimination in all areas where minority groups are subject to harassment, but notably in northern and western Bosnia. UNPROFOR's deployment to this region is crucial. It should be possible to implement this approach based on the consent of all parties to the conflict, which is preferable, either as a 'package' or through separate agreements.

   The advantage of this approach would be its implementation in the short term. It would build on the capacity of the current UNPROFOR troops, and a formal extension of the mandate of these troops would perhaps not be necessary.

4. It is recognized that this approach may at best reduce the level and scope of 'ethnic cleansing'. Failing a cessation of all hostilities, displacement as a result of armed conflict will continue

to occur. UNHCR's second priority therefore remains admission to safety, either in neighbouring States or, especially for those unable to gain admission abroad, in relatively secure regions of Bosnia and Herzegovina. The three points strategy referred to above should equally apply to these regions, thereby improving the safety and material conditions of both the displaced and local population, including minority groups. However, the right to seek asylum abroad must be upheld. The burden of the neighbouring States can and should be alleviated by increased international burden-sharing.

5. In UNHCR's opinion the establishment of one or more clearly delineated 'safe areas' under international military protection should only be a last option. When considering this option, the following considerations would justify utmost caution:

a) *reaction of the parties*
All parties to the conflict have voiced their opposition to the establishment of 'safe areas', or want to use the concept to further their own – military – objectives.

b) *military considerations*
The establishment of military protected areas would require local enforcement action (without producing a cessation of hostilities on all fronts, or even risking to lead to intensified fighting on other fronts). This may apply in particular to city areas under siege or direct threat, if the consent of the parties is not forthcoming (see above). The necessary preparation time severely risks to be used to intensify both the current military offensive and the 'ethnic cleansing'. Once safe areas were established, the complete preservation of security would be doubtful. Terrorist attacks from outside or from within the areas are not to be excluded.

c) *political considerations*
The establishment of safe areas, especially of regional zones in central Bosnia, could result in the consolidation of front lines and thereby of territorial conquests, with serious political consequences. Non-acceptance of this by individuals or groups belonging to one or two party(ies) in the conflict would increase the risk of insecurity referred to above.

d) *human rights and international refugee protection*
Admission to and residence in safe areas should not affect freedom of movement nor *ipso facto* frustrate the right to seek asylum. Denial of asylum and forcible returns of persons having already found refuge abroad would, however, be likely, resulting not only in human drama but also in political dispute

and tension. The establishment of militarily protected, closed areas within ethnic cleansing regions, notably in northern and western Bosnia, would inevitably attract additional 'ethnic cleansing' towards such areas.

e) *impact on durable solutions*
In the absence of a political settlement, protracted camp-like situations would risk being perpetuated, surrounded by enemy forces or territory. The homes of people attracted by the existence of safe areas would risk destruction, so as to frustrate the chances for return. After a certain period of time, demands within the areas concerned for transfer abroad are likely to produce enormous pressure.

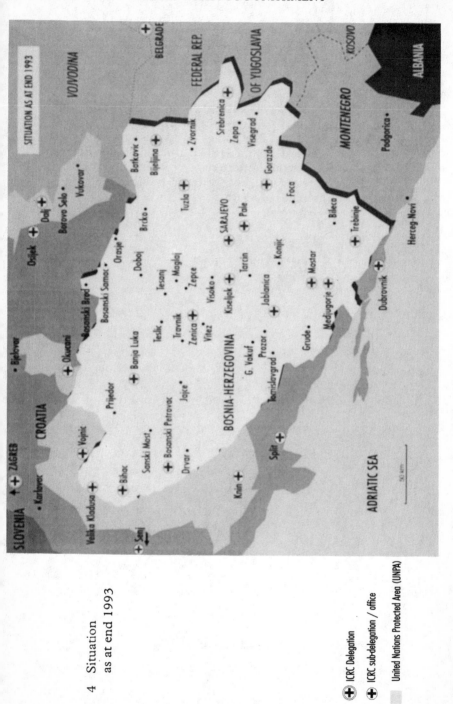

4   Situation
     as at end 1993

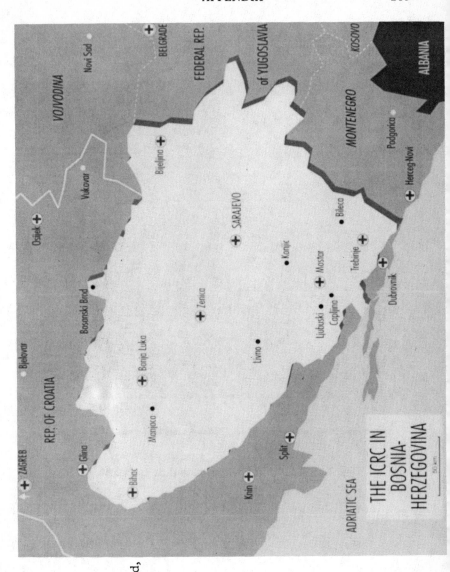

THE ICRC IN
BOSNIA-
HERZEGOVINA

5 Visits since
   activities resumed,
   7 July 1992

Document IX

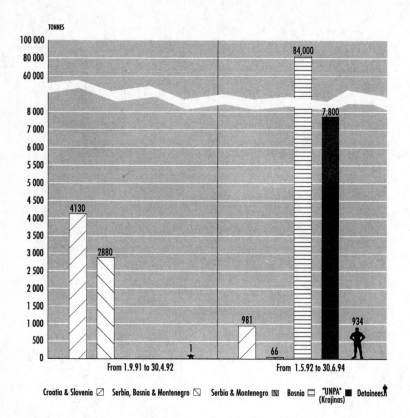

Figure 1 Distribution of relief by region and by category

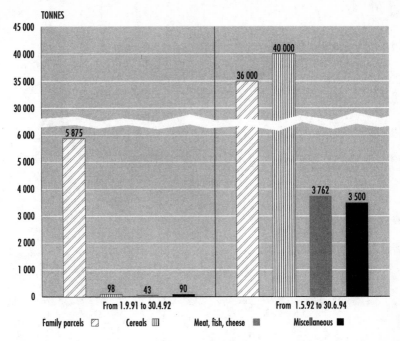

TONNES

45 000
40 000
35 000
30 000
6 000
5 000
4 000
3 000
2 000
1 000
0

5 875
98
43
90

36 000
40 000
3 762
3 500

From 1.9.91 to 30.4.92   From 1.5.92 to 30.6.94

Family parcels ▨   Cereals ▥   Meat, fish, cheese ▦   Miscellaneous ■

Figure 2 Relief by type of merchandise

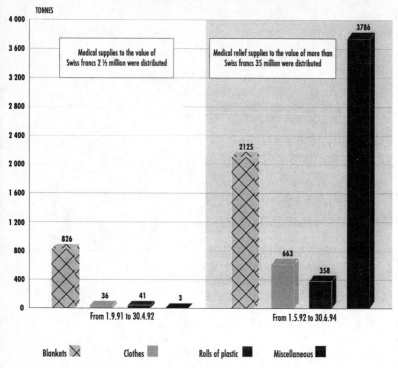

Figure 3 Other relief

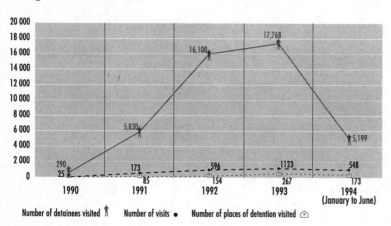

Figure 4 ICRC prison visits 1990–94

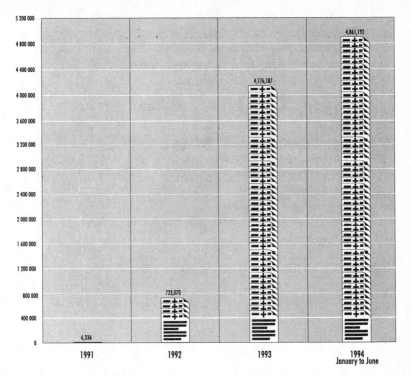

Figure 5 Family messages to and from former Yugoslavia

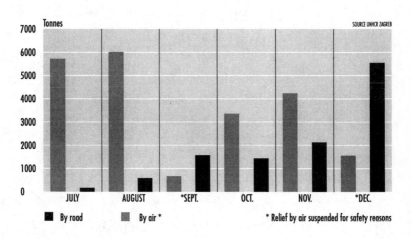

Figure 6 UNHCR relief operations to Sarajevo in 1992

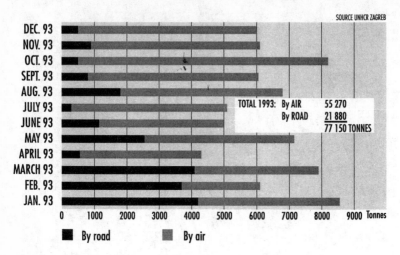

Figure 7 UNHCR relief operations to Sarajevo in 1993

Bibliography

Arsenejevic, Drago, *Voluntary Hostages of the SS*, Editions France-Empire, Paris, 1984.

Biolley, Jacques, *Un génocide en toute liberté*, Wallada, Marseille, and Méandre, Fribourg, 1993.

Carrère d'Encausse, Hélène, *La gloire des nations*, Fayard, Paris, 1990.

Dizdarevic, Zlatko, *Journal de guerre*, Spengler, Paris, 1993.

Feron, Bernard, *Yougoslavie – origines d'un conflit*, Le Monde – Editions, Paris, 1993.

Freymond, Jacques, *Guerres, révolutions, Croix-Rouge*, Graduate Institute of International Studies, Geneva, 1976.

Garde, Paul, *Vie et mort de la Yougoslavie*, Fayard, Paris, 1992.

Gutman, Roy, *A Witness To Genocide*, Macmillan Publishing Company, New York, 1993.

Joxe, Alain, *Voyage aux sources de la guerre*, Presses universitaires de France, Paris, 1991.

Lellouche, Pierre, *Le nouveau monde*, Grasset, Collection 'Pluriel', Paris, 1992.

Médecins Sans Frontières, Populations en danger, Hachette-Pluriel, Paris, 1992.

Nouvel Observateur/Reporters Sans Frontières, *Le livre noir de l'ex-Yougoslavie*, Arléa, Paris, 1993.

Raufer, Xavier et Haut, François, *Le chaos balkanique*, La Table ronde, Paris, 1992.

Rufin, Jean-Christophe, *Le piège humanitaire*, Jean-Claude Lattès, Paris, 1986, et Hachette-Pluriel, Paris, 1993.

Rupnik, Jacques, *et al.*, *De Sarajevo à Sarajevo*, Editions Complexe, Brussels, 1992.

Woodrow, Alain, *Information manipulation*, Editions du Félin, Paris, 1991.

Wynaendts, Henry, *L'engrenage*, Denoël, Paris, 1993.

Principal newspapers, agencies and magazines consulted

Agence France Presse
L'Autre journal
Borba

Chicago Tribune
The Economist
Financial Times
Frankfurter Allgemeine Zeitung
Guardian
International Herald Tribune
Independent
Journal de Genève
Libération
Le Monde
Le Monde des débats
Le Monde diplomatique
Neue Zürcher Zeitung
New York Newsday
Le Nouveau Quotidien
Nouvel Observateur
Oslobodenje
Reuters
Le Soir
Tanjug
Tribune de Genève
Vreme
Die Weltwoche
Die Zeit

Notes

Introduction

1. Communications Director, Comité français pour l'UNICEF, 'Questions sur le droit d'ingérence', *Actualité religieuse dans le monde*, groupe Malesherbes, 15 March 1993.
2. Since the Second World War ICRC delegates have visited more than half a million detainees in 90 countries.
3. Yugoslavia is a party to the 1949 Geneva Conventions and their Additional Protocols of 1977, which it ratified on 21 April 1950 and 11 June 1979 respectively.
4. Except Article 3 common to the Geneva Conventions and Protocol II.
5. *An agenda for peace*, June 1992, p. 1.
6. Ibid., p. 3.
7. Gérard Prunier, writing on Somalia, 'La politique bafouée', *Le Monde des débats*, January 1993.
8. 'Notre dernière illusion', *Le Monde des débats*, January 1993.

Chapter 1 Horror at First Hand

1. The name applied to Serbian nationalist soldiers in the Second World War.

Chapter 2 The Flame beneath the Embers

1. In an article by David Binder entitled 'Yugoslavia Seen Breaking up Soon'.
2. Paul Garde, *Vie et mort de la Yougoslavie*, Fayard, Paris, 1992, p. 304.
3. Xavier Raufer and François Haut, *Le chaos balkanique*, La Table Ronde, Paris, 1992, p. 53.
4. Garde, *Vie et mort*, p. 260.
5. Ibid., pp. 304–305.
6. Jacques Rupnik, 'Aux origines d'une tragédie', *De Sarajevo à Sarajevo*, Editions Complexe, Brussels, 1992, p. 13.
7. By virtue of the principle that the European Community shall be headed by a new president, representing a different Member

State every six months, the president for the period referred to was the representative of Luxembourg, following the representative of Italy and preceding the representative of the Netherlands.

Chapter 3 Summits of Disillusion

1. An interview with the Russian Minister of Foreign Affairs, 14 May 1993.
2. According to the Belgrade daily newspaper *Borba*, referring to the last session of the European Peace Conference, quoted by Henry Wynaendts, *L'engrenage*, Denoël, Paris, 1993, p. 180.
3. Quoted by *Construire* on 13 January 1993, as reported by Jean-Christophe Aeschlimann.
4. Wynaendts, *L'engrenage*, p. 62.
5. Wynaendts, *L'engrenage*, p. 70.
6. For the attention of Ante Markovic, President of the Government of the Yugoslav Federation; Slobodan Milosevic, President of the Republic of Serbia; Veljko Kadijevic, Minister of Defence, Commander in Chief of the Yugoslav Armed Forces; and Franjo Tudjman, President of the Republic of Croatia.
7. The first meeting of plenipotentiary representatives of the Yugoslav Federation, Croatia and Serbia took place on 26 and 27 November 1991, at ICRC headquarters in Geneva.
8. The supreme body of the International Red Cross and Red Crescent Movement, which normally meets every four years. At the International Conference representatives of the states signatory to the Geneva Conventions (nearly all countries of the world) meet with representatives of the ICRC, the National Red Cross or Red Crescent Societies and their International Federation.
9. An organ of the International Red Cross and Red Crescent Movement, charged with supervising the preparation of International Conferences of the Red Cross and Red Crescent.
10. *Annual Report* 1991, p. 135.
11. The umbrella organization of representatives of the ICRC, the National Red Cross and Red Crescent Societies and their International Federation.
12. Appointed on 5 March by the UN Secretary-General at the same time as General Satish Nambiar, Commanding Officer of UNPROFOR, and his deputy, General Philippe Morillon.
13. Alija Izetbegovic, of the Party of Democratic Action, Radovan Karadzic, of the Serbian Democratic Party, and Miljenko Brkic, of the Croatian Democratic Community.

14. United Nations Protected Areas (called Krajina by the Serbs). These areas were placed under the protection of UN forces in April 1992.
15. Resolution 770, on forwarding humanitarian aid, and Resolution 771 on the respect of international humanitarian law.
16. Press release no. 1725, 13 August 1992.
17. Mazowiecki resigned in July 1995.
18. Speech by Cornelio Sommaruga at the press conference of 3 October 1992, press release no. 1728.
19. This commission was known as the Kalshoven Commission, after Frits Kalshoven, the Dutch specialist in humanitarian law later appointed to direct it (see Resolution 780 of 5 October 1992).
20. Resolution of the General Assembly, AG 47/1 of 22 September 1992.
21. See the meeting of the Follow-up Committee of the Conference of 29 July, held in Geneva on 4 December 1992, the UNHCR preparatory document dated 30 November, and the statement by Jean de Courten, the ICRC director of Operations.
22. Communication to the press no. 92/38, 23 December 1992.
23. Sixth extraordinary session of the Islamic Conference of Ministers of Foreign Affairs, Jedda, 1 and 2 December 1992.
24. 'Humanitarisme et Empires', *Le Monde diplomatique*, January 1993.

Chapter 4 Sarajevo 1992: pandemonium

1. Spengler, Paris, 1993.
2. 'Pass on AMTOR' = relay a written communication by radio (AM = amateur, TOR = telex over radio).

Chapter 5 Crimes Without Punishment

1. This title is borrowed from the end-of-mission report, covering the period September 1991–October 1992, made by Thierry Meyrat, head of the ICRC delegation in Belgrade.
2. See above note.
3. Data taken from *Victimes de conflits*, a report made for the World Campaign for the Protection of War Victims, Department of Peace and Conflict Research, University of Uppsala, Sweden, 1991.
4. Letter dated 30 August 1991, to Messrs Mesic of the Socialist Federal Republic of Yugoslavia, Tudjman of Croatia, Milosevic of Serbia and Kucan of Slovenia, giving them simultaneous

notice of the mission to be effected by the ICRC's Director of Operations.

5. He was accompanied by a woman nurse and an interpreter, both of them attached to the ICRC, and by seven buses with their crews of seven drivers, seven doctors and three women nurses from Bjelovar.

6. Emer de Vattel, *Le droit des gens ou principes de la loi naturelle*, Slatkine et Institut Henry-Dunant, Genève, 1983, p. 245.

7. This example is quoted by Charles Zorgbibe in 'La guerre civile', published by the *Annales de la Faculté de droit et des sciences économiques*, Université de Clermont, fascicule 6, 1969, Librairie Dalloz, Paris.

8. 'Evidence Testifies to Mass Execution of 200 Croats in '91', *International Herald Tribune*, 21 January 1993.

9. *Note Verbale* of 12 December 1991.

10. According to Wynaendts, *L'engrenage*, p. 170.

11. Executive Board decision of 27 May 1992.

12. See the Plan of Action of 6 June 1992.

13. On 6 April the twelve states of the European Community recognized Bosnia-Herzegovina, which was admitted to the United Nations on 22 May 1992 at the same time as Slovenia and Croatia.

14. See Ed Harriman's documentary 'A Town Called Kozarac' made in 1993 for British television's Channel 4.

15. Documents assembled by the *Nouvel Observateur* and Reporters sans Frontières, Editions Arléa, March 1993.

16. Ibid., p. 194.

17. Ibid., p. 261.

18. Declaration published on 5 August 1992 by the spokesman of the American State Secretariat.

19. London Conference on former Yugoslavia, 25–28 August 1992.

20. ICRC press release of 3 October 1992 (no. 1728), entitled 'Saving lives in Bosnia-Herzegovina'.

21. Radovan Karadzic for the Bosnian Serbs, Mate Boban for the Croat community, and Haris Silajdzic, Minister of Foreign Affairs of the Republic of Bosnia-Herzegovina.

22. 'Serbia Still Runs 135 Prison Camps, U.S. Thinks', *International Herald Tribune*, 25 January 1993.

23. From July to December 1992 10,800 prisoners were visited. Of these, 8,100 were held by the Bosnian Serbs, 1,600 by the government of Bosnia-Herzegovina, and 1,100 by the Bosnian Croats; 5,500 people were released under ICRC auspices, 2,500 without its participation and 2,700 others are still in custody and receive ICRC visits whilst awaiting release.

24. 'Bosnia's Camps of Death', *Newsday*, 2 August 1992, followed by 'The Rapes of Bosnia', 23 August 1992.
25. Die Grünen, Bundesverband, Bonn; KOFRA e.V. (Kommuni-kationszentrum für Frauen zur Arbeits- u. Lebenssituation), München; Internationale Frauenliga für Frieden und Freiheit (IFFF); Lesbenring e.V., Heidelberg; Frauenanstiftung, Hamburg.
26. Bundesfrauenministerin Angela Merkel; the four main German political parties; the German Red Cross; the governments of Serbia and Bosnia-Herzegovina; the European Parliament; the Secretary-General of the United Nations; the United Nations High Commissioner for Refugees; the CSCE, and the ICRC.
27. *Bosnia-Herzegovina – Rape and Sexual Abuse by Armed Forces*, January 1993.
28. Agence France Presse, 20 January 1993.
29. Rapport général du Comité International de la Croix-Rouge sur son activité de 1912 à 1920, Geneva, ICRC, 1921, p. 152.
30. Drago Arsenijevic, *Voluntary Hostages of the SS*, Editions France Empire, 1984.
31. Co-ordinator of the Special Operation in former Yugoslavia, based in Geneva, in an interview with the author in May 1993.
32. *Chicago Tribune*, 27 January 1993.
33. Press release of 3 October 1992 entitled 'Saving Lives in Bosnia-Herzegovina'.
34. Appeal of 3 October 1992, 'Saving Lives in Bosnia-Herzegovina', press release no. 1728.
35. Resolution 787, reinforcing the embargo on Serbia and Montenegro, condemning all violations of humanitarian law, referring to the Commission of Experts formed on 5 October (Resolution 780) and encouraging humanitarian efforts in general.
36. Jean-Christophe Rufin, *Le piège humanitaire*, Jean-Claude Lattès, Paris, 1986, edition updated in the Pluriel collection, January 1993, 'Humanitarian work and politics since the fall of the Wall', p. 366.
37. The physician responsible for former Yugoslavia in the ICRC's medical division, in an internal memorandum of 21 December 1992.
38. Evaluation reports published in November–December 1992 and January–February 1993, MSF, Paris.
39. 'Notre dernière illusion', *Le Monde des débats*, January 1993.
40. 'Un programme pour sauver les principes humanitaires de la débâcle', *Le Nouveau Quotidien*, 23 June 1993.
41. 'Humanitaire neutre ou juste?', *Le Monde*, 24 February 1993.
42. Interview published in *Le Monde*, 25 May 1993.

43. *Guerres, révolutions, Croix-Rouge*, Graduate Institute of International Studies, Geneva, 1976, p. 57.

Chapter 6 On the Proper Use of Propaganda

1. Tadeusz Mazowiecki's first report on the state of human rights in former Yugoslavia, 28 August 1992.
2. Ivan Colovic, 'The Propaganda of War: its Stratagems', Center for Anti-war Action; round table on breaches of international humanitarian law in the armed conflicts of former Yugoslavia, International Institute of Humanitarian Law, San Remo, 4–6 December 1992.
3. 'Yugoslav War about the Past', 22 November 1991.
4. The UNPROFOR spokesman in Zagreb, quoted by the Agence France Presse (AFP) on 1 April 1993.
5. At the Round Table on the Rights of Journalists and Media Organizations, Ljubljana, Slovenia, 4–5 February 1993.
6. Spengler Editions, Paris, 1993.
7. Jacques Lesourne and Bruno Frappat, 'Information et déontologie', *Le Monde*, 12 February 1993.
8. Alain Woodrow, *Information manipulation*, Editions du Félin, Paris, July 1991, p. 162.
9. Lesourne and Frappat.
10. 'La Défaite des faits', *L'Autre Journal*, No. 4, 1993.
11. 'Ce Bernard Kouchner qui nous agace ...', *Tribune de Genève*, 1 February 1993.
12. 'Bosnia in Color: Television as a Goad of Government', an extract from *Presidents, Television and Foreign Crises*, adapted by the *Washington Post, International Herald Tribune*, 11 May 1993.
13. Véronique Soulé, 13 May 1993.
14. This is a reference to the ICRC's silence on the atrocities of the Second World War, and especially on the Nazi concentration camps.
15. '*L'Etat humanitaire*', a lecture delivered at the International Museum of the Red Cross and Red Crescent, Geneva, 11 May 1993.

Chapter 7 1993 – Brief Chronicles

1. 'Warrior Without Weapons' is the English title of a book entitled *Le Troisième Combattant*, by Dr Marcel Junod, an ICRC delegate. It was published in 1947 and again on the Centenary of the Red Cross by Payot, Paris, 1963.

2. 'To send at any time whatsoever a prisoner into a region where he would be exposed to the fire of the battle area is a breach of the Third and Fourth Geneva Conventions, which the parties have undertaken to respect ...', press release no. 93/5.
3. Isabelle Vichniac, 'Marchandage autour du découpage de la Bosnie', *Le Monde*, 30 July 1993.

Conclusion

1. Jacques Biolley, *Un génocide en toute liberté*, co-edition Wallada, Marseille/Méandre, Fribourg, 1993.
2. Jean-Christophe Rufin, 'La transformation des conflits', in *Populations en danger, Médecins sans Frontières*, collection Pluriel Intervention, Hachette, Paris, 1992, p. 152.

Landmarks 1992

1. Also called the *14th*, when referred to as the cease-fire negotiated on 23 November 1991 in Geneva.

Index